Folklore Fights the Nazis

Humor in Occupied Norway, 1940–1945

Kathleen Stokker

The University of Wisconsin Press

The University of Wisconsin Press
2537 Daniels Street
Madison, Wisconsin 53718

3 Henrietta Street
London WC2E 8LU, England

3   5   7   9   10   8   6   4   2

First published in 1995 by Fairleigh Dickinson University Press

Printed in the United States of America

Library of Congress Cataloging-in-Publication Data
Stokker, Kathleen, 1946–
Folklore fights the Nazis.
280 pp.   cm.
Originally published: Cranbury, N.J.: Fairleigh Dickinson University Press, 1995.
Includes bibliographical references and index.
ISBN 0-299-15444-0 (pbk.: alk. paper)
1. Norway—History—German occupation, 1940–1945—Humor.
2. World War, 1939–1945—Norway—Humor. 3. Norwegian wit and humor.
DL532.S8   1997
940.54′12481—dc21   96-37260

To my father,
George Oluf Stokker (1906–57)

who, like the Norwegians described here,
could find humor in almost any situation.

Contents

To the Reader

What qualifies the jokes in this book as folklore? The fact, mentioned in the first preface, that they have circulated in numerous international variants, both before World War II and since, suggests that they contain the same infectious appeal we associate with folk songs, legends, and tales. To demonstrate this facet of the humor, the book contains a few joke cognates, i.e., jokes that are identical except for slight modifications which make it seem as though a particular witticism originated in the country where it circulated. The book's examples show how the same jokes could ridicule Nazi oppression in Norway, then move on to mock subjugation in Soviet and Romanian Communist regimes (see page 123, page 235, note 14, and page 249, note 7). So far, though, we have said little about the relationship of Norway's anti-Nazi jokes to those that simultaneously spread through the other occupied countries. A few specific examples of these can tell us much about how occupation humor "worked" in general and why it qualifies as folklore.

All of the countries invaded by Hitler's forces could provide jokes similar to the ones presented in this book. The humor traveled in many ways: by word of mouth, via refugees and occupying soldiers; in print, via leaflets dropped by Allied planes, underground newspapers, and related prohibited publications; and over the BBC and other "illegal" radio broadcasts. Danish examples (all from the archives of Copenhagen's Frihedsmuseet Resistance Museum) have been chosen for the present discussion because of the additional light they can shed upon another issue the book briefly raises, namely the equal importance of that which is *not* joked about.

The similarities and differences in Danish and Norwegian occupation humor actually invite a far more detailed analysis than space permits here. Despite the countries' remarkable social, political, and linguistic similarities, the kings of each country—who were brothers—chose seemingly opposite ways of responding to the 9 April 1940 ultimatum that they collaborate with the Nazi regime. While Norway's Haakon VII protested by exiling himself along with the Norwegian government to London, timing and topography prompted Denmark's Christian X to initially adopt a policy of negotiation in an effort to avoid the casualties of open resistance. The similarities in background and differences in response have fascinating implications for the occupation humor that developed in each country. Though currently engaged in studying these, I will confine my remarks here to just a few examples that highlight resemblances in the two countries' occupation humor, before concluding with a striking and highly significant difference between them.

From the vast array of cognate jokes that made the rounds in Denmark and Norway, we might select the example of the witticism quoted on pages 161-62 which in Norway invokes the professed success of Oslo's Viking ships in invading England to deride Hitler's repeated failures to invade England during the fall of 1940. When told in Denmark, this joke featured instead of the Gokstad and Oseberg ships in Oslo, the Ladby ship, excavated in 1934 from a Viking burial mound in the Danish province of Funen; otherwise the jokes are identical:

> Engang i Begyndelsen af Besættelsen kom et Par tyske Officerer for at se Ladbyskibet. Opsynsmanden viste dem rundt og forklarede, hvad de ønskede at se og høre.
> Da de var færdige, sagde den ene af dem, at han ærlig talt ikke syntes, at der var noget særligt ved saadan et Skib, hvortil Opsynsmanden svarede:
> "Det kan jeg ikke forstaa, for med den Slags Skibe har *vi* da to Gange erobret England."
> (Early in the occupation a couple of German officers came to see the Ladby ship. The man in charge showed them around, explaining everything they wanted to see and hear.
> When they were finished, one of them said that he honestly didn't think there was anything special about such a ship.
> To this the man in charge answered, "That's hard to understand since it was with such a ship *we* twice managed to conquer England.")

Some joke cognates reflect lifestyle differences between the two countries. Denmark is a land of bicycles so it is not surprising that the daring role of taunting the Nazis with smart-alect replies, which in the Norwegian humor is played by Bergen's *tjuagutter* (street urchins, see pages 33 and 104), in the Danish humor consistently falls to cheeky bicycle messengers:

> En lille tysk Marine Soldat staar ved Hotel "Phoenix." Et Cyklebud

kommer ned ad Bredgade, og idet han drejer om Hjørnet ved Hotellet
raaber han: "Ved din Mor, at du er her?"
(A little German marine is standing near the Hotel Phoenix. A bicycle
messenger comes down Bredgade Street, and as he turns the corner by
the hotel he shouts: "Does your mother know that you're here?"")

The joke above corresponds to the Norwegian jokes scorning the
youth of the *Hird* (Nazi guard) on pages 128–29, while the one
below expresses the same sentiments as the Norwegian *tyskertös*
jokes described in chapter 3, especially the one on page 65.

En Dag saa et Bud en "dansk" Pige gaa meget kærligt med en tysk
Soldat, hun fik følgende Salut:
"Pass paa, du ikke faar en Unge, du ikke kan tale med."
(One day a messenger saw a "Danish" girl walking very affectionately
with a German soldier. She received the following greeting, "Be
careful you don't have a child you can't talk to.")

Though many of the same stories thus recycled themselves from
country to country, their hearers—not unlike those who give
credence to today's urban legends—often took them for actual and
uniquely occurring local events:

Der gik næsten aldrig en Dag uden en ny Historie. En som skal være
autentisk er denne:
En gammel Dame som gik saa daarligt at hun maatte bruge stok,
snublede da hun var lige ud for en tysk Officer. Han faldt da Stokken
røg ind mellem hans Ben. Den gamle Dame faldt ogsaa og flere hjalp
hende op og spurgte om hun havde slaaet sig, hun svarede nej, men nu
er mit ene Knæ ved at være ømt, saa jeg maa vist holde for i Dag, men
han var ogsaa den sjette.
(Almost no day passed without a new story. Here's one that's supposed
to actually have happened:
An old lady, who walked so poorly she needed a cane, stumbled just
as she passed a German officer. He fell when her cane became entan-
gled with his legs. The old lady fell down, too, and several bystanders
helped her up asking if she had hurt herself. "No," she replied, "but
my knee is getting sore now, so I'd better stop for today. But he was
the sixth one.")

The incident could, of course, also have occurred in Denmark, but
its remarkable similarity to the "invasion day incident" reported
by the Norwegian-American press as having taken place in Norway
(see page 30) reveals it as a story that captures the resistance sentiment that tellers in both countries wanted to celebrate. Meanwhile

the incident itself may never have actually occurred precisely as described in either one.

In all, the occupation humor of Denmark and that of Norway displays tremendous affinities, only hinted at here. Many items seem, like the one above, to have originated in Norway then found increasing response in Denmark as that country's resistance sentiment grew and its official policy of negotiation gave way in 1943 to one of open confrontation. At the same time, significant differences distinguish the occupation humor of each country. One theme that enjoyed widespread popularity in Denmark while being essentially ignored in Norway concerns the plight of the Jews.

Much of the humor mocking the Nazis' outrageous racial policy seems to have originated in Germany. The occupying soldiers probably told these jokes in both countries (see page 219, note 22 and page 224, note 25), but the humor found resonance only in Denmark, where the Jews were fully integrated into the population (see page 49). Two examples from this rich material will have to suffice here:

> Hitler, Goebbels og Goering startede hver sin Vogn fra tre forskellige Steder i Berlin. Paa Potsdammer Platz kørte de alle inde i hinanden med et ordentligt Drøn.
> Hvis var Skylden?
> ???
> Jødernes—selvfølgelig.
> (Hitler, Goebbels and Goering each started a car from three different places in Berlin. At Potzdammer Platz they all collided with each other with an enormous crash.
> Whose fault was it?
> ???
> The Jews'—of course.)

Note the way this joke ridiculing the Nazi tendency to blame all ills on the Jews employs the identical joke mechanism as the item on page 165 which instead mocks the tendency among Norwegians to find universal fault with the British war effort. Perhaps more successful in retaining its amusement to this day is the following portrayal of a Jew making fools of the Nazi elite:

> Hitler, Goering og Goebbels mødes paa "Kaiserhof" for at spise Frokost. Man enes om hver at bestille en Kylling. Dog Goering bestiller to for sin Person.
> Men som saa ofte, faar Maven nok før Øjnene, og der levnes den fjerde Kylling.
> Was nun zu machen! Man enes om, at den første, der passerer forbi

det Vindue, ved hvilket de sidder, skal kaldes ind og gives Kyllingen.

Et Øjebliks Venten, og en Mandsperson passerer. Han kaldes ind. Und das war ein Jude!

Verfluchter Schweinhund, tiltaler Hitler ham, "efter vor Aftale skal Du have denne Kylling, dog kun paa den Betingelse, at alt hvad Du gør ved Kyllingen, gør vi ved Dig. Brækker Du et Laar af, mister Du Dit ene Ben; bryder Du en Vinge, koster det Dig en Arm' og vrider Du Halsen om paa Dyret, faar Din Hals samme Skæbne. Spis saa, Kyllingen er Din, Judeschwein!''

Jøden staar et Øjeblik, tager saa Kyllingen i Hænderne—og giver den et fedt Kys midt paa Gumpen.

(Hitler, Goering and Goebbels met at "Kaiserhof" for a meal. They agree that each would order a chicken, though Goering orders two for himself.

But as so often happens, the eyes can eat more than the stomach, and there's a chicken left over.

What to do? They agree that the first one who passes by the window where they're sitting will be invited in and given the chicken.

After a moment's wait, a man passes. He is called in. And it was a Jew!

"*Verfluchter Schweinhund* [You goddamned son-of-a-bitch]," Hitler addresses him, "according to our agreement you shall have this chicken, but only on the condition that everything you do to the chicken, we will do to you. If you snap off a drumstick, we'll break one of your legs; if you tear off a wing, it will cost you an arm; and if you wring the chicken's neck, your neck will suffer the same fate. So eat; the chicken is yours, *Judeschwein* [you Jewish swine]!''

The Jew stands a moment, then picks up the chicken—and plants a juicy kiss right on its rump.)

The sympathetic treatment Danish occupation humor accords the Jews reflects the concern for their plight shared by the population at large. This concern translated into heroic actions that saved a record 7200 of Denmark's 8000 Jews from Nazi capture, while in Norway—whose occupation humor makes no mention of their plight—a tragically high 50% of the Jewish population never returned from captivity (see pages 48–49 and 213). What a country jokes about, it also takes most seriously.

The quality of humor to express its tellers' deepest concerns makes the jokes and jests, quips and cartoons this book records worthy of preservation and consideration. Norway's occupation humor reflects the will of its people to prevail over domination and to endure adversity. Telling the story of the human concerns of occupied daily life, this material possesses the universal appeal that qualifies it as folklore and which continues to reward today's reader with laughter and a nod of recognition.

Preface

During the five-year period between the 9 April 1940 invasion of Norway by German forces and the 8 May 1945 liberation, Norwegians endured terror, sacrifice, and pain. Many also experienced tremendous exhilaration and unprecedented fellowship. Some demonstrated heroism; others compromised their principles; the vast majority faced the challenge of continuing their daily lives under previously unimagined circumstances.

Bookshelves bulge with accounts of the Norwegian occupation. Yet little has been written about the humor that played a vital role in helping the average Norwegian survive. This book samples that humor; it organizes the anti-Nazi jokes and anecdotes, places them in an historical context, and examines the sentiment behind them. While assessing the wartime role humor played in encouraging resistance, the book ultimately considers the reasons for its enduring significance not only to occupied Norwegians, but to all peoples at all times.

The primary sources of the humor presented here are five private, previously unpublished wartime joke collections, an unexpected and thrilling find. During the summer of 1987 I traveled to Norway in search of occupation humor, and found in the archives of Oslo's Resistance Museum a generous supply of published humor both in the underground press and in postwar joke collections. Still a persistent question nagged me: Had everyday people found meaning in these jokes? The mere fact that this humor was published does not automatically assure that it touched the population on a personal level. But how to discover—fifty years later—whether or not these jokes had made such an impact?

One day toward the end of my stay, I found the answer. Examining the contents of one of the museum's files, I came across a small 4 × 6 inch notebook. On its label the owner had written her name, Sölvi M. Larsen. My pulse quickened as I read the first page with her penciled version of the English national anthem—forbidden in wartime Norway. Turning the page, I knew I had found what I was looking for. Following the heading Vitser (jokes) came twenty-three pages of handwritten variants of familiar occupation anecdotes.

Here was at least one individual who had found this humor sufficiently meaningful to take the time, trouble, and—not least—the risk of writing it down. Had the notebook been found by the Nazis, severe reprisals—even death—would have likely ensued.[1]

The next day during a prearranged interview with the journalist Berit Vikdal, I mentioned the notebook. A tremendous response greeted her subsequent article in *Aftenposten* (The Evening Post), one of Norway's largest dailies. In letters and phone calls people shared jokes they remembered from the occupation. Three of these individuals—Majsol Elvsås, Tore Ellingsen, and Cecilie Schou-Sörensen—possessed similar joke collections. Interviews and extended correspondence followed during which they provided background information not only about the jokes they had recorded but also about the five years of occupation that provide their context.

The fifth source, a diary found in Oslo's University Library kept by Marie Lysgaard Slaatto of Lillehammer, also preserves a great deal of wartime humor. All of the items from these joke collections are included in the pages that follow. Two additional diaries, those of Åslaug Rommetveit (privately owned) and Greta Dahl (recently published by Gröndahl Press in Oslo), subsequently came to my attention; their insights augment the jokes by providing personal perspectives on the occupation experience.[2]

Occasionally this book also draws on jokes from the underground press, from previously published postwar collections, or from other types of occupation literature. The overwhelming majority of material presented here, however, was written during the war years themselves.

Fifty years after the fact, some of these items no longer make sense even to those who had written them down. A quip that "the Germans are now standing in line at the liquor store" ("nå står tyskerne i pol-kö"), for example, seemed utterly inscrutable. Sometime later it was observed that this item was recorded on the same date as the witticism that "The Monolith is Katyn Forest standing on edge" ("Monolitten er Katynskogen på höykant").[3] The latter item clearly referred to the mass grave found in Russia's Katyn Forest near Smolensk containing the bodies of over forty-two hundred Polish officers apparently murdered by Soviet security; the grisly find had conjured in the mind of the joke's originator the vertical column of writhing bodies that comprise Gustav Vigeland's well-known sculpture, Monolitten (The monolith). Given the correspondence of the October 1943 date of the find with the date of the liquor store joke and the double meaning of the word *pol* as not only "liquor store" but also "Pole," the first item seems to be a folk prediction that the Germans would suffer the same fate as the Poles, that is, mass death in Russian hands, a prophecy rapidly reaching fulfillment after the German surrender at Stalingrad (February 1943) had begun turning the tide of Hitler's fortunes.

While the liquor store quip requires a good bit of contextual information and even then may fail to strike a modern reader as particularly witty, a surprising number of the items that follow have retained their humorous impact. Their variety and inventiveness make them worthy of access to all readers, a goal the present annotated survey aims to achieve.

Some may puzzle over the term *folklore* in the book's title. Indeed not all of the items presented here exhibit the characteristic of "multiple variants" resulting from the "oral transmission of a compelling idea" that defines an item as folklore. Examples having a single, fixed form—such as the children's book *Snorri the Seal* or the Christmas cards described in chapter 5, belong instead to the category of "popular culture." The great majority of the jokes, quips, and anecdotes, however, do qualify as folklore.[4] They circulated in multiple versions and existed in various dialects all over the country. Arising in one specific place, they traveled by word of mouth, being subtly reshaped by new tellers and adapted to new places and situations. Like folk songs and folk stories, many of these jokes have crossed international boundaries and transcended the limits of time—being told in other countries both long before and after Norway's World War II occupation. Some, like the postage stamp joke in chapter 2, have recently circulated in our own country.

Since many of the jokes do have cognates in other lands and cultures, their original language versions (including all idiosyncracies of spelling and syntax) have been included for the purpose of potential comparative study and because the humor of many items resides in their language. Quotations from Norwegian language diary passages and secondary sources are, on the other hand, presented in English. Unless otherwise stated, all translations are the author's own.

* * *

Many individuals and institutions have assisted in the creation of the present volume. First and foremost are the diarists and joke collectors upon whose observations the book is based, and among them I especially thank Majsol Elvsås, Cecilie Schou-Sörensen, and Åslaug Rommetveit for their patience. I am also grateful for kind assistance received at Norway's Hjemmefrontmuseum, the

University of Oslo's Krigtrykkssamling, the University of Bergen (from Ragnhild Ullern), and the University of Trondheim's division of specialized collections (Avdeling for spesialsamlinger).

As a reader of an earlier version of the manuscript, Jane Jakoubek, Associate Dean, Luther College, Decorah, Iowa provided particularly astute commentary. Another shaper of the work has been the thought-provoking responses audience members have offered during presentations of this work in various parts of the country. Similarly rewarding have been the helpful replies of the Norwegian and Norwegian-American public to various queries in the Oslo dailies *Aftenposten* and *Verdens gang* (World events) as well as in the *Viking* and *Norseman* magazines. Well remembered, too, are the individuals, too numerous to name, who have kindly provided jokes, postcards, and books, and thereby contributed invaluably to the material presented between these covers; for their continuing correspondence and assistance Tore Argren, Vidar Steen-Hansen, and Svein Tonning deserve special thanks.

Luther College's Interlibrary Loan and Computer Services departments have provided vital assistance during all phases of this work, and I acknowledge with profound appreciation the generous financial support this project has received from Luther College, the National Endowment for the Humanities, the Midwest Faculty Seminar, and the Norwegian Consulate. The personal interactions reflected throughout the pages that follow account in large measure for the enormous satisfaction work with this fascinating material has brought me and I hope that readers, too, will find pleasure in it.

The Diarists

Sölvi M. Larsen, the compiler of the original joke notebook found in Oslo's Resistance Museum, was about twelve years old when the occupation began and living in Oslo. She brought her collection to the museum along with the wartime papers of her father, a plumber, shortly after the museum's inception in 1970.[1]

Solveig Maj Christerson now goes by the name of *Majsol Elvsås* and lives in Moss in Eastern Norway. Born on 22 May 1929, she was eleven years old when the occupation began and living in Bergen. During the early months of the occupation, she kept a notebook of jokes she heard at home, mostly from her mother's twenty-one-year-old brother, who she believes suggested she collect them. Though she has since written several newspaper articles, songs, and poems, she is a physical therapist by profession. In addition to the joke notebook from 1940, she kept a diary during 1943, some of whose entries were read on a 1980 Norwegian radio program.

Åslaug Rommetveit was born on 18 March 1924 and lived in the western Norwegian town of Bryne during the occupation. Sixteen years old when the occupation began, she was a pupil at Rogaland Business High School, where her diary tells that anti-Nazi humor circulated by way of notes passed in class. Both passionate anti-Nazis, she and her mother several times housed fugitives attempting to escape Norway. Having coincidentally begun a diary on 1 April 1940, she felt compelled to continue by the dramatic events that began unfolding in the wake of the 9 April invasion. Before the end of the occupation she had filled four thick books in which she also saved illegal flyers and other anti-Nazi propaganda. The material provided the basis for a 1990 Norwegian radio program; excerpts of her diaries have also appeared in a local magazine.

Cecilie Schou-Sörensen (b. 17 August 1916), now of Fredrikstad in southeastern Norway, was living in Oslo during the occupation and was twenty-three years old when it began. As part of her wartime diaries she kept a section of jokes—amounting to 170 items in all. A member of the prominent factory-owning Schou family, she was hired by the University of Oslo as the president's secretary in 1942. While neither she nor her mother actively participated in resistance activity, they did read and help circulate illegal newspapers. Not sure why she started writing down the jokes, apart from a general desire to "get things down on paper," she never dreamed her diaries would be of interest to anyone besides herself.

The son of *Elsa "Bibs" Ellingsen* (b. Elsa Sophia Larssen) sent me a typed collection of jokes assembled by his mother and titled: "Norges smil gjennom tårer" (Norway's smiles through tears). She was born in Kristiania (Oslo) on 30 January 1904 and was thirty-six when the occupation began. Her joke collection seems to contain more items relating to international politics, a perspective which may reflect her more mature age at the time of the occupation.

Marie Lysgaard Slaatto (b. 1926), whose diary was found in the Oslo University Library, was fourteen years old and living in Lillehammer when the occupation began. Her older brother was involved in producing one of the underground news sheets and provided the jokes she has recorded. She began her diary on 11 May 1940, about a month after the invasion, motivated—like Rommetveit—to keep a record of the unbelievable events taking place around her.

Greta Dahl (14 October 1904–1 June 1988) lived in Narvik, a Norwegian place-name that received worldwide attention as British and French Allies fought to gain a foothold there in 1940. Like Elsa Larssen, she was in her thirties during the war years and also demonstrates a more mature perspective. Her diary distinguishes itself by expressing remarkable sensitivity to the sufferings of individuals on both sides of the conflict. Having kept diaries since girlhood and until her death, it was only natural that she also kept one during the occupation. She wrote her observations in twenty-nine individual notebooks, finding them easier to hide in a hurry. Like the other diarists, she wrote her observations as a private aid to memory, without thought of later publication. Unlike the others, though, a portion of hers has previously appeared in book form, published by Gröndahl Press in 1990. The original is in Narvik's Red Cross War Museum.[2]

The spontaneous creation and personal intention of these joke notebooks and diaries add much to their value. Unlike memoirs produced after the war and intended for publication, they provide an unself-conscious view of the occupation experience. Kept by women, the diaries and the joke notebooks that provide the substance of this book focus not so much on the concerns of soldiers or policymakers, but on the vital details of daily life as experienced by the ordinary people of Norway. Their entries vividly retain impressions, emotions, and attitudes often unavailable in other sources and they accurately reflect the fabric of fear and uncertainty, hope and aspiration these individuals felt during one of the most dramatic periods of Norway's history.

Introduction

While the phenomenon of Norway's occupation humor has certainly not gone unnoticed,[1] its exact nature and the significant role it played in developing a resistance mentality among the Norwegian people have remained largely unexamined. The role of occupation jokes in maintaining morale seems obvious, but beyond making people feel better, wartime humor granted a voice to those deprived of free speech, discouraged the undecided from a hasty attachment to Nazism, and helped the initially amorphous group of individuals opposed to Nazism to develop a sense of solidarity (Skodvin 1969, 167). This volume, in addition to presenting the humor and explaining its context, demonstrates how resistance humor accomplished these vital tasks.

Postwar accounts of the Norwegian occupation have tended to suggest that Norwegians spontaneously and unanimously resisted Nazism as of the 9 April 1940 invasion. Accounts from the early war years, however, reveal a different truth, emphasizing a paralyzing uncertainty in the wake of the invasion. In fact a 12 April 1940 report by the German Wehrmacht (Nazi Army) highlights the Norwegian civilian population's surprising lack of resistance.

> In the entire occupied area there is for the most part no hostility. . . . Often helpfulness, especially from Norway's Red Cross, who saved critically wounded Germans. Willing help by countless drivers. No appreciable difficulties from the Norwegian authorities. No passive resistance. [Quoted in Nökleby 1989, 114]

A 13 August 1940 entry in Slaatto's diary notes, moreover, that quite a few Norwegians became collaborators.

> Norway is crawling with traitors; they have no love of country and join the Nazi Party just to get good jobs.

On 4 November 1940 she again reports that there are "loads of traitors."

Given the tendency of postwar memoirs to oversimplify the com-

17

plexity of the dilemma Norwegians faced, one may wonder how anyone could have sympathized with the invaders. During the early weeks and months of the occupation, however, the sides were far from clearly drawn. For one thing, Nazi ideology in many respects resembled the sentiments of prominent patriots like Björnstjerne Björnson who only a few decades earlier had succeeded in infusing Norwegians with sufficient national pride to prompt passage of the 1905 referendum in favor of independence from Sweden. Perceived deficiencies in Norway's prewar society, her crushing military defeat that could be blamed on the former government, and the Allies' early ineptness against the highly efficient and apparently unbeatable Germans, with whom—it was argued—only a Norway headed by the Nazis could establish peace, all contributed to confuse the situation.[2]

As the war progressed, this confusion diminished. A mythology developed, probably assisted by the jokes themselves (see chap. 12), that the only response of "good Norwegians" to Nazism was resistance. Growing Nazi terrorism and subsequent revelations of Nazi atrocities reinforced understandable tendencies to forget or repress any ambiguity in one's original view, perhaps similar to the way in which time has rearranged many Americans' perceptions of their own initial stance on the conflict in Vietnam.[3]

Not only is the Norwegians' initial confusion understandable, but its very existence makes the role of occupation humor all the more significant. Had these jokes merely manifested an already-established mentality of collective resistance, they would retain their interest as historical documents, but not their status of having influenced that history. Given the hesitation and uncertainty that many Norwegians actually felt, however, the jokes' vital role in encouraging resistance by portraying resisters as positive role models and emphasizing Nazi stupidity and cruelty was crucial, and no doubt kept many of the confused and hesitant from following the more materially rewarding path of joining the National Socialist party.

In addition to denigrating the Norwegian Nazis and German occupiers, the humor disseminated information and attitudes about war developments not available in the censored media. Its wry comments about shortages, restrictions, terrorism, and other wartime hardships raised consciousness as it fanned indignation about the extent of Nazi political, spiritual, and material oppression. In its own time this heightened awareness prevented an unthinking infiltration of Nazism into Norwegian society. To our time, resistance humor brings the legacy of accurate documentation, as it allows us, fifty years later, to gauge the popular view of the propaganda and personalities, hopes and hardships of war-torn Norway. Ultimately this humor tells of the triumph of the human spirit; it demonstrates that even in the face of undernourishment, jail sentences, and death threats, a large segment of the Norwegian population somehow found the will to transcend adversity with a smile.

Folklore Fights
the Nazis

1

The Humor of Contempt

It was Norway's strategic position that prompted Hitler's surprise invasion of the country on 9 April 1940. The German war effort depended on an unhindered supply of Swedish iron ore which could be exported year-round via the ice-free north Norwegian port of Narvik. The capture of Norway also opened the Atlantic to the German Navy and assured German control of the Baltic Sea.

In the early hours of 9 April, the Germans struck several Norwegian cities simultaneously, landing men in Kristiansand, Arendal, Egersund, Stavanger, Bergen, Trondheim, and Narvik. Only the attack on Oslo did not go as planned. The heavy cruiser *Blücher* had entered Oslo Fjord on its way to the capital, but was sunk near Dröbak by the Norwegian guns and torpedoes of Oscarsborg fortress.[1] The resulting delay in invading Oslo allowed the Royal Family and government ministers to escape before German backup forces could land at the Oslo airport.

Determined to remain neutral and unprepared for armed conflict, Norway's military resistance managed to last almost two months, but could not endure. In southern Norway fighting lasted only a matter of weeks, but in Narvik, British and French forces landed and managed to hold the city. Before they could drive the Germans over the border to Sweden, however, they had to withdraw: the magnitude of Hitler's attack on France required their presence there instead. The Allied forces left Narvik in early June; on 7 June the king and his government left Tromsö for exile in London, and Norway was forced to surrender on 9 June.[2]

Shock and confusion characterized the period following the invasion and capitulation. The Norwegian campaign made the Germans look competent and powerful while the Allies appeared disorganized and impotent. British troops had come to help Norway, but, lacking training and proper equipment, their efforts proved futile; even before their precipitous and disastrous withdrawal from Narvik, they had left the towns of Åndalsnes and Namsos in flames.[3]

Preinvasion opinion had run high that no foreign power, including Britain, should be allowed to compromise Norwegian neutrality. On that very basis Foreign Minister Halvdan Koht had as recently as 6 April rejected a British plan to mine Norwegian ports in order to stop the German transport of Swedish ore. He also pointed out that of twenty-one notes of protest sent to foreign governments, the largest number had gone to England.[4] Though it was more or less tacitly understood that Norway would not fight against Britain, Germany appeared to many to be the less likely to threaten Norwegian neutrality,[5] a position the Germans took pains to emphasize in their official invasion-day memo to the Norwegian government. Claiming support for Norway's ardent desire to be protected from war on her own soil, the memo blamed Britain's 8 April mining of Norway's coastal waters for violating Norwegian neutrality and for inviting Germany's retaliatory invasion.[6]

Contrary to romanticized reports that Norwegians spontaneously and unanimously resisted the German invasion, opinion was divided during the summer of 1940 and included strong sentiment for collaboration with the occupiers along with only the early stirrings of resistance.[7] It was in this climate that the first occupation jokes began to circulate. The exile of the king and the government to England had put an end to the possibility of neutrality, and the government had seemingly bound its fate to the side least likely to win. Britain's poor performance during the fighting and suspicions that she had drawn Norway into the war did little to enhance her image.

In contrast to the atmosphere of despair and uncertainty engendered by these circumstances, occupation humor projected conviction and certainty in its venting of unmitigated hatred for the invaders and for their Norwegian collaborators.

> Kan du si meg forskjellen mellom nazistene og en bötte mökk?—Bötta. [Larsen, Schou-Sörensen][8]
> (Do you know the difference between the Nazis and a bucket of manure?—The bucket.)

It told in no uncertain terms of the rage provoked by the sight of the green-clad German soldiers.

> Nordmennene er blitt farveblinde. De ser rödt når de ser grönt. [Schou-Sörensen, Christerson][9]
> (Norwegians have become color blind. They see red when they see green.)

This chapter will sample some of the themes and mechanisms of this early humor of contempt and consider how it reflected and helped shape the changing opinion.

Asserting widespread popular aversion to Hitler's adulation of the Aryan race, one joke claimed:

> Ingen vil höre radio lenger, de spiller bare "Arier". [Ellingsen]
> (No one wants to listen to the radio any more; all they play is *Arier* [wordplay meaning both "operatic arias" and "Aryans"].)

Puns such as this one dominate Norway's anti-Nazi humor as do formulations similar to the "Saddam Hussein = So damn insane" puns popular during the 1991 Gulf War.[10] Typical is the following one recorded by Schou-Sörensen about the hated and feared German Nazi propaganda minister Joseph Goebbels (1897–1945) whose name rhymes with the Norwegian word for "cad," "delinquent," or "vandal": Göbbels = Pöbbels. Another wordplay termed the barracks built for the German soldiers *pakkhus;* i.e., houses for "riffraff" or "trash."[11]

A more extended pun employed the image of washing.

> Tyskerne har tatt fra oss all sepen fordi de trenger så meget til å renvaske seg med, og til å bakvaske engelskmennene, men det gjör ingenting for vi skummer allikevel. [Schou-Sörensen]
> (The Germans have taken all our soap because they need so much to *renvaske seg* ["wash themselves clean," i.e., clear their names; restore their reputations] and to *bakvaske* ["backwash," i.e., "slander"] the English. But it makes no difference, for we're still foaming [i.e., at the mouth with anger].)[12]

The joke alludes not only to the Germans' postinvasion propaganda campaign designed to justify their own actions and to impugn the British war effort,[13] but also reflects a basic reason for the Norwegians' hatred of their occupiers, namely the shortages caused by their presence.[14] Memoirs from the period describe the galling effect of

> having to watch [the occupiers] walk in streets that were ours, swagger around our shops and send home goods we needed for ourselves, paid for by money they had taken from us. [Kuhnle 1945, 83]

On 19 August 1942 the diarist Greta Dahl comments: "The soldiers here are fat as pigs. When they go home on vacation, they lose weight in a hurry." This common observation inspired the single most widespread item of wartime humor, published by the illegal newspaper *Hvepsen* ("The wasp"—so-called for its intention of "stinging" the Nazis) in December 1940 accompanied by the following text:

> Below is a drawing that clearly characterizes recent developments. Seen the CORRECT way, the picture shows the German soldier on April 9th. Turn the picture upside down and you see the typical German soldier in December 1940:[15]

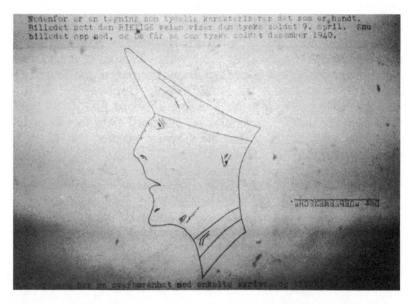

Seen *right side up:* the German soldier as he appeared on 9 April 1940; *upside down:* the way he looked by December 1940. From *Hvepsen,* December 1940.

At the same time Greta Dahl realizes the cause of the occupiers' apparent greed. "Here they get all the things they've had to do without for years in Germany" (22 November 1940). Understandable or not, the shortages of food, fuel, and fiber created hardship and ill will. It also aroused such a flourish of anecdotes and jokes that they require their own chapter (see chap. 8).

THE COLD SHOULDER

To express their anger, many Norwegians treated the occupiers with undisguised contempt, a circumstance the humor repeatedly reflected and encouraged.

On an Oslo street a German soldier stopped a passerby to ask the way to a certain office. Without looking at the soldier, and with disdain in his voice, the man replied he did not know. Incensed by the Norwegian's haughty tone, the German exploded:

"All you Norwegians are shameless in your manner toward us Germans. You treat us as if we were dogs!"

"We do not treat our dogs in a shameless manner," said the Norwegian. [Olav and Myklebust 1942, 9]

Because public transit brought Norwegians into close contact with both their German occupiers and the Norwegian collaborators, it provided a uniquely suitable forum for the expression of anti-Nazi sympathies, as the following joke demonstrates:

To anleggsarbeidere kommer på toget mellom Oslo og Drammen. I en liten kupe er det to ledige plasser. I dören heiler den ene av arbeiderene. Passasjerene ser meget brydd ut. Da snur han seg til sin kamerat og sier: "Kom kal," her er bare jössinger!!" [Ellingsen]

(Two railroad workers get on the train between Oslo and Drammen. A small compartment has two vacant seats. In the doorway one of the workers gives the Nazi salute. The passengers look really uncomfortable. Then he turns to his companion and says: "It's ok. They're all *Jössings!*")

The term Jössing denoted those opposed to Nazism and originated among Nazi sympathizers as a derisive term. It derived from the Jössing Fjord (near Stavanger) where the British had boarded the German ship *Altmark* on 16 February 1940 and released some English prisoners of war.[16] The editor of Sweden's pro-Nazi paper *Sverige fritt* (Sweden free) subsequently coined the word "Jössings" to designate the "cowardly Norwegians who didn't shoot the British in Jössingfjord," and it became the usual way for Nazi sympathizers to vilify their antagonists as pro-British traitors. Those to whom they applied the appellation, however, quickly defused its original negative connotation by adopting the name and using it with pride.[17] They also provided it with their own content, as Schou-Sörensen records.

Jössing = *J*eg *Ö*nsker *S*taten *S*tyrt *I*följe *N*orges *G*runnlov
(Jössing = I want the state ruled according to Norway's Constitution.)

Rather than being pro-English traitors, the Jössings saw themselves as opponents of the Nazi "New Order," who desired a return of the prewar regime and of Norwegian independence.

To air their hostility, the Jössings adopted the habit of changing their seats on public transportation if a German soldier or Norwe-

Passengers avoiding sitting next to a German soldier. From Finn Bö, *Forbuden frukt*, 1946. Reprinted with permission from Aschehoug Forlag, Oslo, Norway.

gian Nazi sat down next to them. In an effort to discourage this anti-Nazi display, the authorities placed placards on the trams proclaiming that

> Passengers who demonstrate against the German military or members of the NS [Nazi party] by changing places will be expelled at the nearest station. [Bö 1946, 46]

The Jössings had a ready response to this tactic, too: now they refused to sit inside the carriage, preferring the discomfort of standing on the tram's overcrowded back platform to risking sitting beside a German or NS member. In retaliation Nazi authorities issued new placards, this time announcing that it was "Forbidden to stand as long as seats are available," and threatening that "Those who do not obey will be asked to leave the tram and subjected to punishment" (Bö 1946, 55).

The clandestine press openly encouraged the Jössings' display of contempt, known as *isfronten* (the ice-front).

> What the Germans suffer most from here in Norway is the coldness they feel from the people, and their exclusion from contact. Let them

Det er

FORBUDT

å stå i vognen så lenge det finnes sitteplasser. De som ikke etterkommer påbudet blir fra idag bortvist fra vognen og straffet.

———

Das Stehen in dem Wagen

IST VERBOTEN

solange es noch Sitzplätze gibt. Wer dem Gebote nicht Folge leistet, muss den Wagen verlassen und wird bestraft.

Oslo, 4. mai 1944.

Politipresidenten i Oslo.

A bilingual Nazi poster threatening punishment for not sitting when seats are available. From Finn Bö, *Forbuden frukt*, 1946. Reprinted with permission from Aschehoug Forlag, Oslo, Norway.

feel this chill to their very marrow. [*Vi vil oss et land*, (We want for ourselves a country) 1 October 1940]

Humor about the "ice-front," meanwhile, emphasized its ubiquity, portraying it as a characteristic of everyone, from very young to very old.[18]

> The four year old daughter of Inge Ringnes [one of Norway's most famous pianists] was traveling from Slemdal to Gulleråsen. Seeing that one section of the tram had only Germans in it, she stood in the doorway and commented loudly, "Well, we certainly can't sit in here." [Schou-Sörensen]

> Invasion day incident: A Nazi officer brushed past a little gray-haired, aristocratic-looking old lady. She raised her cane and knocked off his hat, berating him loudly for showing so little respect toward his elders. Embarrassed, he apologized, but she continued her tirade until he fled. The little old lady went on about her business chuckling to herself, "Well, we'll each have to fight this war as best we can; that's the fourth hat I've knocked into the mud this morning." [*Decorah posten*, (The Decorah post, a widely circulated Norwegian-American newspaper) 6 June 1941][19]

Emphasizing how thoroughly anti-German sentiment had permeated Norwegian culture, the little boy in the following anecdote automatically adopts a derogatory term as a generic noun for the German soldier:

> En dame kom inn på trikken med sin lille sönn. Det var trangt på trikken og vanskelig å få plass. En tysk offiser hjalp den lille gutten til rette. Hvorpå gutten ser henrykt på sin mor og sier: "Det var et snilt svinebest det, mama." [Schou-Sörensen][20]
> (A woman got on the tram with her little son. It was crowded and hard to find a seat. When a German officer helped the little boy get settled, the boy looked ecstatically at his mother and said: "That was a nice *svinebest* [brutal, ruthless person], mamma.")

The child had certainly not been taught to expect any sort of humanity, let alone kindness, from the occupiers, and his attitude provides both the intended humorous effect while giving an inadvertent glimpse into the loneliness that duty in the North must have brought many a German soldier. Though humor tends only to show the Norwegians' hatred of the occupiers, a 24 December 1940 entry in Greta Dahl's diary indicates that behind the overtly demonstrated cold shoulder treatment, some felt genuine sympathy for the human being inside the uniform.

It is so sad to see the Germans' unhappy faces. It's as though they're begging for mercy. . . . This will be a Christmas of doing without, but the poor Germans are even worse off than we are.[21]

While individual Norwegians may have empathized with the difficult position of the German soldiers, a growing number followed the developing normative pressure not to show it, and Jössing humor, itself a form of propaganda, also reflected the politically correct cold shoulder directive.[22]

Politics and Daily Life

Some humor moved beyond the personal sphere to reflect more critical political issues, such as Hitler's usurping of territories by invading Poland on 1 September 1939; Norway and Denmark on 9 April 1940; Luxembourg, the Netherlands, Belgium, and France on 10 May 1940:

Når en simpel mann stjeler kalles det tyveri.
"   "   fin   "   "   "   "   kleptomani.
"   et land   "   "   "   Germany. [Schou-Sörensen]
(When a poor man steals, it's called thievery.
When a man of means steals, it's called kleptomani(a).
When a country steals, it's called Germany.)

Repeating the kleptomania image but adding a play on the World War II fates of the other two Scandinavian countries, another witticism told:

Sverige skal heretter hete Transitania.
Danmark "   "   "   Underdania.
Tyskland "   "   "   Kleptomania. [Schou-Sörensen]
(Sweden will hereafter be named Transitania.
Denmark "   "   "   "   Underdania.
Germany "   "   "   "   Kleptomania.)

Schou-Sörensen explains that *Transitania* refers to Sweden's allowing Germany to transport soldiers through Sweden to Narvik, while *Underdania* (cf., *underdanig* = "subservient") refers to Denmark's initial policy of negotiating with the occupiers, instead of resisting, in an effort to preserve peace.[23]

The theme of Hitler's hegemony also appears in a popular punning riddle which asked:

> Hvorfor Hitler bruker Brylcrem? Fordi han vil ha Schweiz. [Schou-Sörensen, Larsen, Ellingsen]
> (Why does Hitler use Brylcreem [a popular men's hair treatment]? Because he wants to have *Schweiz* ["Switzerland" but also a homonym of *sveis,* i.e., "well-groomed hair"].)

The following more extended joke also attained broad circulation:

> To damer sitter på en kafé i sentrum. En tysk offiser henvender seg til den ene og ber om å få ta en stol ved hennes bord.
> Hun svarer ikke.
> Spörsmålet blir gjentatt.
> Intet svar.
> Den andre damen spör hvorfor hun ikke svarer.
> "Det er vel ikke noe å svare på. Når de har tatt hele landet, kan han vel ta den stolen også." [Ellingsen, Olav and Myklebust 1942]
> (Two ladies are sitting at a cafe downtown. A German officer comes up to one of them and asks if he might take a chair at her table.
> She doesn't answer.
> The question is repeated.
> No answer.
> The other lady asks why she doesn't answer.
> "There's nothing to answer, is there? When they've taken our whole country, he can certainly take that chair too.")

The next joke similarly commented on the tendency of Nazi and Fascist regimes to take what was not theirs:

> En jössing kom til en nazist som hadde bilder på veggen av Jesus, Hitler og Mussolini. Jesus hang mellom de to.
> -Jaså, sa jössingen-er dette de to röverne som han ble hengt mellom? [*Karikaturens Krigs-humor* n.d., 22][24]
> (A Jössing was visiting the home of a Nazi. On the wall were pictures of Jesus, Hitler and Mussolini, with Jesus in the middle.
> "Oh," said the Jössing, "are those the two robbers he was hung between?")

The inner workings of Norwegian politics also supplied grist for the humor mill. On 25 September 1940 the Hitler-appointed German Nazi party veteran Josef Terboven (1898–1945) took exclusive charge of Norway's government.[25] As his first Official Act (Stats-akt) he replaced the Storting (Parliament) and government minis-ters with thirteen mostly Nazi appointees, to be known as the Konstituerte statsråder (Constituted commissioners). Folk wit not only dubbed this group the Prostituerte statsråder (Prostituted commissioners), but also publicized the group's salary as 18,000 crowns—"plus a supplement of 30 pieces of silver" (Schou-Sörensen). The allusion to Judas' betrayal of Christ for that same amount leaves no doubt about the regard in which the Jössings held these commissioners.[26]

Though enough humor specifically motivated by actual war de-velopments exists to warrant three entire chapters (9, 10, and 11), even more often it is the basic concerns of daily life that permeate the occupation jokes.

Vi får flesk til jul allikevel,—svina blir i landet. [Schou-Sörensen]
(We'll be having pork for Christmas after all,—the swine [i.e., Ger-mans] will still be here.)

Wartime humor tended to express itself in the already estab-lished themes, rhythms, and motifs of a given locality. In Bergen, for example, the tjuaguttene (street urchins) occupy a prominent role in all kinds of humor, in the occupation jokes as well.

Nu kan ikke tjuaguttene i Bergen leke krig lenger. For ingen vil være tysker. [Christerson]
(Now the street urchins in Bergen can't play war anymore. No one wants to be a German.)

En tysk offiser som har hört at tjuaguttene i Bergen gir så rappe svar, spör en: "Har du sett en bil full av apekatter kjöre forbi?"
"Ka hva det då? Har du dotten a'?" [Christerson][27]
(A German officer who has heard about the sassiness of the street urchins in Bergen asks one of them: "Have you seen a car full of monkeys drive past?"
"What's the deal? Did ya fall off?")

Humor from Trondheim frequently plays on the linguistic features of Trönder dialect,[28] and occupation jokes are no exception.

To små gutter i Trondheim gikk på gaten og pratet om Hitler, etc. Da sa den ene: Ja, dersom æ hadde jebursda'n min i samme måned som'n Hitler, så ville æ heller gå å hæng mæ. [Schou-Sörensen]
(Two little boys in Trondheim were walking down the street talking

about Hitler, etc. One of them said, "Well, if I had my birthday the same month as Hitler, I'd rather go hang myself.")

Not captured in the translation is the abundant æ-sound characteristic of the Trönder dialect which makes "I," "hang," and "myself" rhyme.

> I Trondheim får man bare kjöpt halve flasker på Vinmonopolet for der har de ikke "heil å sell." [Schou-Sörensen][29]
> (In Trondheim you can only buy half-bottles at the Vinmonopol [liquor store] for they have no *heil å sell* ["whole (ones) to sell," which in the Trönder dialect with its characteristic dropping of the final syllable is a homonym of the Nazi greeting *Heil og sæl*].)

Having considered some general traits of occupation humor, we move on to one of its most ubiquitous modes: wishful thinking.

DELIGHTING IN DEATH AND DESTRUCTION

Folklore frequently indulges in wishful thinking and Norwegian wartime humor is no exception. The Jössings particularly enjoyed imagining the occupiers' annihilation.

> Det ringte opp en til det kontoret som plasserte tyskere i privathjem julaften og sa han kunne ta noen hos seg. Ja, hvor mange? 1, 2, 5, 10? Enda flere? Hvor mange kan De ta da? Jeg kan ta alle sammen jeg. Hvem er De da? Jeg er Faen jeg. [Schou-Sörensen]
> (Someone phoned the office in charge of placing Germans in private homes for Christmas Eve and offered to take a few.
> "Well, how many? 1, 2, 5, 10? Even more? How many can you take?"
> "I can take them all."
> "And what is your name?"
> "This is the Devil speaking.")

> Tormodseter ble spurt om han ville begrave en tysker. Han er litt döv, la hånden til öret og spurte: Hva, en tysker? Gjerne alle sammen. [Schou-Sörensen, dated October 1942]
> (Tormodseter [a local minister] was asked if he would bury a German. He is a little hard of hearing and, placing his hand behind his ear, answered: "What, a German? Sure, I'd be glad to bury all of them.")

Suspected of muttering anti-German thoughts to himself as he walked along the street, a man was brought in for questioning by the Gestapo.

"I am out of work," he explained, "and I was only telling myself that I'd rather work for ten thousand Germans than for one Englishman."

So pleased were the Germans by this reply that they offered to help find him a job. What was his trade?

"Oh," he answered. "I'm a grave-digger." [Olav and Myklebust 1942, 30]

Much of the occupation humor arose as spontaneous reactions to specific situations. The following anecdote, for example, came in the wake of the clergy's break with the Quisling government beginning in February 1941 and their subsequent replacement by Nazi ministers:[30]

I Ullern menighet ble sokneprest Smith avsatt av nasi-myndighetene eller la ned sitt embede. En Blessing-Dahle ble innsatt som sokneprest av nasistene, men få eller ingen gikk til hans gudstjenester.

Organisten i Ullern kirke, Geburg Aasland, var blind, og kunne vanskelig annet gjöre enn å bli sittende på sin orgelkragg. Det ble fortalt, at som han intonerte skulle han på orgelet ha streifet innom: "Hadde jeg vinger så ville jeg fly. . . ." [Mads Almaas, letter to author, 17 January 1993][31]

(The Nazis replaced Pastor Smith of the Ullern congregation with the Nazi minister Blessing-Dahle, but almost no one went to his services. Ullern church organist Geburg Aasland was blind and had no choice but to keep his job at the church. They say that when he played the prelude, however, he'd include the song: "If I had wings, I would fly away. . . .")

While this incident may very well have happened just as reported, other items are jokes that use factual circumstances merely as a point of departure. The following item, for example, reflects the Nazi system of conscripted labor which forced workers from the occupied countries to take work in German factories in order to maintain their production levels in the absence of German citizens who had left to fight at the front. It also alludes to a complaint Hitler actually received from the German Nazi army commander Hermann Goering (1893–1946) about the decline in German discipline.

Hitler og Göring er uenige om samholdet i Tyskland. Det blir foretatt noen pröver på fabrikker. Hitler leverer en revolver til en arbeider og sier: "Skyt 5 mann!!"

"Nei, min Förer, det kan jeg ikke, det er mine arbeidskamerater." Ved neste fabrikk gjentar de pröven. Mannen, som får revolveren, skyter 5 mann som han blir bedt om.

"Hvem er De da mannen min?" spör Hitler.
"Jeg?—Jeg er Olsen fra Norge!" [Ellingsen]
(Hitler and Goering disagree about the solidarity of support in Germany. Some tests are made at factories. Hitler hands a revolver to a worker and says: "Shoot 5 men!!"
"No, my Führer, I can't do that, they are my fellow-workers."
At the next factory they repeat the test. The man given the revolver shoots 5 men as he is asked.
"Who are you, my good man?" Hitler asks.
"Me? I'm Mr. Olsen from Norway!")

No less grotesquely, the following two items (one a constructed joke and the other an anecdote possibly based on an actual incident) also express Jössing delight in the occupiers' death:

En jössing möter en god venn. Han ser på vennens stövler og sier: "Det var noen fine stövler du har!"
"Ja, jeg tok knekken på en tysker og tok stövlene hans. Det skulle du også gjöre."
En uke gikk, og de to vennene möttes igjen. No hadde vennen også fine stövler. På spörsmål hvor han hadde vært så lenge, svarer vennen: "Ja, du skjönner jeg måtte pröve 18 par." [Ellingsen]
(A Jössing meets a good friend. He looks at the friend's boots and says, "Those are terrific boots you've got there!"
"Yes, I killed a German and took his boots. You should too."
A week went by and the two friends met again. Now the friend also had a fine pair of boots. To the question of where he had been for so long, he answered: "Well, you see, I had to try 18 pair before I found these.")

Det ble vist på kino hvordan engelskmennene bombet i Tyskland: barnehjem. Hvorpå en roper höyt: Det er riktig, ta dem mens de er små. [Schou-Sörensen]
(A film was being shown at the movies of the English bombing Germany: orphanages. Someone in the audience calls out: "That's right, get them while they're young.")

In addition to surveying some typical mechanics, themes, and categories of wartime humor, this chapter has considered the confusion and despair actually felt by the majority of Norwegians in the wake of the German invasion. This confusion finds little expression in the decisively anti-Nazi tone and sentiment of the emerging humor that began both shaping and being shaped by the once neutral nation's growing pro-British and anti-German opinion. Beyond the contempt for the Nazis and German occupiers in general, occupation humor heaped particular hatred upon the Nazi leaders Adolf Hitler and Vidkun Quisling, as chapter 2 will show.

2

Quisling and Hitler Jokes

VIDKUN QUISLING (1887–1945): WHAT'S IN A NAME?

Because of his negotiations with Adolf Hitler for the German invasion of his own country, the name of Vidkun Quisling has internationally come to mean "collaborator with one's country's enemies, traitor."[1] Quisling had founded Norway's Nazi party in 1933 and served as its leader since that time. The party never achieved much representation in the Storting (Parliament) and was decidedly on the wane as the 1930s drew to a close, weakened by election defeats and internal conflict.[2]

In December 1939 Quisling went to Germany and obtained an audience with Adolf Hitler. Quisling emphasized to the German leader the significance for Germany of having a base of support in Norway and claimed that Britain already had an agreement with Norway for free passage in the event of war. Asserting that Norway had fallen under the influence of Marxists and Jews, Quisling proposed that his Nazi party take over the government by means of a German-assisted coup. Hitler promised Quisling's party financial support, but avoided making any commitment with regard to a Norwegian invasion, though immediately after the visit he did mandate that the German defense staff study possible operations to be taken against Norway. In March 1940 as Hitler made final plans for the invasion, he neither assigned Quisling a role in it nor did he inform him in advance of the attack (Kersaudy 1987). On his own initiative Quisling forced his way to the microphones of the Norwegian Broadcasting Company on the evening of 9 April as soon as the Germans were in possession of Oslo. He declared himself prime minister and foreign minister of the new "National Government" and ordered that all resistance to the German occupiers cease. To most Norwegian listeners it must have seemed that the German plan was that Quisling would be Hitler's man in Oslo (Andenæs, Riste, and Skodvin 1989), and Quisling propaganda did

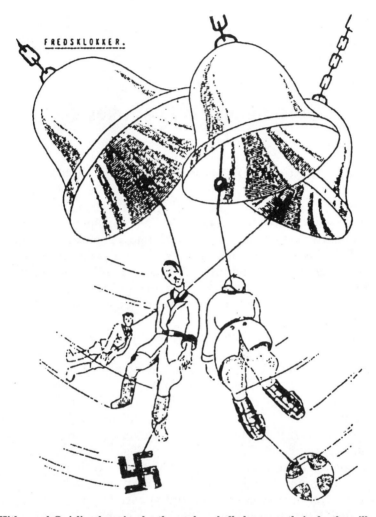

Hitler and Quisling hanging by the neck as bell clappers; their deaths will allow the "Bells of Peace" to ring. From *London-nytt*, 30 December 1943. Artist: Per Alveberg, who had been arrested one month before it appeared for previous subversive drawings.

its best to promote this notion. Folk wit, too, tended to portray greater accord between Quisling and Hitler than actually existed. In point of fact, however, Quisling's National Government enjoyed only a very brief reign, being dismissed after a mere six days when the Germans saw the degree of resentment it aroused among the majority of Norwegians.

Hitler needed calm in order to keep the wheels of industry and political administration turning in support of the German war effort. Toward this end, on 19 April, he appointed the seasoned German Nazi official Josef Terboven as Reichskommissar and sent him to Oslo to straighten out the situation. During the first part of the summer, negotiations proceeded for a National Council (riksråd) to govern Norway. This plan had the advantage that Norwegian citizens could avoid being directly governed by either Quisling or Terboven, and it provided a body that would look after Norwegian interests and put her on an equal footing with Germany. The plan called for the Reichskommissar to withdraw and for subsequent relations between Germany and Norway to be handled through diplomatic channels. Terboven had plans of his own, however; he intended to create a new NS that would exclude Quisling and through which he could obtain power over the riksråd.

Terboven succeeded in getting the Storting to agree with the establishment of the riksråd, but had considerably more trouble getting them to depose the exiled government and the king. Finally on 27 June, though, a parliamentary majority moved to request that Haakon abdicate. In a widely circulated speech, the king refused (cf., chap. 4). As the summer progressed, Norwegian opinion gradually shifted toward stronger support for the king and against the riksråd.

Suddenly on 25 September, the entire situation changed: Terboven proclaimed a New Order; he declared that the king and the government were deposed, that all political parties except the NS were illegal, and that negotiations for a riksråd had failed. In its place he appointed konstituerte statsråder (cf., chap. 1) drawn mostly from Nazi ranks, who would report directly to him. Though Quisling remained the head of the Nazi party and in 1942 appeared to be appointed the head of government receiving the title of minister president, Terboven actually continued to be in charge of occupied Norway throughout the war, answerable only to Hitler.

Though Quisling thus had far less power than popularly supposed, his name gained rapid international circulation.[3] The February 1942 issue of the underground newspaper Eidsvoll (named for the place where Norway's constitution had been drafted in 1814), sardonically reports "with pride"

that no Norwegian's name has previously swept the globe as has Quisling's. Hardly a person in Australia, Alaska or Siberia remains unaware of the Quisling name. Street urchins around the world use it as an insult; linguists study the new words created from his name; Churchill has even characterized the great Mussolini as the "Italian Quisling." [*Eidsvoll*, no. 1, 1942]

A related anecdote told that a Frenchman asked a Norwegian colleague: "What's the name of your Quisling? Ours is named Laval"[4] (Bö 1946, 34). Ragnvald Blix[5] captured this elevation of "Quisling" from name to concept (as well as Quisling's actual lack of individual identity let alone power) in his January 1944 cartoon, one of the best-known items of Norwegian occupation humor, captioned "In Audience with Hitler."

"Quisling in an audience with Hitler." "I am [a] Quisling." "And what's your name?" Artist: Ragnvald Blix (Stig Höök), Göteborgs Handels-och Sjöfarts-tidning, January 1944, republished in Blix, *De fem årene*, 1945. Reprinted here with permission of Gyldendal Forlag, Oslo, Norway.

Focused on the goal of conducting a Nazi revolution in Norway, Quisling and his party viewed themselves as the protectors of Norwegian interests against foreign control, whether British or German. Their ultimate aim was Norwegian independence.[6] In order to benefit from the assistance of the Norwegian Nazi party, Germany initially gave lip service to these ends, but never lost sight of the true goal of incorporating Norway into the greater German Reich.

Meanwhile Quisling and his party established in the "New Norway" institutions based on those in Hitler's Germany, including a Hird, an armed guard recruited to protect Nazi speakers at public meetings, not unlike the German Brown Shirts. Because of these activities, the majority of the Norwegian population along with Jössing humor regarded the Norwegian Nazis as agents of the occupiers and therefore to be despised. Occupation humor directed its contempt especially at the Norwegian Nazi leader and expressed itself in rather earthy tones, associating the whistling sound of Quisling's name with the words *fisling* (farting) and the *hvisling* (hissing) of a snake. Jokes extend the scatological theme by suggesting that his name was literally "lower than shit" and demonstrating people's refusal to bear it or, by implication, any part of his ideology.

> En bonde kom opp i departementet og sa at han gjerne vilde bytte navn.
> "Hvad heter De da?"
> "Vidkun Lortbekken."
> "Hm. Ja, da er det forståelig nok at De gjerne vil ha et annet navn. Og hvad hadde De tenkt å kalle Dem i stedet da?"
> "Jeg hadde tenkt å kalle meg *Ola* Lortbekken." [Bö 1946, 35; variant: Kristiansen 1945, 15]
> (A farmer came to the Department and said he wanted to change his name.
> "What is your name then?"
> "Vidkun Shitcreek."
> "Hm. Yes, I can certainly see why you'd want to have another name. What did you plan on being called instead?"
> "I was planning to take the name *Ola* Shitcreek.")

Like the Gulf War's "Saddam Hussein = So damn insane" formulation mentioned in chapter 1, wordplays on Quisling's name made the rounds. The name's similarity to the word *usling* (scoundrel) attained particular popularity: *Vidkun Quisling = Vidkjent Usling,* i.e., "widely known scoundrel" (Larsen, Schou-Sörensen). Ellingsen has a slightly more elaborate derision of his title, transforming *Vidkund Quisling fra Nasjonal Samling* (Vidkund Quisling of the Nazi party) into *Vidkjent Usling fra sans og samling* (Wellknown scoundrel who is out of his mind).[7] The Quisling/*usling* wordplay also underlies a Blix drawing from December 1940.

The newspaper *Ringerikeblad* (Ringerike news) even managed to get the "Quisling/*usling*" wordplay into a front-page banner headline, identifying the Nazi party leader as *Vidkun ¾uisling.* Professing himself innocent of evil intent, the editor Oscar Hassel-

The boy defaces a Quisling poster to read "scoundrel" and receives "Norwegian Justice." Artist: Ragnvald Blix (Stig Höök) Göteborgs Handels- och Sjöfarts-tidning, December 1940, republished in Blix, *De fem årene*, 1945. Reprinted here with permission from Gyldendal Forlag, Oslo, Norway.

knippe disarmed the local Nazi Press director's subsequent threats to clean out "that nest of Jössings at *Ringerikeblad*" by inviting him for a visit during which he coolly demonstrated how easily such an "error" could occur given the storage of rarely used typefaces like *Q* and *Z* near the foreign characters and fractions (Hasselknippe, letter to author, 1 September 1989).

The association of *usling* with Quisling's name received added, though inadvertent, impetus when the Nazi treasury issued a new two-crown note called a "Quisling"; folk wit immediately dubbed the one-crown note an *usling,* so that two *uslings* made one *Quisling*—Quisling was twice a scoundrel (Schou-Sörensen).

Besides these new twists, folk wit employed ways both tried-and-true to express contempt for Quisling. The following joke, for example, has attached itself to oppressive leaders around the world since the invention of the postage stamp:

Et rykte forteller at vi skal få nye frimerker med Quislings bilde på, men utsendelsen av disse er utsatt fordi en ikke vet hvilken side en skal spytte på. [Ellingsen]

(Rumor has it that we're getting new stamps bearing Quisling's likeness, but distribution has been delayed because no one knows which side to spit on.)[8]

Like occupation humor in general, Quisling jokes frequently employ the mechanism of wishful thinking, sometimes finding satisfaction in the mere utterance that Quisling might leave.

Hört fra London: Quisling var nylig i Bergen, bodde på Hotell Norge. Da han dro til foredragssalen ropte mengden: "Nå reiser Quisling fra Norge." [Schou-Sörensen]
(Heard from London:[9] Quisling was recently in Bergen and stayed at the Hotell Norway. When he left the hotel to deliver a lecture, the crowd yelled: "Now Quisling is leaving Norway!")

The January 1941 issue of the underground newspaper *Hvepsen* (The Wasp) reported this example:

The Nazi Party has published a calendar which truly can be said to symbolize the New Time.[10] Quisling's picture is on the cover, which it says "MUST BE TORN OFF" to get into the NEW YEAR.

Perhaps the most outspoken wish for Quisling's departure circulated after the death of Propaganda Minister Gulbrand Lunde in an October 1942 auto accident.[11]

Hvorfor flagges det på halvstang? Fordi Vidkun Quisling ikke var med. (Why is the flag flying at half-staff? Because Vidkun Quisling wasn't along.) [Trondheim diary, 17 November 1942]

The Norwegian Judas

Deriving directly from Quisling's negotiations with Hitler, the theme of betrayal is perhaps most characteristic of the Quisling jokes.

Hvet du hvorfor Quisling har reist til Tyskland?
???
For å fornye förerkortet. [Larsen]
(Do you know why Quisling went to Germany?
???
To renew his *förerkort* ["driver's license" and "license to be the *förer* or leader," cf., German Führer].)

Quisling visited Hitler a total of eleven times between 1939 and 1945, far more than most other local "Führers." The trip referred to in this joke may be his December 1940 journey to Berlin to explain away his disappointing performance in recruiting members for the Nazi party. He managed to win new confidence from those in power ("renew his license") by suggesting the formation of a Norwegian fighting force which came to be known as Regiment Nordland.[12] The *förer* wordplay recurs with some frequency in occupation humor because of both Hitler and Quisling's fondness for the vaunted title. Punning on it served to soften the appellation's intimidating specter.[13] Another wordplay emphasizing Quisling's treason told:

> Quisling fikk tittel av landhandler da han solgte Norge. [Schou-Sörensen]
> (For selling his country, Quisling received the title of *landhandler* ["grocer," "country seller," i.e., one who runs a country store, but in this context also "one who sells (out) his country"].

With the Nazis' persistent propaganda lectures as a backdrop, the following widespread joke also employs the traitor theme:

> Quisling kommer inn i foredragssalen. Alle reiser seg, gjör hilsen og sier i kor: "Vi er for Quisling." Quisling bukker, hilser og sier," Jeg er for-Eder." [Larsen, Schou-Sörensen, Slaatto]
> (Quisling enters the auditorium. All rise to their feet, give the Nazi salute and say in chorus: "We are for Quisling."
> Quisling bows, salutes and says, "I am *for Eder*" ["for all of you," but also a homonym of *forræder* = "traitor"].)[14]

Folk wit saw a clear parallel between Quisling and Judas, and references to the "thirty pieces of silver" Judas received for betraying Christ abound in the Quisling jokes.[15] Perhaps the best-known example is the mock stamp produced by the Voss artist Arne Taraldsen in December 1943, depicting Quisling's head in a noose.[16] The stamp's text echoes Björstjerne Björnson's frequently sung 1868 poem of praise to "The Norwegian Sailor": Vår ære og vår makt har hvite seil oss brakt (Our honor and our might have been earned by our sails so white). The stamp's rendition reads: Vanære og forrakt har Quislings færd ham brakt (Dishonor and disdain are the wages of Quisling's reign). The stamp's face value of "30 pieces of silver" eloquently articulates the depth of that disdain (Christerson).[17]

In another Judas allusion, the cover-drawing of Ottar Ramfjord's

Quisling's head in a noose on a mock stamp worth "Thirty pieces of silver," and bearing the text: "Dishonor and disdain are the wages of Quisling's reign." Artist: Arne Taraldsen, distributed by British aircraft, December 1943.

postwar humor collection, *Okkupasjons humor,* depicts Quisling as a butcher preparing to slice up a joint of meat that resembles the map of Norway. Hitler, as his customer, requests a portion worth "thirty pieces of silver."

THE LITTLEST PRESIDENT

Terboven's plans to remove Quisling from Nazi leadership had to yield to pressure from certain powerful individuals in Germany who insisted on Quisling's continued prominence. On 1 February 1942 Quisling's final accession to power occurred amid much staged fanfare at Oslo's Akershus Castle when Terboven undertook his second Official Act (Statsakt) and appointed him Ministerpresident (minister president),[18] responsible for organizing a "National Government" which would function until the end of the war. The press was forced to announce the event with banner headlines and with a jubilant commentary proclaiming: "A new day has dawned for Norway! This is the greatest day in Norwegian history" (Luihn 1960, 86). Quisling installed himself in the Royal Palace and issued a decree that as Ministerpresident he now possessed the authority which the Constitution had formerly accorded to both the king and the entire Storting (Parliament).

Deflating the bombast, Greta Dahl comments:

> February 3, 1942: The Norwegian flag has been flying at the city hall, telegraph building and market place for three days now. It was raised on Sunday when Quisling became the German Prime Minister of Norway. Everyone was supposed to participate, but that was a fiasco, as just about everyone stayed home. A few cowardly souls went to the movie theater where speakers were rigged up to broadcast the farce from Akershus. Now we're just waiting for our men to be called up. I've heard that all boys over the age of 15 years will be sent to Germany for Work Service, and all men between 18 and 55 will be drafted. It all seems so unreal, I have refused to believe it as long as possible. Uff, sometimes things look so dark and dreary.[19]

Folk wit tried to dispel this despondence, and—recognizing the truth that Quisling's new appointment was mere window dressing[20]—developed its own version of Quisling's strange-sounding new title. Calling him Minstepresident (littlest/least president), Jössings soon devised numerous witticisms and anecdotes to deride his inflated self-image.

Quisling, as the butcher, prepares to slice off a piece of Norway for Hitler in exchange for "thirty pieces of silver." From the cover of Ottar Ramfjord *Okkupasjonshumor,* 1945. Reprinted here with the permission of Lærdal Medical, Stavanger, Norway.

Ministerpresidenten har prostrata, hans nye tittel er ministerpissetrengten. [Schou-Sörensen]
(The Minister President has prostate trouble: his new title is *ministerpissetrengten* [Minister Needs to Pee].)

En nordmann, en svenske og en danske kom sammen og snakket om hvem som var flinkest til å lappe folk igjen. Dansken sa: "Jeg kuttet en gang armene av en fyr hjemme i Danmark og satte nye på, og nå er han verdens beste bokser!" "Jamen jeg har kuttet benene av en fyr, jeg. Og nå når jeg har satt nye på, er han blitt verdens beste fotballspiller," sa svensken. Så sa nordmannen: Alt det der er bare blåbær, hjemme i Norge kuttet jeg hodet av en fyr, og satte i stedet kålhode på, og nå er han Norges ministerpresident!" [Christerson]
(A Norwegian, a Swede and a Dane were talking about which of them was best at patching people back together. The Dane said, "I once cut the arms off a guy back in Denmark and attached new ones, now he is the best boxer in the world!" "Well, I cut the legs off a fellow and after I attached new ones he became the best football player in the world," said the Swede. Then the Norwegian said, "That's nothing. Back in Norway I cut the head off a guy and replaced it with a cabbage and now he is Norway's Minister President!")

While folk wit saw through the ruse, Quisling regarded his elevation to minister president as just the chance he needed to achieve his plan for a Riksting (National Assembly), by which Norway's most important organizations were to be subordinated to the Nazi party in order to form the basis of a new corporate state. This would give him sufficient power to achieve the peace treaty he sought with Germany that would recognize his regime as sovereign and independent of the occupying power. Though Quisling persisted in this hope until 1944–45, Hitler rejected it already in the fall of 1942, when Quisling's attempts to reform the organizations of teachers, clergy, laborers, and other groups by replacing their leaders with Nazi commissioners, resulted in the wholesale resignations of their memberships. German leaders now wrote Quisling off as a political failure and rebuffed all further attempts to discuss the Riksting, a circumstance captured in the following rhyme recorded by Ellingsen:

1942 Riksting/1943 Ingenting (1942 Riksting/1943 Ingenting [*Ingenting* = "Nothing"].)

In the wake of this failure, Quisling's policies became increasingly desperate, and in October and November of 1942 he began venting his rage at the Jews. The property of all fourteen hundred

Jews in Norway was to be confiscated, and all male Jews over fifteen years of age were to be sent to concentration camps. Unlike Denmark's Jews, who through early warning and widespread popular assistance largely managed to escape before being rounded up, 50 percent of Norwegian Jews never returned. While in Denmark, the government, public opinion, civil service and administration obstructed German plans to eradicate the Jews, in Norway the Jews' lack of cultural and social integration into the non-pluralistic society seems to explain why the Norwegian Jewish community suffered the greatest losses of any Scandinavian country (Abrahamsen 1991, 1–6). Indeed the Jössing resistance movement seems to have shown no more mercy toward their plight than did the Nazi party (Christensen 1988, 107), a conclusion to which Jössing humor also leads, given its lack of attention to the subject. Since tension over unresolved issues is a primary mechanism of humor, the absence of the Jews or their situation in these jokes suggests lacking concern about them.[21]

The growing desperation and madness of Quisling's policies whether in persecuting the Jews or other groups is suggested in the prominence of insane asylum jokes in which Quisling appears as the central character.[22] One proposes dementia as a necessary prerequisite to showing Quisling any respect.

På et sinnssykeasyl ventet man en dag besök av Quisling, som skulde komme og inspisere. Pasientene stod oppstilt på geled og hadde fått beskjed om at de skulde strekke hånden opp og rope "Heil og sæl".

"Föreren" kom, og alt gikk etter oppskriften inntil han kom til siste mann i rekken. Han lot plutselig være å hilse.

"Hvorfor hilser ikke De?" spurte Quisling.

"Nei, jeg er ikke gærn, jeg," svarte mannen, "jeg er vokter her." [Bö 1946, 22]

(An insane asylum was awaiting a visit of inspection by Quisling. The patients stood in rows at attention and had been instructed to lift their right arms and shout, *"Heil og sæl."*

The "Führer" arrived, and everything went according to plan until he got to the last man in the row. This man was suddenly not saluting.

"Why aren't you saluting?" Quisling demanded.

"I'm not crazy," the man answered, "I'm the custodian.")

Another asylum joke suggests that Quisling himself is going insane.

Major Quisling once visited an insane asylum. Drawing an inmate into conversation, the Nazi puppet boasted, "I am Vidkun Quisling!"

"Never heard of him."

"What! Have you never heard of Vidkun Quisling, the greatest Norwegian since King Harald Fair Hair?"[23]
"Take it easy, old man," said the inmate sympathetically. "That's
how it started with me too." [Olav and Myklebust 1942, 27]

Finally, in a rather tasteless incident that certainly shows the
contempt many felt for Quisling, but also demonstrates the degree
to which the hatred engendered by war can play havoc with humane sensibilities, the Nazi newspaper *Fritt folk* (Free people) reported on 9 September 1941 that a sign had been placed on the
Quisling family grave in Gjerpen Cemetery reading, Deposit Gar-
bage Here (Quoted in Höidal 1989).

ADOLF HITLER (1889–1945)

Jokes about Adolf Hitler began spreading in Germany at least
as early as 1933.[24] Their name—Flüstervitze (whispered jokes)—
reflects the repressive nature of the German regime, where this
humor had to be circulated with far greater caution since it represented a subversive, minority view in a country where the majority
supported the charismatic leader.[25] While in Norway, too, the repressive policies of the occupiers and Nazis necessitated joke tellers to exercise caution, the regime in power did not enjoy majority
support. As a consequence the Norwegian jokes could afford a
more outspoken, combative tone (as will be discussed later), and
could circulate more openly. While many of the jokes told about
Hitler came to Norway by way of the German occupiers, the following one clearly originated in Norway:

Two children were brought to Beistad church for baptism. "My son
shall be named Vidkun Adolf," said the first father. The pastor chris-
tened the infant accordingly.
    "We are a Norwegian family," said the second father, "and we have
chosen a Norwegian name for our son, so would you please change the
baptismal water before proceeding?" [Olav and Myklebust 1942, 10][26]

As with the Quisling jokes, the theme of popular contempt domi-
nates, and frequently Hitler and Quisling jokes are cognates (i.e.,
the same joke but with different names), as is the following one of
the Quisling name-change joke cited in the previous section:

Adolf Schmutz sökte Hitler om å få bytte navn. Ja, Schmutz var jo
ikke så svært pent navn, så det ble innvilget. Takk, sa han, men det
var fornavnet han ville bytte. [Schou-Sörensen]

(Adolf Schmutz applied to Hitler for permission to change his name. Well, Schmutz wasn't such a nice name, of course, so permission would be granted. Thanks, said the man, but it was actually the first name he wanted to change.)

EXTERMINATION AND EXCREMENT

So strong was the contempt for Hitler, according to folk wit, not even the Devil could stand him.

En dag sto det på et gjerde: Fa'en ta Hitler! Neste dag var det tilföyet: Jeg vil ikke ha'en. Hilsen Fa'en. [Schou-Sörensen]
(One day someone had scrawled on a fence: "The devil take Hitler!" By the next day someone had added: "I don't want him." [signed] the Devil.)

Even more graphic in their contempt are the jokes associating Hitler with excrement.

"Vet du at Hitler er tryggest på dö?"
"?"
"Jo, for da har han den brune masse bak seg." [Larsen]
("Do you know that Hitler is most secure on the toilet?"
"?"
"Because then he has the brown masses behind him.")

The brown masses alludes to Hitler's brown-shirted guard, about whom the joke registers unequivocal disgust. In the next two items it is the Führer himself who is equated with excrement:

Nede i gaten satt en liten pjokk og lekte med noe man på godt norsk kaller hestemökk. Han tok "ball" på "ball" fra det opprinnelige, forövrige nokså store haugen og la dem skiftevis i to andre hauger, idet han sa: "En for Göring—en for Hess,—en for Göring-o.s.v."
 Hirdmann Brakknas stoppet og så på denne pussige leken, og han kunne ikke dy seg for å komme med et spörsmål: "Enn Hitler da?" Gutten tittet opp—litt forbauset over å ha fått tilhörer, og svarte, idet han målte hirdmannen med öynene: "Så stor lort ha æ itj' foinne einnå." [Kristiansen 1945, 52]
(Down the street a little boy was playing with something known in good Norwegian as horse shit. He took "ball" after "ball" from the original, rather large pile and placed them alternatively in two other piles, saying: "One for Goering—and one for Hess,—one for Goering, etc."
 Brakknas, a member of Quisling's Hird, stopped and watched this

curious game, then couldn't help asking: "But what about Hitler?"
The boy looked up—a little surprised at having attracted an audience.
Looking the *Hird* member up and down, he answered: "I haven't found
a piece of shit that's big enough.")

En gang Hitler var på reise i fly over Tyskland, ble han svært nödig,
og da flyet ikke akkurat var av den störste type, fans det ikke et slikt
sted hvor man kunne få gjort det nödvendige. Man rådet ham da, som
siste utveg, å bruke luen sin, og så kaste den ut etterpå.

. . . .

En tid senere kom det en lastebil kjörende med voldsom fart inn i en
tysk landsby, og så gikk det som löpeild gjennom gatene at Hitler var
död! Det skulle være noen tömmerhuggere som hadde funnet Hitlers
offiserlue med hjernemassen i! [Kristiansen 1945, 85]
(Once when Hitler was on a plane trip over Germany, he had to relieve
himself, but as the plane was not very big, it had no place to accomplish
this necessary task. As a last resort, he was advised to use his cap and
then throw it out.

. . . .

Some time later a truck speeded into a German village, and soon word
was spreading through the streets like wild fire that Hitler was dead!
Some lumberjacks had allegedly found Hitler's uniform cap filled with
his brains.)

These jokes' fastidiousness about mentioning the words "toilet"
and "shit" suggests that in their own time they made an even more
powerful statement of their tellers' contempt.

Deflating the Superegotist

Like the Quisling jokes, Hitler humor played upon Der Führer's
inflated self-image, often characterizing him as having a Messiah
Complex.

Stauning kom til St. Peter og sa han ville ha hans plass for han hadde
så meget lenger skjegg. St. Peter gikk til Vår Herre og klaget. "Ta det
med ro," sa Vår Herre. "Der nede er det en mann med bare en liten
bart som vil ha min plass." [Schou-Sörensen]
(Danish Prime Minister Stauning[27] came to St. Peter demanding to
replace him since he had a much longer beard. St. Peter went to God
and complained. "That's nothing," said God. "There's a man down
there with just a little mustache who wants to take my place.")

Stalin, Hitler og Chamberlain diskuterer om hvem som er den
mektigste.

"Jeg er mektisk," sier Chamberlain, "for jeg har flest folk under meg."
"Nei, jeg er mektisk," sier Hitler, "for jeg har mest land under meg."
"Nei, jeg er mektisk," sier Stalin, "for det har Gud sagt."
"Nei, det har jeg ikke det," sa Hitler. [Larsen]
(Stalin, Hitler and Chamberlain are arguing about which of them is most powerful.
"I'm the most powerful," says Chamberlain, "for I rule over the greatest number of people."
"No, I'm the most powerful," says Hitler, "for I rule over the most land."
"No, I'm the most powerful," says Stalin, "for God told me so."
"I did not," said Hitler.)

Other jokes belittled Hitler's accomplishments and emphasized his humble origins.

Hvet du hvorfor Hitler har fått jernkorset?
???
Alle—kan få det. [Larsen]
(Do you know why Hitler has received the Iron Cross?
???
Everyone—can get it.)

One of the most frequent reminders of the Nazi presence was the ubiquitous Hitler salute,[28] marketed in Norway as Den norske hilsen (The Norwegian Salute), said to go back to the Vikings. A poster ordered for display in all public offices as of January 1941 proclaimed:

The ancient Norwegians greeted each other with an up-raised right hand. *Heil og sæl* was their salutation. This is the custom among free men. This greeting has been revived in Norway by those Norwegians who want to regain our country's freedom and independence [i.e., the Nazis]. *Heil og sæl* and the upraised right hand is the new Norwegian greeting. This is the custom among Norwegians today.[29]

Besides replacing *god dag* (hello) when people met in person, *heil og sæl* (essentially a wish of "health and good fortune") was also to be used in closing written correspondence. Popular wit, of course, had a ready response, like the rhyme scribbled on a post-card found in the War Archive (Krigtrykkssamling) of Oslo's University Library: Heil og sæl, lyg og stæl (Lie and steal). Another way of cutting the intimidating Hitler salute down to size was to allude to Der Führer's early years as a frustrated artist.

> Vet du hva Hitler hilsen egentlig er forno?
> Nei.
> Det er resultat av malerkosten. [Larsen]
> (Do you know what the Hitler salute really is?
> No.
> It's the result of the paint brush.)

The Hitler-as-painter motif reminded listeners of the eighteen-year-old Hitler's humiliating failure to be admitted to the Vienna Academy of Fine Art and his subsequent miserable struggle to eke out a livelihood by painting designs for postcards and advertisements while drifting from one municipal lodging to another. Jokes denigrating Hitler in this way circulated in various forms and helped reduce the impact of the propaganda idolizing him.

> Kan du si meg likheten mellem Hitler og en död katte?
> ?
> Begge har sluttet å male. [Larsen, Schou-Sörensen]
> (Can you tell me how Hitler is like a dead cat?
> ?
> Both have stopped å male [the word means both "meowing" and "painting"].)

Folk wit also likened the Hitler salute to a urinating dog.

> Kan du si meg likheten mellem en bikkje og Hitler?
> Nei.
> Hitler löfter på armen og bikkja på benet. [Larsen]
> (Can you tell me how Hitler resembles a dog?
> No.
> Hitler lifts his arm and the dog his hind leg.)

Another joke told of a popular revue artist (probably Einar Rose; see chap. 7), making his first appearance after release from a German prison.

> Wearing a German uniform, he marched stiffly to the center of the stage, faced the audience, and raised his arm in Nazi fashion. A number of German officers present rose, clicked their heels together and saluted in return. With his arm still outstretched, the comedian's face broke into a smile as he remarked: "That's how high my dog jumped yesterday." [Olav and Myklebust 1942, 15]

Besides downgrading the Hitler salute, this joke empowers the anti-Nazi comedian both physically and emotionally to manipulate the German officers in the audience. A more elaborate wordplay deriding the salute told:

> En skomaker i Halden ble NS og forsömte deretter totalt sitt arbeide, hvoretter byens borgere skrev fölgende brev til ham: Skomaker bli ved din lest,—hel og sål. [Schou-Sörensen]
> (A cobbler in Halden joined the NS and subsequently fell far behind in his work, whereupon the town's citizens wrote him the following note: Shoemaker stick to your trade—heel and sole.)

The pun plays on the well-known saying Skomaker, bli ved din lest ("Shoemaker, ·stick to your last," i.e., don't become embroiled in something you don't understand), disapproving the cobbler's NS membership while also ridiculing the *heil og sæl* salute by reducing it to the mundane.

Amid the laughter and derision, however, folk wit did not lose sight of the terrible danger posed by Hitler, and it created opportunities to contrast this peril with the image Hitler projected of himself as a savior, pointedly making unfavorable comparisons between him and genuine heros such as Mahatma Gandhi (1869–1948), whose peaceful hunger strikes transformed India.

> I India suiter *1* mann for hele folket, men i Europa sulter hele folket for *1* mann! [Christerson]
> (In India one man is starving for all the people, but in Europe all the people are starving for one man!)

A 19 November 1942 entry in Greta Dahl's diary makes the relevance of this quip's hunger motif painfully clear.

> I saw a little, thin, pale girl with her face covered by sores. Her eyes were so large and innocent, I wanted to cry. That little face continues to haunt me, so that even the music I'm listening to sounds like children whimpering. To think that poor, innocent children have to suffer so that some history-crazed bandits can rule the world into such misery! That little face, deformed by ugly scars, will torment me for the rest of my life. This god-damned war!

Given the vehemence of her sentiment, it comes as no surprise that, both in reality and in humor, the ultimate desire was for Hitler's death.

Hitler, Göhring og Mussolini var ute og flöy sammen og så falt flyet
ned da de var over Atlanteren. Hvem ble reddet? Europa. [Schou-
Sörensen][30]
(Hitler, Goering and Mussolini were out flying together, but the plane
crashed while they were over the Atlantic. Who was saved? Europe.)

Hitler og Göring var engang ute og bilte sammen. Da de passerte gjennom en landsby kjörte de ihjel en gris. Göring syntes han måtte gå til
bonden og beklage det inntrufne. Han ble inne både vel og lenge og
ble traktert riktig godt. Da han kom ut igjen spurte Hitler hvorfor han
ble så lenge. Jo, det var stor begeistring i stua over det jeg fortalte, sa
Göring, og jeg måtte endelig spise med.
    -Hva fortalte du da? spurte Hitler.
    -Jeg sa at nå var grisen död. [Hansen and Baggethun 1945, 45]
(Hitler and Goering were once out driving. Passing through a village,
they ran over a pig. Goering thought he should find the farmer and
apologize for what had happened. He was gone a very long time and
received very fine hospitality. When he returned Hitler asked why he
had stayed so long.
    "Well, there was much celebration in the house over what I told
them," Goering replied, "and finally I had to join in."
    "What did you tell them?"
    "That the pig was dead.")[31]

3

Fraternizing with the Enemy: The Tyskertös

Even more despised than the Nazis, their leaders, and the occupying soldiers were the Norwegian women who befriended them. The term *tyskertös*[1] remains, in fact, one of the most loaded expressions among occupation survivors, perhaps because of the extra strong feelings sexuality arouses when in service to the enemy (Hjeltnes 1987, 63). As many as 50,000 Norwegian women had some sort of erotic contact with the German soldiers. While most Norwegians formerly regarded their actions as "the feminine gender's tragic betrayal," more recent observers have tried to explain the women's behavior, pointing out among other things that given the presence of 300,000 occupying soldiers, it would have been unnatural had such relationships not arisen (Senja 1986).

At the time, however, these women's conduct so outraged national sentiment that when the occupation ended, citizens took matters into their own hands and beat them or shaved their heads.[2] Greta Dahl notes in her diary on 13 May 1945 that "Women who have gone with Germans are being made to clean the barracks, under a constant barrage of torture from the Norwegian soldiers supervising them." Many others were "arrested" by citizens who turned them into the police; most were fired from their jobs and excluded from respectable social circles.

Several of Slaatto's 1940 entries trace the development of the *tyskertös* phenomenon. On 26 July, she comments somewhat objectively:

> There are quite a few Germans here in Lillehammer. Some women (prostitutes) associate with them, but there are also many who remain aloof and refuse to speak to them.

Less than a month later (13 August) the fourteen-year-old observer complains indignantly:

> More and more women *(töser)* are starting to go out with the Germans. They even do so openly. Uff, I get so mad every time I see any of them, I just want to scold them.

Tyskertös. **Artist: Oddmund Kristiansen. From** *Jöss!* **1945. Reprinted here with the permission of Lærdal Medical, Stavanger, Norway.**

Finally on 5 November, in frustration over both the situation and the authorities' repression of reaction to it, she seethes:

> We have to watch these girls going with the Germans, but can't say a word! If we did, we'd be locked up and on bread and water.

Annoyance over the *tyskertösene* prompted the editor Oskar Hasselknippe, to comment in *Ringerikeblad* (Ringerike news) that autumn: "I mangel av skinnkåper er enkelte damer begynt å gå med svinepelser." (Lacking fur coats, some ladies have begun going with *svinepelser* [literally "swine-furs" = SOBs].) The quip struck a responsive chord, and much to Hasselknippe's surprise and consternation, it reappeared—with its source acknowledged—in several underground news sheets, but fortunately without reprisal (Hasselknippe, letter to author, 1 September 1989).[3]

Popular preoccupation with the *tyskertös* phenomenon is also attested in the interpretation given to the ubiquitous Nitedal brand matchboxes, imprinted during the occupation with the image of a running horse; these were said to illustrate the secret message encoded in the manufacturer's name read backward: Slik löper alle damene etter tyskerne i Norge (This is how all the ladies are running after the Germans in Norway).[4]

Before long, full-blown narrative jokes arose.

-Du pappa?
-Hva er det?
-Du. -Nå tror jeg mamma er blitt orntli interessert i å lære tysk.
-Det var da morsomt! -Men hvordan kan du tro det?
-Jo! -Men nå må du ikke si det, pappa, for jeg tror det skal være en overraskelse til deg. -Da du var bortreist i forrige uke hadde mamma og Gefreiter Scheinefroh tysktime hele natten og da han gikk om morgenen hörte jeg mamma si: "Det som du har lært meg i natt vil jeg aldri glemme, og vi skal gjenta det så ofte vi får anledning; men vær forsiktig så ikke min mann får anelse om det." [Kristiansen 1945, 37]

("Dad?"
"What is it?"
"I think Mom's awfully interested in learning German."
"Oh? What makes you think so?"
"Well,—but you mustn't let on that you know, Dad, because I think she wants to surprise you. When you were gone last week, Mom and Corporal Scheinefroh had German class all night long and when he left in the morning I heard Mom say: "I'll never forget what you taught me last night, and we'll repeat it as often as we can, but be careful my husband doesn't find out.'")

Like the drawing on the next page, some of the humor ridiculed the eagerness and lack of discretion with which these women threw themselves at the German soldiers.

To dager etter okkupasjonen hadde en tös allerede fått fatt i nummeret og telefonerte:
-Hallo, e' de' vernemaktå. Kan eg få snakka me' han Kurt? [Imsland 1946, 94]
(Two days after the invasion, one tart had already managed to get

« Fifty-fifty »

The loose morality of the *tyskertös*. From: Oddmund Kristiansen, *Jöss!* 1945. Reprinted with the permission of Lærdal Medical, Stavanger, Norway.

hold of the Germans' telephone number and called it asking, "Hello, Occupation Forces? May I speak to Kurt?")

Kurt being such a common German name, the girl had assured herself a response.

As in so many anti-Nazi jokes, puns proliferate in the *tyskertös* items. Using the double meaning of "chicks" that exists in both Norwegian and English, the next two witticisms also reflect the wartime food shortages (to be more thoroughly discussed in chap. 8):

Hvet du hvorfor det ikke er egg i by'n!?
Nei.
Fordi på landet har tyskerne eggene og i by'n har de hönene. [Larsen]
(Do you know why there's no more eggs in town?
No.
Because in the country the Germans have the eggs and in town they've got all the chicks.)

Det er ikke nok at tyskerne har eggene våre, men de skal ha hönene
til å fly etter seg også. [Larsen]
(It's not bad enough that the Germans have taken all our eggs, but
they've got the chicks running after them too.)

Several wartime jokes play on the Nazi party name NS as a homonym of *en ess* meaning "an ace." The synonymous meaning of
Norwegian *dame* as both "Queen" (in playing cards) and "lady"
provided the ingredients for jokes about the *tyskertös*.

Det går ikke an å spille kort lenger—Kongen er i England, knektene
har tatt damene og da er det bare NS igjen! [Ellingsen]
(You can't play cards any more. The King is in England, the Jacks
[soldiers] have taken all the *damer* ["queens/ladies"] and all that's left
is *NS* [one ace//the Nazi party].)

Military Software

The *tyskertös* humor could be rather racy in times considerably
less explicit than our own. Greta Dahl mentions in a 21 November
1942 diary entry that the girls "usually are called *tyskermadrassene*
(the Germans' matresses) while a well-circulated riddle asked:

Vet du forskjellen på en hirdgutt og ei hirdjente?
Nei.
Jo, hirdgutter ligger på magen for tyskerne. [*Karikaturens krigs-humor*
n.d., 28]
(Do you know the difference between a *Hird* boy and a *Hird* girl?
No.
Well, the *Hird* boys fight for the Germans on their stomachs.)

Frequently this humor derived its effect from the juxtaposition of
military terminology with the girls' less-than-official function.

Det er bare lov å ta brystbilleder nå fordi det er forbudt å fotografere
militære mål. [Larsen]
(Only pictures from the waist up are allowed, because it's illegal to
photograph military targets.)

Vet du hvorfor damene har sluttet med å bruke pil på strömpene?
?
Fordi pilene viser til ofentlige tilfluktsrom. [Larsen][5]
(Do you know why women have stopped using arrows on their hoisery?
?
Because the arrows point to public shelters.)

"**Photographing military objectives is forbidden.**" From Georg Svendsen's anonymous, undated *Krigenshumor samlet av Mr. George.* Publisher: Tell Forlag.

Nu må alle gå med mörke bukser.
Hvorfor det?
Man må blende alle forlystelses-steder. [Larsen]
(Now everyone has to wear dark trousers.
Why?
All places of entertainment are supposed to be blacked out.)[6]

By equating these women's sexual favors with public places, the jokes emphasized the easy virtue of the *tyskertös.*

BOTTOM OF THE HEAP

In addition to having loose morals, the *tyskertösene* of folk wit were generally undesirable and stupid.

De norske pikene som går med tyskerne kalles surru-gattin. [Schou-Sörensen]
(The Norwegian girls who go with German soldiers are called *surro-gattin* = "surrogates.")

The term brings to mind the surrogate coffee and other below-par foodstuffs with which people had to make do in wartime (see chap. 8). Poor quality clothing also abounded, as flimsy cellulose garments replaced the real thing, a circumstance the following quip reflects:

Da en norsk tös i Fredrikstad fikk barn med en tysker, sa folk at det bare var surrogat. Det ble som selluklærne borte i vannet, når det ble vasket. [*Karikaturens krigs-humor* n.d., 10]
(When a Norwegian *tös* in Fredrikstad had a child with a German, people said that it was only a surrogate and, just like celluose clothes, would dissolve in the wash water.)

The next joke denigrates the *tyskertös'* morality while also deriding her intelligence:

Ei bondejente kom til doktoren og fortalte at hun skulde ha barn med en tysker.
"Hvor er faren hen da?" spurte doktoren.
"Je veit itte. Han har vörti borte."
"Har'n vörti borte? Vet De ikke hvad han het da?"
"M-jo, je syns han sa 'Alf Widerse'n' da'n gikk." [Bö 1946, 27]
(A farm girl told the doctor she was pregnant by a German soldier.
"And where is the father?" the doctor asked.
"I don't know. He's gone away."
"Gone away? Don't you know his name?"
"Well, when he left I think he said 'Alf Widerse'n.'")[7]

So much stupidity begs the question, which—according to folk wit—at least one German couldn't help asking:

"Er der bare dumme damer i Norge?" Får svar: "Det er bare dumme damer som går med dere." [Christerson]
("Are there only stupid women in Norway?" He received this reply: "No, only the ones who go out with you Germans.")

Another joke similarly uses the *tyskertös* theme to mock the Germans themselves, here deriding the loose morality of the *tyskertös* while at the same time provocatively professing Norway's allegiance to Germany's arch enemy, Britain, who the joke suggests will eventually prevail.

En norsk *bra* pike hadde snakket med en tysker som syntes at de norske damers moral var så dårlig. Hun svarte at det er ikke damene, men tösene som er sammen med tyskerne, damene sitter hjemme og venter på engelskmennene. [Schou-Sörensen]
(A Norwegian *good* girl was conversing with a German who thought the morality of Norwegian women was frightfully low. She answered that the ladies don't go out with Germans; they're at home waiting for the English men.)

Besides being stupid and of easy virtue, folk wit held that the *tyskertös* could be rather advanced in years.

En dame var sammen med en tysker og de hadde det svært hyggelig sammen, da han tilslutt ville betale henne sa hun:
"Jeg har av alderstrygden jeg, takk." [Schou-Sörensen]
(A woman is out with a German and both are having a really nice time. At the end of the evening when he offers to pay her, she says: "No thanks, I get enough from my pension.")

Not young, smart, or beautiful, the *tyskertös* of Jössing humor also lacked a clear concept of patriotism, disdaining anyone who would stoop so low as to collaborate with the enemy while somehow being blind to her own complicity.

En norsk såkalt "feltmadrass" er kommet tilbake fra den tyske födsels-klinikken i Oslo, hvor hun har fått barn med en tysker. Hun beretter til en venninne:
"Vi var 35 som lå der, og vi hadde det så greitt.—Og vet du, det var en som var NS, men henne snakket vi jo ikke med." [Ramfjord 1945, 20]
(One of the so-called Norwegian "field matresses" returns from the German maternity clinic in Oslo, where she has given birth to a German baby. She tells a friend:
"There were 35 of us in the home and we really had a nice time. One of the women was a Nazi, but of course we didn't talk to her.")

Though the *Jössings* occasionally dealt harshly with the German-friendly women, who might be found naked in the streets with their heads shaved or swastikas painted on their breasts, more often this treatment was merely threatened because of the severe reprisals likely to befall its actual perpetrators. As Greta Dahl's 25 April 1941 entry affirms, however, the urge to punish these women remained strong.

One evening as the chorus was leaving practice they met a Norwegian girl in the company of two German marines. "Take a good look at her, so we'll be able to recognize her," one of the singers yelled to the others, despite the strict punishment he risked for doing so.

Whether or not they carried through their veiled threats, their utterance exemplifies the harsh psychological treatment these women often had to suffer, and which the next two anecdotes also reflect:

På kaien i Stavanger gikk et blottende ungt byens pikebarn med en tysk offiser. Et par iltre smågutter kretset bak dem og begynte å gi luft for sitt mishag:
Dritjenta! Dritjenta!
Offiseren ble hellig fortörnet, gjorde helt om og viste de forbausede småguttene en diger revolver.
Det ble bare "et öyeblikks pause". Så sprang en av småkarene fram, blottet et magert bryst og ropte:
-Skyd! Hvis du tore!
Offiseren stakk revolveren i hylsteret igjen og fortsatte sin spasertur med jenten.
Men bak dem vokste svermen av gutter som skrek og huiet:
-Der går han så ikkje torde skyde! [Svendsen n.d., 17–18]
(On the dock in Stavanger one of the local young things was strolling along with a German officer. A couple of hot-headed boys circled behind them airing their displeasure, *"Dritjenta! Dritjenta!"* [Filthy—litterally "shitty"—girl].
Furious, the officer turned on his heel and surprised the boys by drawing an enormous revolver.
After only a moment's pause, one of the boys ran up to the man, bared his bony chest and yelled, "Shoot! If you dare!"
The officer replaced the revolver in its holster and continued his stroll with the girl.
But behind them a growing swarm of boys jeered and heckled, "There's the one who didn't dare shoot!")

I Bergen skal endel soldater og gaster innskribes fra andre havner. Endel av de aller "tidligste" småtösene fra Bergen er der og tar avskjed med vennene sine. En av dem har vondt for å rive seg lös, hun klenger seg til vennens brede bryst og skriker höyt.
Da sier en tjuagutt bakerst i hopen på bryggen:
-Ikkje gråt du mor, du får han igjen te' somren—som makrell!
[Svendsen, n.d., 17]
(In Bergen some of the earliest little *tösene* are saying farewell to their German boyfriends who are about to ship out to another port. One girl has a particularly hard time tearing herself away and clings to her boyfriend's broad chest, sobbing loudly.
Suddenly from the back of the crowd on the dock comes the voice of a street urchin:

"Don't cry, my dear, you'll get him back this summer—as mackerel!")[8]

While most of these jokes and anecdotes suggest the Norwegian women's eagerness for liaisons with the German soldiers, others flatly deny this complicity and portray the liaisons as arising from German coercion. Some of these items came in response to Heinrich Himmler's Lebensborn-directive, whereby it became the "sublime task" of women of "good blood" to bear the children of the German soldiers. Himmler had established the German Lebensborn (Spring of Life) organization in December 1935 with the purpose of replenishing German stock through such regulated extramarital procreation, ensuring a large number of children with the "right" Aryan features, such as a high forehead, blue eyes, and blond hair. An SS document found in Norway declares:

> It is expressly desirable that the German soldiers conceive as many children as possible with Norwegian women, regardless of whether it is within or outside of the bonds of matrimony. [Kjendsli 1986, 46]

Two jokes deriving from the policy of encouraging German soldiers to impregnate Norwegian women told:

> Vi får ikke egg fra Vestlandet mere fordi hönsene vil ikke egge opp for tyskerne. [Schou-Sörensen]
> (We aren't getting eggs from West Norway any more because the chicks won't put out for the Germans.)[9]

> Episode fra Undergrunden under flyalarmen: En sykepleierske går rundt og roper stadig: "Er det noen gravide her?"
> "Kjære Dem da, ta det med ro, vi har jo bare vært her 10 minutter enda." [Schou-Sörensen]
> (Episode from the subway during an air-raid: A nurse is going around constantly calling out: "Are any of you pregnant?"
> "Take it easy for heaven's sake, we haven't even been here ten minutes yet.")

In addition to these two jokes, Schou-Sörensen has collected a couple of anecdotes that also propound German coercion as a reason for the international couplings.

> A nurse is walking home in the evening, a German follows her; neither one speaks. He follows her up the stairs, but she manages to squeeze through the door without him. The next day she gets a notice that

if she doesn't apologize to the German, she'll have to go to jail for three months.

A man and woman were walking outside of Oslo's Glassware Shop one evening, when a German car stops. The German slugs the woman, pulls her into the car and they drive to the Hotel Regina. Fortunately she has a flashlight with which she hits the German between the eyes so his glasses shatter and blood flows. She runs out, finds a Norwegian policeman and hides in a doorway while he hails a paddywagon to drive her home.

Whether motivated by force or free will, relations between Norwegian women and the German occupiers contributed to a Norwegian wartime birth rate that reached record highs, especially in the number of children born outside marriage. Between 1941 and 1945, 7.37 percent of all births occurred extramaritally, compared to 6.3 percent during the years 1936–40 (Hjeltnes 1987, 62). About this situation, Greta Dahl comments on 11 October 1943:

A terrifyingly high number of Norwegian women have been pregnant by the Germans, especially here in Narvik. . . . If it's a little German boy, it's a great honor, but there's much less interest in a little girl since they don't make good cannon fodder.[10]

On a lighter note Greta Dahl recorded the following anecdote on 8 April 1944:

Sitting aboard the Ofoten railroad on the way home to Tårstad, I've been listening to a young couple out in the corridor. He was teasing her about how crazy Norwegian women are about the German men. "Just look at the 60 thousand *tyskerunger* (German kids) that have been born here in Norway. What do you think has caused that?" [The woman responded,] "Do you suppose it could be the food?" Everyone had a good laugh.

Further emphasizing the high pregnancy rate among the *tyskertös-ene*, the phrase "going with a German" becomes in the following joke a generic term for being pregnant:

To småjenter satt og lekte. Da sa den ene-
  -Har katta deres fått onger nå'a?
  -Nei, de' har a ikke de'!
  -Jo, de' har a de' så, for mora mi sa de!
  -Det er lögn! sa den andre småjenten, kom her så skal vi höre å mora mi sier!

Hun ropte opp til 3dje etasje så det ljomet:
-Mor! Er vist det sant at katta vår har flyi me' tyskerane? [Svendsen n.d., 28]
(Two little girls were playing when the one said, "Your cat has had kittens now, hasn't she?"
"No, she hasn't."
"She has too! My mother said so!"
"That's a lie!" said the other little girl. "Come on, let's ask my mother." She hollered resoundingly up to the third floor:
"Mom! Has our cat been going with the Germans?")

Prevention was not unknown, but the means were not easy to obtain. Both German and NS authorities regarded birth control (or "maternal hygiene," as it was called) as immoral; they labeled facilities for its distribution "abortion clinics," and had them shut down. German soldiers were supplied with condoms for the prevention of venereal disease and received strict orders to use them, but they tended to neglect their use in established relationships (Senja 1986, 43).

In all, it is estimated that approximately 9,000 wartime babies were born having a Norwegian mother and German father, while only 400 marriages between Norwegian women and German soldiers took place during the occupation period (Hjeltnes 1987, 62–63). The long bureaucratic process required for marriage played a role in creating this situation; in 1941, for example, 139 Norwegian-German marriages were performed while 884 applications awaited a decision (Senja 1986, 48).

Quite early in the occupation the Germans recognized their responsibility to the children of these unions. As a result of the relatively friendly relations that had prevailed between the Norwegians and their occupiers during the summer and fall of 1940, quite a few Norwegian women were expecting children by German soldiers as of the spring of 1941. Worsening relations between the Norwegians and the occupying forces put these girls at risk of being thrown out of their homes and shunned by friends and relatives (Senja 1986). The Germans addressed this problem in February 1941, and established Norway's first Lebensborn home shortly thereafter. Most of the German-Norwegian children born during the occupation arrived at one of several of these homes, located in Oslo, Trondheim, Östfold, Brumunddal, Bergen, and Bærum as well as in several tourist hotels. They also appeared in Jössing humor.

Holms hotell på Geilo blev en tid brukt som födehjem for norske kvinner som skulde ha barn med tyskere.

En dag da to av hjemmets "gjester", som begge var i den 8de måned,
kom vraltende bortover veien, mötte de kontordamen på Ustaoset ho-
tell, frk. Siri Carlsen. Frk. Carlsen hadde et belte om livet i rödt, hvit og
blått, som tydeligvis skar den germanske rases forplantersker i öinene.
Den ene av dem pekte på beltet og sa med dyp forakt:
"Se på hu' derre som lissom skal være nasjonal på magan!"
"Tenk om De hadde vært like nasjonal i maven," sa frk. Carlsen.
[Bö 1946, 57]
(Holms Hotell in Geilo was used for a time as a maternity home for
Norwegian women made pregnant by the Germans. One day as two
"guests" of the home, both in their eighth month, came waddling down
the road, they encountered Siri Carlsen, the secretary of Ustaoset Ho-
tell. Miss Carlsen was wearing a belt in Norway's national colors of red,
white and blue, and this sight clearly irritated these two progenitors of
the Germanic race.
One of them pointed at the belt and said with deep disdain: "Look
at her—trying to be patriotic on her stomach."
To which Miss Carlson replied, "Imagine if you had been equally
patriotic in your stomach.")

After the war some of the mixed couples married. No exact
figures exist, but it is thought that approximately one thousand
marriages between Norwegian women and German men took place
both during and after the occupation. Some of these couples settled
in Norway; more went to Germany. Of these, a few remained
abroad, while others eventually returned to Norway (Hjeltnes
1987, 63). The lack of exact statistics concerning these women
testifies to the official policy of ignoring their predicament; researchers did not begin studying these relationships until forty
years after the war.

The April 1986 founding of Norges Krigsbarnsforbund (The Norwegian Association for War-Children) suggests that the time has
finally come to begin addressing this situation. Intending to assist
children wanting to find their German fathers or Norwegian moth-
ers, the organization's efforts have met with an immediate and
enormous response. No doubt the psychological need to finally
share their stories with sympathetic people of similar background
provides a compelling reason to contact the association since the
treatment accorded these innocent children in postwar Norway
has otherwise often been extremely cruel, sometimes going beyond
shunning and name-calling to physical harm. Little research has
been done on the children, either, but the tragedy of their plight
has gradually emerged in literary and film productions, notably

Marit Paulsen's *Liten Ida* (Little Ida) (1979), Herbjörg Wassmo's *Huset med det blinde glassveranda* (The house with the blind glass veranda) (1981), Berit Waal's *Krigsbarn—en syklus i dikt og prosa* (Children of war—a cycle in poetry and prose) (1981), and Veslemöy Kjendsli's *Skammensbarn* (Children of shame) (1986).

4

Humor's Response to Nazi Repression and Cruelty

On 26 September 1940 Åslaug Rommetveit told her diary:

> As of today German authorities have replaced the King and Storting [Parliament]. All political parties in the country are forbidden. Only the Nazi Party [NS] will continue to exist. Disquiet prevails and resentment smolders among people all over the country.

This smoldering resentment found varied and sometimes surprising expression. That fall, for example, some Oslo students decided that wearing a paper clip in the lapel would signify solidarity. *Binders* is Norwegian for "paper clip," so wearing it suggested: Vi binder sammen—"we bind together, united we stand." The Nazi police attempted to discourage this demonstration, occasionally resorting to violence and arrests, but, notes the diarist Schou-Sörensen:

> No sooner did they forbid the paper clip demonstration, than people began carrying combs protruding from their breast-pockets to signify: *Vi greier oss selv* [We'll manage by ourselves, i.e., without German "help"—a pun based on the double meaning of the verb *å greie* as both "to comb" and "to manage"].)

It was also common, she writes, to pass the lapel through its buttonhole in order to "stick out one's tongue" at the Germans or to wear the face of one's watch on the underside of the wrist to proclaim: Ned med den nye tid ("Down with the New Time"—i.e., down with Nazism). Some men wore matchsticks in their hat bands to suggest Vi er opplyst: ("We're enlightened; you can't fool us"— *opplyst* means both "lit up" and "enlightened, informed").

STOCKING CAPS AND SUBVERSIVE SLOGANS

One of the most effective anti-Nazi demonstrations was the wearing of red woolen stocking caps during the winter of 1940–41. Myrtle Wright, an Englishwoman detained in Norway during the war, noted in her diary:

> The unanimity with which youth suddenly wore the *nisselue* (the Norwegian name for caps worn by gnomes) did not pass unnoticed by the authorities and was recognized by the NS as a demonstration against them.

With Hitler's June 1941 invasion of Russia (see chap. 10), all red clothing became suspect and simply wearing that color could lead to arrest, since the Nazis regarded it an expression of support for the Soviet Red Army. The police department had trouble finding room for all the confiscated red clothing, and their rapidly growing supply of toggery led to jokes about women coming to the police department asking directions to the dress department. Anecdotes of confrontations between the Nazis and their stocking cap-clad opponents also multiplied (see chap. 8 for more), like this one recorded by Schou-Sörensen:

> A Nazi woman removed the *nisselue* from a young girl on the Holmenkollen tram. The girl didn't react, but as she exited the tram, she snatched the lady's hat and got off with it.

Quisling decried the "absurd" anti-Nazi demonstrations for undermining Norway's best interests, and on 8 July 1941 Propaganda Minister Gulbrand Lunde—not otherwise credited with a strong sense of humor—ridiculed those individuals

> who go around wearing paper clips, whether because they think they're a piece of stationery, or plan to be sent in the mail, . . . it reminds us of [Ibsen's play] *Peer Gynt* in which an insane asylum inmate fancied he was a pen. [Nökleby 1985, 117]

Reverting to the Nazis' proverbial humorlessness, Lunde continued,

> One could of course be tempted to laugh if it weren't so tragic that people in Norway really are carrying on with this foolishness while the whole world is in upheaval. [Nökleby 1985, 117]

Notwithstanding Lunde's seeming dismissal of the demonstrations as "idiotic pranks," the Nazis took the Jössings' jokes and demonstrations very seriously and in no small measure invested them with extra power by overreacting to them. The overreaction went so far, notes Christerson, that if individuals went without a stocking cap in cold weather, this too was regarded as a demonstration: it was a *nisselue* they were *not* wearing! About these demonstrations and the Nazi overreaction to them, another survivor says:

> What was done often seemed ridiculous, but it had the effect of uniting all the opposition forces. These were acts that if ignored by the authorities would have had no effect, but because the Regime protested so vigorously, these little things became important symbols of resistance. [Haakon Holmboe quoted in Sharp ca. 1958, 6][1]

In the Nazi view, however, the demonstrations and jokes *had* to be taken seriously, for, as the Nazi politician Robert Ley asserted, "It is suicide to allow them." Particularly emphasizing the danger of anti-Nazi jokes, he concluded,

> Immediate action must be taken against anyone telling such stories, whether on the train, in cafés or elsewhere. [Interview in the Norwegian and Danish Nazi newspaper *Politikken* (Politics), 23 February 1943]

Certainly the Nazis harmed their own cause by overreacting, but their assessment of the jokes' power was accurate. Besides allowing those opposed to Nazism the opportunity to announce their views, the humor permitted individuals to distance themselves psychologically from Nazi ideology, thereby defusing both its seductive appeal and intimidating threat. Participating in the demonstrations and seeing others do so developed a feeling of identity and solidarity among the diverse opponents of Nazism. Nurturing their will to continue resistance activity, it also assisted in the identification and formulation of specific resistance goals (Skodvin 1969, 167).

Slogans and passwords also played a key role in encouraging resistance. Schou-Sörensen notes the popularity of KLUMP, which stood for Kongen leve ut med pakket (Long live the king; out with the riffraff). The king referred to in these slogans, Haakon VII, became the most significant emblem of Norway's resistance, despite Hitler's efforts to prevent just this eventuality. A week before the invasion (2 April 1940), he had issued a directive that the monarch be prevented from escaping at all costs (Kersaudy

1987, 49), but the sinking of the *Blücher* and the ensuing delay in attacking Oslo defeated this plan (see chap. 1). On 13 June, six days after the king had departed for exile in England, the Germans demanded that the Norwegian Storting assemble and vote to depose both the king and the government (see chap. 2). To their subsequent letter urging his abdication, Haakon replied on 8 July, that since the approval had not been the product of free deliberation, it could not release him from his duty to the Norwegian constitution. To abdicate, he said, "would go against everything I have regarded to be my duty as Norway's king since I came to Norway almost 35 years ago" (Skodvin 1990, 52). Haakon's announcement was broadcast on London radio and circulated by flyer from hand to hand. Together with his 7 June departure-day promise to stake everything on the effort to maintain Norway's sovereign status and to regain her freedom and independence, Haakon's refusal helped define resistance objectives and ultimately made his name synonymous with defiance and hope.[2]

To counteract the power of this persuasive royal image, the Nazi-controlled press permitted only the view that Haakon had deserted Norway in her hour of greatest need.[3] As part of his 25 September 1940 speech declaring the New Order, Terboven announced that the Royal Family had forfeited their right to ever return to Norway. The traditional prayer for the king and his house was omitted from the liturgy of the Lutheran State Church and possessing likenesses of any member of the Royal Family or making positive reference to them became illegal acts, subject to severe reprisal. A majority of the Norwegian people nevertheless found increasingly inventive ways to flout these strictures, as the following January 1941 entry in Slaatto's diary indicates:

> Another thing many are being arrested for is wearing one-öre coins with the H7 insignia. Along all the ski trails and on a great many fences it says, "Long Live the King" etc. since no one can know who has written it—luckily![4]

Others showed more overt opposition by tearing down the ubiquitous Nazi propaganda placards. Slaatto's entry continues:

> my bother Nils has been expelled from school for two weeks for having torn down an NS poster. A girl from his class had seen it and reported him.

The growing peril of being turned in for such actions is confirmed by this Rommetveit entry, also from January 1941:

It's a little more dangerous at school now. There are certain "striped" pupils who threaten to tell if we sing or say something illegal.

"Striped" *(stripede)* designated those individuals who couldn't decide which position to support and opportunistically took advantage of both sides.

Jokes and Repression

Schou-Sörensen used her diary to record several incidents that reflect the growing climate of repression.

A large number of high school students from Oslo Cathedral school were arrested in November for turning their backs to Goebbels the day he came to Oslo.

The story of SSU: Seven boys started an organization called SSU— the *S*wine *S*hall [get] *O*ut ["Out with the pigs," i.e., the Germans]. They claimed it stood for: Summer, Sun and Outdoor-life. Tostrup [a prominent Oslo jewelry firm] made an emblem for them. A girl had obtained one of these and wore it along with the flags of Norway, England and France. A German saw this and went to Tostrup, got the names of those who owned these emblems and now they're all in jail.

The repression of free speech, of course, also provided an opportune theme for jokes and witticisms.[5]

Fiskemannen i gården roper: "Fin fisk idag, Di, fin feit fisk, likeså feit som Göhring." Han ble satt inn i 14 dager. Da han så kommer ut roper han igjen: "Fin, feit fisk, likeså feit som for 14 dager siden." [Schou-Sörensen, Slaatto]
(The fish monger at the outdoor market was calling, "Fine fish today, nice fat fish, just as fat as Goering." He was put in jail for two weeks. When he got out, he called, "Nice fat fish, just as fat as two weeks ago.")

The following pun satirizes the Germans' continual confiscation of materials deemed necessary for their war effort; it also reflects the tellers' awareness of the war's intrusions on their language, imposing alien, wartime meanings on formerly more pleasant peacetime expressions:

Det siste våpen tyskerne har beslaglagt er en av Frelsesarmeens bösser. Men så har de til gjengjeld lagt ut sure miner i Pilestredet. [Schou-Sörensen]

(The latest weapon confiscated by the Germans is one of the Salvation Army's *bösser* [meaning "collection containers," but also slang for *börse* = "gun"]. In return they have laid *sure miner* in Pilestredet. [*Sure miner* means "frowns," while *miner* means "mines," in the sense of "explosives"; Pilestredet is the street in Oslo where the Salvation Army had its headquarters.])

Other wordplays reflect a preoccupation with the conformity, intolerance, and restrictions that characterized life in occupied Norway, such as these responses to Terboven's 25 September 1940 announcement banning all political parties except the NS:

Det er forbudt å skrive Larssen med 2 s'er. Alt skal være NS. [Ellingsen (whose birth name was Larssen)]
(It is forbidden to write Larssen with two -s'es. Everything has to be *NS* ["one -s," homonym of NS].)

Alle kaniner skal innleveres, de har for lange örer. [Ellingsen]
(All rabbits are to be confiscated, their ears are too long.)

Tyskerne har arestert en 6 års gutt fordi han har fått engelsk syke. [Larsen]
(The Germans have arrested a 6 year old boy because he has contracted rickets [known in Norwegian as *engelsk syke* (English disease)].)

Aiding these individual assaults on Nazi ideology, members of one occupational group in particular managed to arouse resistance sentiment in their articles.[6]

JOURNALISTS' RESPONSE TO REPRESSION

Though press censorship had begun immediately with the 9 April invasion, during the first months of the occupation, active Jössings continued to write almost daily articles with uncamouflaged patriotic content. Probably the best-known example was the September 1940 article by the Stavanger journalist Trond Hegna. Writing in response to the portion of Terboven's 25 September speech advancing Nazism as Norway's only hope for a bright future, Hegna declared:

If any of us should be asked to trample ideals we cherish . . . to adopt a new way of life we scorn, there is only one course to take. If this is the New Order, our answer is: No Norwegians for sale. Several hundred

Norwegians have already sacrificed their lives for something they held sacred. It is also sacred to us.

Hegna's article struck a responsive chord; Rommetveit reports that the authorities had supplied the newsstands' copies of this issue with a sign stipulating, Not for Norwegians, but by the time the paper had been seized and Hegna arrested (he would spend the rest of the war in captivity), many Jössings had already heard and enthusiastically adopted Hegna's slogan of No Norwegians for Sale.

Other print-demonstrations were more subtle, and Nazi censors often missed them until well after publication. Readers attuned to just the right "wave length," however, picked up even the most carefully concealed messages. As already noted in chapter 2, *Ringerikeblad*'s editor Oskar Hasselknippe found typographical "errors" particularly suitable for defying the Nazis. When his paper was compelled to carry a lead article declaring that "in this war the Germans are utterly superior in men and cannons *(menn og kanoner)*," the printed copy read: *"menn og kaniner"* (men and rabbits). Forced to carry the description of the local Nazi organization's meeting, the newspaper editor retaliated by mangling the Nazi greeting and reporting that the meeting had concluded with a threefold *heil og sau (sau = "sheep")* for the Führer (Hasselknippe, letter to author, 1 September 1989).

Though *Ringerikeblad* suffered no reprisals for these "errors," the authorities put a quick end to Hasselknippe's humor column with its mock-serious debates about whether the "Organization for the Advancement of Beards and Moustaches" should admit members having only a mustache, but no beard (such as Hitler). A formal letter arrived from the Press Directorate which prohibited this discussion due to the danger of its "being understood as a mockery of certain symbols of the ruling party" (Letter to author, 1 September 1989).

Acrostics (poems in which the first letters of the lines form words) provided another effective means of smuggling a secret message, clandestine demonstration, or encouraging greeting into the otherwise censored press. Schou-Sörensen records a well-known example in which the Nazi-controlled *Tidens tegn* (Signs of the time) on 30 January 1941, printed a poem whose first letters spelled out, "God Save the King." Not to be outdone, the Nazis recruited another poet to write an acrostic whose initial letters would read *Heil og sæl.* The latter appeared in the 3 February 1941 *Tidens tegn,* signed by the same name as the first and accompanied by an explanation about the poet's having experienced a change of heart as he now supported the Nazi cause (Bö 1946, 110–11).

The Nazi magazine *Hirdmannen* (The guardsman) for 24 October 1942 printed a poem purportedly submitted by a young female Hird member. The poem seemed to drip with praise for the handsome, proud, and brave young men in the Waffen SS (Armed SS), but upon publication, the first letters of each line clearly spelled out the inflammatory slogan Leve kongen (Long Live the King) (Bö 1946, 112).

Typographical tricks took other forms as well. Schou-Sörensen tells that the sports newspaper *Norges idrettsblad* (Norway's athletic news) carried a list of names purporting to be winners of a skiing contest, but whose initials spelled out Gid faen tok Hitler (May the devil take Hitler), roughly the equivalent of "God damn Hitler," a rather strong oath for the times.

SKIRENN

GUTTEKLUBBEN FRAM

'har holdt et morsomt slalåmrenn. Resultater:

Over 13 år: 1. Gunnar Iversen, 2. Didrik Ferrem, 3. Arve Eriksen.

Under 13 år: 1. Nils Teigen, 2. Ole Kolberg, 3. Harry Iversen, 4. Terje Løveng, 5. Erik Reinertsen.

"Aesopian language" used to convey the message *Gid faen tok Hitler* (The devil take Hitler) in the initials of the boys' names. *Norsk Idrettsblad,* here reprinted from Finn Bö, *Forbuden frukt,* 1946, with permission from Aschehoug Forlag, Oslo, Norway.

Personal ads could also serve to camouflage Jössing messages. In 1942, *Aftenposten* carried the notice of a Nazi office-worker, nature-lover, and man of simple needs, who hoped to meet an enterprising single Norwegian woman for the purpose of immediate matrimony:

Ekteskap. Kontorm. og nazist, grei, elsker naturen, lever enkelt, vil ekte norsk ensom dame med egen driftskap. Nu straks. B.m. "1808 Ca. 30 år". [Bö 1946, 112]

Once again, quite a different message emerges from the words' initial letters, namely Kongen leve, ned med NS: "Long live the king; down with the Nazi party."

According to Bö, people carried these newspaper clippings in their wallets both to maintain their own morale and to share with others who might not have seen them.[7]

Even more daring was the poetry printed in *Hardanger,* a newspaper edited by Olav Kolltveit. Toward the end of July 1941, for example, Bjarne Slapgard's poem "Olsok" appeared, ostensibly praising Olav Haraldsson, the king killed at Stiklestad on 29 July 1030, and who subsequently became Norway's patron saint, annually celebrated on the date of his death which became known as St. Olav's Day or Olsok. The poem pleads with the king to "Come home, come back home to Norway" and uses St. Olav's traditional appellation Perpetuus Rex Norvegiae (Norway's eternal king), all in a thinly veiled reference to the exiled king Haakon VII. The reference did not pass unnoticed. A 7 August 1941 letter from the authorities threatened that any further attempts to carry propaganda for the "former king or other fugitives" would put an end to the newspaper. The letter also noted *Hardanger*'s previous record of "sabotaging" the articles sent them by the State Press Office and suggested that in the paper's own best interest it begin showing more goodwill (Letter in Utne Folkemuseum, Hardanger).

This letter did not end the matter, however. Soon the editor Kolltveit received a summons to appear before the Ortskommandant (local Nazi commander) in Odda. Berating the poetry carried by the newspaper, the Kommandant demanded the addresses of two authors in particular: Bjarne Slapgard and Per Sivle, in his view "the greatest sinners against the New Time and the New Norwegian State!" Kolltveit objected that neither one posed a threat: Slapgard was the passivist director of the Hardanger Folk High School, while Sivle—dead since 1904—unfortunately had a more uncertain address, having committed suicide in the bathtub. "Some think he ended up in Hell, but others believe he received forgiveness and went to Heaven," said Kolltveit and invited the Kommandant to take his choice. The German had a sufficient sense of humor to laugh, Slapgard reports, "and that's how both Kolltveit and I escaped imprisonment" (Slapgard, letter to author, 14 December 1991).

It didn't always end so well. *Ringerikeblad*'s ¾uisling "typo" (see chap. 2)—along with several other disagreements with both the local press authorities and the NS—ultimately had tragic consequences for its editor, Kaare Filseth, who was executed during a 19 September 1944 State of Emergency proclaimed in Ringerike (Hasselknippe, letter to author).

ILLEGAL LISTENING

Though the Nazis had immediately taken over the Norwegian broadcasting company, most Jössings listened to the alternative Norwegian language radio broadcast established in London by the exiled Norwegian government. Besides ridiculing the Nazis' racist policies, the following well-known joke reflects the popularity of these 7:30 P.M. broadcasts:[8]

> Tre feil i följende setning: En jöde spiser en nazihjerne kl 19.30. 1) En jöde spiser ikke svin, 2) en nazi har ikke hjerne, 3) klokka 19.30 hörer han på radio. [Schou-Sörensen, January 1944]
> (Three errors in the following sentence: "A Jew is eating a Nazi brain at 7:30 PM." 1) A Jew doesn't eat swine, 2) a Nazi has no brain, 3) at 7:30 PM he is listening to the radio.)[9]

The strong interest in the BBC broadcasts persuaded the authorities to confiscate Norwegian radios in the fall of 1941.[10] District by district between 1 August and 10 September 1941 Norwegians were forced to give up their one remaining link to the outside world, leaving them stripped more than naked, as the Blix drawing below eloquently portrays.

Some observers say this confiscation prompted more than a few

The psychological effect of radio confiscation. Artist: Ragnvald Blix (Stig Höök), Göteborgs Handles- och Sjöfarts-tidning, September 1941. Republished in Blix, _De fem årene_ (1945). Reprinted here with permission of Gyldendal Forlag, Oslo, Norway.

Norwegians to join the NS, since party members could legally keep their radios.

No other occupied country experienced such a pervasive deprivation of listening rights,[11] and the situation immediately gave rise to several narrative jokes, one of which told of two old friends meeting in one of the ubiquitous wartime queues.

-It's a long time since we met, said the one. Won't you visit me this afternoon? If you'll come before half past seven you can get the news bulletin.

-Sss, said the friend, alarmed, -somebody might hear you; which in fact, anybody could because the man had spoken at the top of his voice.

The same evening the two friends sat before the fire, talking of this and that. Just before half past seven the police arrived.

-Was it correct, the police sternly asked, that guests were invited to listen to the wireless here?

-Well, said the police fumbling with their weapons.

-It's not time yet, pointed out the host. A minute later the host gave the sign. He kicked aside the carpet and laid his ear to the floor. The police followed his example and could hear the well known voice of the Norwegian broadcaster in London, Mr. Öksenvad.

-Who occupies the floor below, thundered the police.

-A member of the *Hird,* answered the host with a smile. [Thomsen 1945, 30–32]

Jössings found other ingenious ways to continue listening to the broadcasts,[12] and humor glories in recounting—and exaggerating—the extent of the illegal listening.

En stund etter at det var meldt fra at kundene på Vinmonopolet måtte ha med seg tomflasker for i det hele tatt å få utlevert fulle kom det på et av utsalgene inn en kar som ikke hadde noe tomgods med seg.

-De må ha med tomflaske, sa ekspeditören.

-Hva et det for noe töys?

-Vet De ikke det? Det har vært bekjentgjort i avisene og i Oslo Kringkasting!

-Oslo! sa kunden med et bredt hånflir, nei hvis De vil at vi skal få greie på slikt, så må De da sende det ut over London mann! [Svendsen n.d., 23]

(A while after it was announced that State Liquor Store customers had to bring in empty bottles in order to receive full ones,[13] a fellow came into one of the outlets without any empties.

"You have to have an empty in exchange," said the clerk.

"I've never heard of such a thing."

"You haven't heard? It's been announced in the newspapers and on the Oslo broadcasting station!"

"Oslo!" said the customer with a derisive laugh. "If you want us to know about such things, you've got to broadcast it on the London station!")

Schou-Sörensen records an anecdote that makes the same point more subtly.

A man thought his son had been killed while piloting a plane to England, and he arranged a memorial service at his home. Just before it was to begin, he heard on the London broadcast that his son had been captured there;[14] but he didn't dare say anything and had to go through the whole memorial service charade. A twinkle in his brother's eye told him, however, that he, too, knew the son had survived and silently they pressed each others hands, while neither dared utter a word.

A related anecdote, also recorded by Schou-Sörensen, like the "empty bottle" joke, makes "illegal listening" seem almost universal.

A couple was going to hold a service for their son who they thought had been killed. The day before they heard on the London broadcast that the son had been taken prisoner. None of those invited came to the service the next day.

THE UNDERGROUND PRESS

Despite the extent of illegal listening, confiscation of the radios transformed the underground press. Beginning already during the summer of 1940, these handwritten, hastily mimeographed or typed circulars originally existed to counteract Nazi propaganda by means of humor, irony, and satire;[15] indeed several items presented in this book originally appeared in these news sheets. Their mast-heads alone suggested and encouraged resistance: Mens vi venter (While we wait), Vi vil oss et land (We want for ourselves a country), Alt for Norge (Everything for Norway—King Haakon's motto), For konge og fedreland (For king and fatherland), Norge vort land (Norway, our country), Hjemmefronten (The homefront: the name of Norway's resistance forces).[16] With the radios' confis-cation, however, the newspapers' chief function became carrying summaries of the BBC war news and names like London-nytt (London news) and London Radio joined the fray.

Meanwhile the danger of having anything to do with the underground press grew increasingly acute. The 1 June 1942 issue of *Hjemmefronten* (The homefront) could plead:

> DON'T BE SO AFRAID THAT YOU BURN THIS NEWSPAPER. Remember the work that lies behind it. It is your DUTY to pass it on.

But by 8 July 1942, *Jössingposten* (Jössing post) felt it necessary to warn, "be extra careful with the newspaper," and the 20 November 1942 issue of *For konge og fedreland* (For king and fatherland) appealed to its readers

> more than ever before [to] show the very greatest caution in receiving, reading and passing on our newspaper.

The Climate of Cruelty

The change in tone came in response to a 12 October 1942 ordinance that exponentially increased the danger of engaging in any form of resistance, by stipulating that

> Whosoever deals in propaganda for an enemy government or produces, obtains or spreads communications or other items harmful to German interests, or listens to other than German or German-controlled radio broadcasts will be punished by death, in less serious incidents or when extenuating circumstances prevail, by imprisonment or jail. Anyone possessing any item of anti-German propaganda must immediately turn it in to the nearest German or Norwegian police authorities. Violators will be punished by death.

Not surprisingly, the repression that culminated in this ordinance also had an effect on wartime diarists. Already on 7 February 1942, Rommetveit writes:

> Oh, there is so much I would like to write down and preserve for later. But I simply don't dare. Don't want to be jailed just because they chance to come across these books.

In a May 1991 letter to the author, Rommetveit tells of having to wrap her diaries in oilcloth and bury them in the yard to keep them from discovery, and Greta Dahl comments similarly in a 2 March 1943 entry:

> I must say that these diaries are beginning to burn me. It would be horrible if they were found. I'm planning to sew them into a heavy

blanket we keep at the foot of the bed in cold weather, although, they do search beds, too.

On 2 November 1943 she laments:

My beloved diary! You're more dangerous to have in the house now than an English paratrooper. Rumors are raging about coming raids, so many treasured papers have probably turned to ashes these last few days. Others have perhaps been buried in lead boxes. I have kept you under my pillow at night so you'll be handy if something occurs to me early in the morning.

On 22 April 1945 she comments:

Now I've got to fish out this dangerous book from its hiding place to add a few things. We have some SS members (so-called Norwegian) in town, and they're snooping around examining things. . . . Women have had their purses searched. It's especially weapons and illegal papers they're after.

The diaries of these two women also confirm the seriousness of the threats. Rommetveit reports on 23 April 1944:

Now the Germans are undertaking a rash of house-searches in the middle of the night. They demand to see passports at the most unexpected locations. On Saturday evening a local youth was shot for not carrying a passport.[17]

And on 27 and 29 June 1945 Greta Dahl writes:

So many gruesome things are happening these days, I can hardly breathe. . . . Their methods make me want to vomit.

HUMOR'S RESPONSE TO CRUELTY

Even in the face of such atrocities, folk wit continued to inform and embolden, to raise morale and inspire anti-Nazi solidarity. One of the best-known incidents of Nazi terrorism occurred on the Lofoten island of Austvågöy on 4 March 1941, prompted by an Allied attack. Approximately 550 British and 52 Norwegian commando soldiers had gone ashore and attacked the Nazi-controlled fish production plants and herring oil factories in the towns of Svolvær and Stamsund, sinking several German and German-

controlled ships in the process. The forces took 213 German prisoners and 12 NS members back to England along with 314 Norwegians who needed or desired an escape from Nazi-controlled
Norway.

Upon hearing of the raid, Terboven flew to Svolvær and took
immediate steps to punish all those directly or indirectly involved:
he ordered all the properties of those who had fled to England and
of those who had helped the British during the raid to be burned
to the ground; those found guilty of helping the British were to be
arrested and severely punished, and the island's entire population
was to be fined 100,000 *kroner* (ca $14,000) for reparations.

Despite the severe reprisals, humor was not among the casualties.[18] A 26 June 1941 article in the underground newspaper *Alt for
Norge,* titled "Leve det gode humor" (Long live good humor)
attested:

A sense of humor has not disappeared despite the harsh blow fate has
dealt Svolvær. After the visit of the British fleet with Norwegian sailors
on board, the Germans decided to show who was really the boss here
in Norway. Toward this end, they posted a photograph of Hitler beside
the main street. One day some young boys gathered and, led by one
of their friends, goose-stepped up the street like a little platoon of
German soldiers. When they reached Hitler's picture, the friend commanded, "Left face, spit." Whereupon the photograph assumed a cor-
responding appearance. Now guards have to stand watch over the
picture. . . .

Nor did humorists allow the Lofoten raid to be forgotten. One
of Arne Taraldsen's December 1943 mock stamps (see footnote 16
in chap. 2) shows a gigantic Norwegian marine emerging from the
sea and stuffing panic-stricken Germans into a sack. The text
reads, "Lofoten, March 4, 1941" and the stamp has a value of 20
öre plus a 20 öre (2.8¢) "contribution to the fine."

Even the general state of emergency declared in Oslo in September 1941 evoked a humorous response, though the bleakness of the
situation would seem to have precluded any such possibility.

Wednesday September 10, 1941 was a gray, rainy day in Oslo, and
from the early morning hours an unusually large police detachment
had been patrolling the streets with steel helmets, clubs and machine
guns. From the walls of the buildings and fences shone newly hung
posters by the German authorities: Reichskommissar Terboven had
declared a state of emergency . . . resistance would be "broken by
armed force." Anyone who opposed these regulations would be shot
by firing squad. [Chr. Christensen 1965, 24]

A mock stamp "commemorating" the Lofoten raid of 4 March 1941. A giant Norwegian marine dispatches German soldiers. Its value is 20 öre plus a 20 öre "contribution to the fine." Artist: Arne Taraldsen, 1943.

Two private citizens, Viggo Hansteen, a lawyer for the Labor Organization, and Rolf Wickström, a union member, were executed to deter further acts of defiance. Being the first civilian executions, these killings are recalled by many survivors as the most shocking of the entire occupation (Mogens 1945). Still folk wit proved capable of rising to the occasion. Schou-Sörensen reports that on the posters listing various specific infractions and proclaiming for each one: "You will be shot if you . . ., You will be shot if you . . . , You will be shot if you . . . ," someone had scrawled: *Skutt blir du hvis du ikke allerede er skutt!* ("You will be shot if you haven't already been shot!")

The quip suggests the Nazi regime's characteristic lack of humane correlation between the seriousness of an infraction and the brutality with which it was punished, and several narrative jokes play on the same theme.[19] One told of a farmer who had received a threatening letter about his failure to produce enough eggs.

Han skrev tilbake og sier: "Har forelagt skrivelsen for rette vedkommende, men da de ikke ville svare, er de no stillet for standrett og skutt!" [Ellingsen][20]
(He wrote back saying, "Have submitted your document to the individuals concerned [i.e., the hens], but inasmuch as they refused to comply, they have been court martialed, placed before a firing squad and executed!")[21]

Another mocked the brutal methods of the Gestapo, the German secret police.

Responding to a loud knock on the door a Norwegian asked fearfully, "Who is it?"
"It is the Angel of Death," came the ominous reply.
"What a relief!" responded the Norwegian. "I thought it was the Gestapo."

This chapter has traced the growth of the Jössing response to the repressive atmosphere that had descended upon occupied Norway after Terboven's September 1940 assumption of power, and it has surveyed the various means employed in fighting back, including wearing symbolic clothing, smuggling subversive messages into the censored press, illegally listening to London radio broadcasts, and reading underground news sheets. First and foremost, the Jössings employed the weapon of refusing to show their fear. Confronting their oppressors rather than dwelling on their oppression became

5

Answering Back: The Growth of Anti-Nazi Solidarity

Both despite and because of Nazi cruelty and reprisals, more and more Norwegians found ways to express their opposition to the "New Order's" domination. This chapter examines a few of the more unique demonstrations of this growing anti-Nazi sentiment: a subversive children's book, underground Christmas cards, and regime-mocking magazine covers. Though not jokes per se, these alternative forms of protest circulated widely and complement the jokes in theme and method. The chapter concludes with a consideration of how Norwegian occupation jokes compare with those of other repressive regimes.

SNORRI THE SEAL: A CHILDREN'S BOOK GOES UNDERGROUND

In November 1941 a deceptively innocent-looking children's book appeared on the Norwegian market. *Snorre sel* (Snorri the seal), written and illustrated by Frithjof Sælen, tells of "the vainest little seal in the Arctic Ocean," who ignores his mother's advice that "to live in peace one must constantly be on guard." Instead Snorri spends his time dreamily admiring his beautiful coat in blissful ignorance of the enemies poised to attack him.

The situation resembles Norway's pre-9 April 1940 attitude toward the war in Europe and her complacent assumption of being left in peace since she herself posed no threat.[1] The book's second illustration, likening the ice floe on which Snorri sits to a map of Norway, dispels any doubt that the author intended this parallel.

Snorri's enemy Brummelab, a lip-smacking polar bear who has Stalin's gleam in his eye, represents the Soviet Union. Notwithstanding the latter's ultimately indispensable role in turning the tide of Hitler's fortunes in favor of the Allies, the Soviet Union

Snorri the seal jumps from an ice floe resembling the map of Norway. From Frithjof Sælen's "fable for children and adults," *Snorre sel,* 1941. Reprinted here with permission of Frithjof Sælen.

represented a threat at the time of Sælen's book. The Soviets had attacked Norway's Scandinavian neighbor Finland in September 1940, usurped the Baltic states as well as territory in Romania, and entered a mutual nonaggression pact with Germany to divide up Poland.[2]

Snorri receives many warnings from Uncle Bart the kindly walrus, who represents England and whom Sælen draws with a characteristically British mustache. Despite Bart's warnings, Snorri

allows himself to be lulled into complacency then suddenly is star-
tled to discover Brummelab's hot breath on his face seconds before
the polar bear plans to devour him.

Snorri just barely escapes being Brummelab's dinner. But by
jumping into the sea to save himself, he also manages to get into
even deeper trouble. He finds himself in the realm of Glefs, the
killer whale, who initially hides his evil intentions by playing on
Snorri's vanity and admiring his beautiful coat, just as German
propaganda had exalted the Norwegians' Aryan features and
claimed that they had come as friends. Finally realizing his folly,
Snorri cries out for help, but having neglected to let his mother
and Uncle Bart know where he was going (an allusion to Norway's
lack of an articulated foreign policy), he sadly realizes they won't
know where to find him.

A pair of sea gulls, Sving and Svang (who share more than initials
with the Nazi SS)[3] add to Snorri's problems by constantly reveal-
ing Snorri's hiding places both to Brummelab and to Glefs. Sport-
ing the red and yellow colors of the Nazi party and having a "false
gleam" in their eyes, the gulls incessantly screech, *Skui, skui,* an
allusion to the inescapable Nazi *heil og sæl* salute. Promising Glefs,
"if you want steak, we can get it for you," the treacherous pair
reflect not only Quisling's aid in luring Norway into Germany's
grasp, but also the abundance enjoyed by the occupiers and their
Norwegian collaborators as others endured crippling shortages and
rationing. At the same time, Glefs's own plan of polishing them off
when he is finished with Snorri reveals an awareness of the German
exploitation of the Norwegian Nazi party for her own ends while
ignoring the party's own goal of Norway's ultimate sovereignty.[4]

Cornered on an ice floe by Glefs, Snorri again remembers Uncle
Bart's warnings and feels "almost angry" that his uncle isn't there
to save him, reflecting the impatience many Norwegians shared in
their view of Britain's inept assistance (see chaps. 1 and 9). Sælen,
like Snorri, holds out hope that Britain would eventually come to
Norway's rescue, however. Uncle Bart, he asserts, is stronger than
anyone else in the entire Arctic Ocean; it just takes him longer to
get sufficiently riled.

Snorri swims for his life to escape Glefs and in the nick of time
finds a hole in an iceberg just the right size to admit him, while
excluding Glefs. The hole turns out to be a tunnel through the
iceberg and when Snorri reaches the other end, he finds Uncle
Bart. The walrus in the meantime has had his teeth sharpened (an
allusion to Roosevelt's March 1941 Lend Lease Act that supplied

Britain with sorely needed weapons). Now Bart is ready to fight and the two of them make a plan to defeat Glefs.

Snorri swims back through the tunnel and emerging from its opening, starts teasing the enormous Glefs. The whale can stand being mocked by the little seal no better than Norway's German occupiers could tolerate the Jössings' derision (a circumstance further portrayed by some shrimps that constantly gnaw at Glefs's teeth). Just as the occupiers empowered Jössing demonstrations by overreacting to them, Glefs lunges furiously at the taunting Snorri with the result that Snorri once again escapes through the tunnel while Glefs becomes hopelessly lodged in the opening. Bart has meanwhile swum around the iceberg's perimeter toward Glefs, whom he now attacks and defeats.

Sælen's message was astonishingly prophetic. At a time when England had achieved few military successes and Hitler's armies had yet to lose a single field battle, the story dared to suggest England's victory and Germany's defeat. It moreover endorsed acts of passive resistance such as those described in chapter 4. Finally it suggested that like the iceberg's tunnel, the long, dark, and uncertain passage of Norway's occupation period eventually would end in sunlight.

It is thus little short of amazing that the book, provocatively subtitled, "a fable in color for children and adults," initially not only escaped censorship, but actually received high praise in the Nazi-controlled press. The German-language *Deutsche Zeitung in Norvegen* (German newspaper in Norway) reviewed it favorably, while the Norwegian Nazi organ *Fritt folk* (17 November 1941) extolled Sælen as "the Norwegian Walt Disney," and assured readers that "both adults and children will enjoy making this book's acquaintance."

By the time the Nazi authorities tried to confiscate the book in December, all 12,500 copies printed had been sold. Although the Jössings quickly caught on to Sælen's hidden messages, the authorities did not summon Sælen for interrogation until January 1943.[5] During the three-hour hearing, Sælen denied intending any anti-Nazi message and asked with feigned innocence if they would also "ban the Brothers Grimm." The Nazis released him and he continued his resistance work, becoming by 1944 a leader of the West-Norwegian branch of the military resistance organization (Milorg). Soon Sælen's anti-Nazi efforts forced him to flee to England. There he presented a copy of his book to King Haakon VII, whose forbidden monogram he had also managed to smuggle into one of the book's illustrations (24).

Snorre sel lifted morale laid low by the hardships of war. It was one of the very few occupation publications that managed to escape censorship long enough to spread the hopeful message that Norway would emerge from her plight and that the seemingly invincible Nazi-German war machine could be defeated.[6] But Sælen also told Norwegians some less pleasant truths, scolding them for their naïveté and lack of faith in Britain (the vindicated Uncle Bart ill-conceals his disgust with Snorri for having "gotten lost") and sounding repeated, emphatic warnings against trusting the Nazis. Postwar accounts of the Norwegians' spontaneous and unanimous anti-Nazism notwithstanding, these were warnings the author clearly felt his contemporaries needed to hear.[7]

Anti-Nazi Card-Tricks

The year 1941 stands out as a time when the will to overcome wartime hardships and to resist the occupiers passed new milestones. We find this growing resolve reflected with surprising accuracy in an unusual venue: that season's Christmas cards. Flagrantly violating the November 1941 flag ordinance which reserved the right to display Norway's colors exclusively to members of the Nazi party, the Stavanger firm of Aasmund Lærdal produced a series of cards dominated by outsize Norwegian flags.

One card shows mischievous *nisser* cunningly raising the flag, while in another the flag plays backdrop to three *nisser* joyfully ski-jumping. In a third, three laughing *nisser* sit atop a horse that sports an enormous *syttendemaislöyfe* (17 May ribbon), alluding to severe wartime restrictions on the celebration of Norway's traditionally jubilant Constitution Day. All the cards wish the recipient, "God *norsk* jul" (Merry *Norwegian* Christmas) rather than the usual "God jul!"—and pointedly suggest a desired return to Christmas as it used to be: without uninvited guests.

Other 1941 Christmas cards poked fun at the increasing food shortages Norwegians suffered as the Nazis fed the occupying troops and exported goods to Germany (see chap. 8). Flouting Nazi restrictions and expressing a defiant sarcasm about these war-induced hardships helped many Jössings find a much-needed sense of mutual support and solidarity against a shared adversary, and this in turn enabled them to put up an increasingly united resistance front.

A Christmas card wishing recipients "Merry *Norwegian* Christmas" and featuring the forbidden *nisses* and out-size Norwegian flags. 1941. Artist: unknown. Reprinted with permission of Lærdal Medical, Stavanger, Norway.

THE NEFARIOUS NISSE

The 1941 Christmas cards' most concerted attack on Nazi authority came in the very act of depicting the *nisse*. Already in fall 1940 the Nazis had found the *nisse* a threatening symbol, as the following letter—written on NS party letterhead—attests:

> During a visit at the office of Supply Director Wik today I noticed he had a *julenisse* hanging on the wall over his desk. I regard this symbol [as] a demonstration and fail to see how a public servant can be permitted to have such an item hanging in his office. I asked him to remove the *julenisse*, but he refused to do so. I therefore request that the State Police visit Mr. Wik's office immediately to confiscate the *julenisse* and that they report Mr. Wik. [Hjeltnes 1987, 111]

As discussed in chapter 4, wearing the *nisselue* had been an important early demonstration of anti-Nazi sentiment, and punishments for wearing it had grown increasingly severe during 1941.

Alluding to the Nazi confiscation of the hats, one illegal card drawn by the children's book illustrator Vigdis Rojahn (b. 1902) shows the German "crow"—a derision of the Reichsadler (the eagle symbolizing the Third Reich)—trying to tear the *nisselue* from a Norwegian equipped with a *tine* (traditional food box) and *kringle* (pastry). The image suggests that the resistance sentiment expressed by the *nisselue* was as much part and parcel of authentic Norwegian cultural identity as these other ancestral items, and that this cherished national heritage now stood in equal danger of being snatched away by the invaders.

As one might expect, word of the subversive cards traveled fast, and people flocked to buy them. But when Nazi authorities noticed the activity, they descended on both the printer and the stores to confiscate the entire series. To prevent cards already sold from arriving at their destinations, the Nazis issued a directive on 22 December 1941 to postmasters throughout the country that they confiscate any of them found in the mails.[8]

How much the Christmas cards' daring expression of defiance meant to like-minded Norwegians is attested by the number of these cards still found in archives and private collections throughout Norway, despite the severe penalties threatened for possessing any form of anti-Nazi propaganda. The following diary entry makes the point explicitly:

> In times like these, when it is an utterly hopeless task to express a hint of obstinacy in our dear Norwegian fatherland—this country

A crow (caricaturing the eagle of the Third Reich) tries to nab the Norwegian's red stocking cap. Artist: Vigdis Rojahn, 1942.

which has become one big concentration camp—there are nevertheless those who still dare to take action, and in the most varied and unbelievable ways irritate those in power and encourage the rest of us to persevere and to believe in liberation. [Trondheim diary]

MAGAZINES AND THE ART OF DARING

The specific act of defiance to which this diarist refers appeared on the cover of *Magasinet for alle* (The magazine for everyone), no. 19, 23–30 May 1942. At first seeming innocent enough in its depiction of a farmer plowing his field, a closer look reveals that

the worms here know their fate. From the depths of the soil they gaze up in tearful anxiety toward the destiny that awaits them. [Trondheim diary]

In their writhing, the worms form the letters *V* (Vidkun) *Q* (Quisling) and the bird's wings bear an "unmistakable resemblance" to the American armed forces insignia:

the heavenly promise to us of the peace that will come from the American planes. Yes, those worms have good reason for the large tears and the frightened looks. [Trondheim diary]

The diarist goes on to point out that the squiggles in the upper left-hand corner spell out *Ne(d) me(d) NS* (down with NS) and *Leve H7* (Long live Haakon 7), and he also manages to find Haakon VII's insignia hidden in the horse's reins and collar.

During the winter of 1942–43 another magazine, *Norsk ukeblad* (Norwegian weekly) published a series of daring covers. The one for December 1942 depicts Stalin as a blacksmith hammering a horseshoe which a little boy holds with considerable pain in a pair of tongs. The boy resembles Hitler, and in the horseshoe symbolism German censors correctly saw references to the Don River bend in which the Germans had recently suffered the humiliation of having trapped Soviet soldiers only to watch them escape. When interrogated about the cover's meaning, however, the editors professed innocence, and no reprisals followed.

Norsk ukeblad's 20 February 1943 cover brought more serious repercussions. This one ostensibly portrays a father teaching his little son to skate, but the father has Hitler's mustache and the son bears a striking resemblance to Quisling. The boy can't seem to stand on his own two feet and hangs like a helpless puppet in his

Terrified worms, writhing into the initials _V_[idkun[_Q_[uisling], about to be devoured by a bird whose wing feathers resemble the U. S. armed forces insignia. From the cover of _Magasinet for alle_, 23–30 May 1942. Artist: Unknown.

An allusion to Hitler's loss to Stalin's forces at the bend of Russia's Don River. From *Norsk ukeblad*, **5 December 1942. Reprinted with permission of** *Norsk ukeblad*, **Oslo, Norway.**

father's arms while a *nisselue*-wearing Jössing girl laughs at their antics.[9] In response, Nazi authorities stopped the production of *Norsk ukeblad,* confiscated the magazine's money, closed down its offices, and sent the editor and illustrator to Oslo's Grini prison camp.[10]

THE QUICK-WITTED, ANTI-NAZI PUT-DOWN

As discussed in chapter 4, Norwegian occupation jokes mirrored and augmented these alternative anti-Nazi demonstrations by articulating the same readiness to defy oppression. Frequently the humor achieved this goal by employing quick-witted, anti-Nazi put-downs, which could be relatively innocent:

> En tysker spurte om veien. Får til svar: "Har De noget i mot at at jeg svarer på engelsk?"
> "Å neida."
> "I don't know." [Christerson]
> (A German asks for directions and gets the answer, "Do you mind if I answer in English?"
> "No, not at all."
> [In English]: "I don't know."

Or might sometimes be rather rude:

> -Kannst du den Weg nach Trolla sagen?
> -Ha du no foinne veien te Norge, så får du piskan toilli finne veien te Troilla å! [Kristiansen 1945, 12]
> ([In German]: "Can you tell me the way to Trolla?"
> "If you found your way to Norway, you can sure as hell find your way to Troilla, too!") (Some "poetry" has been lost in translation.)

A study of Norway's occupation humor conducted by the author in 1991 demonstrates that the quick-witted anti-Nazi put-down in fact became the standard of Norwegian occupation humor (Stokker 1991), as exemplified in the following joke:

> På Frydenlunds bryggeri er det opplagring av innleverte radio apparater. Et NS medlem kommer inn på kontoret for å hente sin radio: "Heil og sæl, jeg skal hente min radio!" "Leve Kongen!—Förste dör til höyre." [Ellingsen]
> (Confiscated radios are being stored at Frydenlund's brewery. An NS member comes into the office to retrieve his set, "*Heil og sæl,* I'm here to pick up my radio!" "Long live the king!—First door to the right.")[11]

Hitler's difficulties with Quisling as Norway's ostensible Nazi ruler are mocked on the cover of *Norsk ukeblad,* **20 February 1943. Reprinted with permission of** *Norsk ukeblad,* **Oslo, Norway.**

Unintimidated by his Nazi customer, the clerk not only refuses to acknowledge and return the Hitler salute, but he also dares to respond with the inflammatory Jössing slogan.

The refusal to be intimidated by the occupiers also suffuses the next joke:

> På et offentlig kontor skulle det henges opp et bilde av föreren. Ved-kommende spurte vaskekonen som holdt på der, om bildet hang rett. "Jeg har bare med lorten på golvet å gjöre jeg," sa hun. [Schou-Sörensen]
> (A picture of Hitler was being hung in a government office. The official hanging the picture asked the cleaning woman working there if he'd gotten the picture straight.
> "I only deal with the dirt that's on the floor," she replied.)

Whether clerk or cleaning lady, the protagonists of these jokes serve to suggest the Jössings' deep-seated unwillingness to change their way of life for the sake of the occupiers or to show that the occupiers' presence in any way inconveniences them.[12] The following joke conveys the same message:

> En gang det gikk flyalarm i Bergen kom en tysker bort til en torvkone som sto og glante opp i luften. Han befalte henne å gå inn, men hun sa: Det er'kje meg dem er etter, det er Dokker. [Schou-Sörensen][13]
> (Once when an air-raid alarm sounded in Bergen a German approached one of the outdoor-market's female fish mongers who stood staring up at the sky. When he ordered her to go inside, she replied: "It's not me they're after, it's you Germans.")

These jokes manifest the conviction articulated by the journalist Arne Skouen in June 1943: "Thou shalt not show oppressors that their oppression is oppressive" (148).[14]

In an exuberant reflection of the same spirit and amid dire death threats to anyone who provided assistance to those attempting escape to England, the following joke gained popularity:

> A Gestapo agent stormed into the home of a fisherman's family. "What has become of your boat?" he demanded brusquely. Looking the intruder straight in the eye, the fisherman's wife replied: "Is it my job or yours to keep watch on this coast?" [Olav and Myklebust 1942, 26]

ANSWERING BACK WITH IMPUNITY

The distinctive character of Norwegian resistance humor emerges with particular clarity when compared to the humor of

other repressive regimes. Jokes from the former Communist regimes of Russia and Romania have been chosen as examples because of the availability of a large sample in English translation.
Such a comparison reveals that while the Norwegian material has
a predilection for portraying Norwegians delighting in overtly disrespectful replies to Nazi authorities, the humor of the former
Communist regimes tends toward almost the exact opposite
mechanism of highlighting the individual's terror of expressing *any*
opinion that could possibly be construed as critical of the regime.

> Two Rumanians are on a bus. One is sitting down; the other is stand-
> ing. The man sitting asks:
> -Are you a member of the Communist party?
> -No, I am not.
> -Are you in the military?
> -No, I am not.
> -You mean you are not a government or party official of any kind?
> -No, I am not.
> -Then get the hell off my foot! [Banc and Dundes 1986, 24–25][15]

> Popescu talks with his friend.
> -You know what happened to me last night? I came home and found
> my wife in bed with a Russian officer.
> -What did you do?
> -Tiptoed out, of course. I was lucky. He didn't see me. [Banc and
> Dundes 1986, 107]

The subversive rejoinder, when present at all in Eastern Bloc humor, tends to be maneuvered into the mouths of the authorities
themselves, as in the next two examples:

> Two friends were chatting as they walked along a street when one of
> them exclaimed: "We have a rotten government!"
>   A secret policeman appeared from nowhere and grabbed the friend.
> "You are under arrest for making a treasonous remark against the
> government!"
>   "But I didn't say *which* government," protested the offender.
>   "That explanation won't do," the secret policeman retorted. "There's
> only one rotten government and you know it!" [Ruksenas 1986, 115]

> It is October 1944. A man comes to the police station to make a
> complaint.
> -Two Swiss soldiers have looted my house and raped my wife and
> daughter.
> -What do you mean, Swiss soldiers? There isn't a single Swiss soldier
> in Romania.

-I tell you they were Swiss soldiers.
-Think again. Weren't they perhaps Russian soldiers?
-You said it, sir, not me. [Banc and Dundes 1986, 32]

Alternatively, the subversive rejoinder of Communist humor could be given by Radio Armenia.

Question to Radio Armenia:
"Is it possible to build Communism in a randomly taken capitalist country, for example, Holland?"
Answer:
"It's possible, but what did Holland ever do to you?" [Draitser 1978, 13]

The Norwegian material portrays instead the oppressed taking the upper hand, deprecating the occupiers to their faces and refusing to be intimidated or even to alter the slightest details of their life-styles in deference to German regulations:

En bergensk kjuagutt sitter på trappa en dag i 1941, og ser i et av "TIMES" siste nummer. En tysk offiser ser dette og spör i en skarp tone hvor han har fått avisen fra. Gutten ser foraktelig på ham og svarer: "Eg har ikkje fått han. Eg holder han". [Ellingsen, Christerson]
    (A Bergen street urchin was sitting on the steps one day in 1941, reading a recent issue of the London *Times*. A German officer sees this and angrily demands to know who has given it to him. Looking at him with contempt, the boy responds, "No one gave it to me. I subscribe.")[16]

Besides reveling in the boy's disobedience of the Nazi ban on reading the *Times* (London), the joke implies the refusal even to give up the convenience of having it delivered. The extra irony of the subscriber's being a street urchin adds the insulting implication of the Nazis' impotence in enforcing their own restrictions. For many, of course, reality was far different, as diarists' reports of raids, searches, and seizures attest. But by laughing at the inconveniences, hardships, and even atrocities of occupied daily life, the jokes provided solace for the privations actually suffered, while also communicating the more profound hope that the Norwegian way of life—as defined in her constitution and in the form pursued prior to the 9 April invasion—would endure and emerge unscathed from under the Nazi heel.[17]

6

Adjusting the Image of the Übermensch: Humor's Antidote to Nazi Propaganda

Poster Wars

In a November 1942 essay from his series about life in occupied Oslo, the journalist Arne Skouen observed:

> We weren't so busy pasting up posters before 9 April 1940, but an essential part of the New Order is the ceaseless scream . . . [with] the walls of every building in town having become howling megaphones, . . . [and] shrieking as though possessed. [Skouen 1943, 7–8]

In the absence of the confiscated radios (see chap. 4), Nazi authorities regarded posters as their most effective means of spreading party ideology. The enormous resources expended and their state-of-the-art production methods—including professional artistic and marketing experts—make the resulting lithographs impressive even by today's standards.[1] Often strikingly beautiful and compellingly articulate, some of these posters employed Viking symbolism to convey the message that the Nazi party aligned itself with traditional Norwegian values and ideology.[2] Other posters emphasized Britain's culpability in Norway's occupation (see chap. 1), or warned of the threat of Bolshevism (see chap. 10). In all, about three hundred different designs appeared. They were printed in large editions and in several different sizes for uses ranging from placards for display in collective transport, public offices, and on outdoor electrical poles to postcards, postage stamps, and color slides for cinema advertisements. The designs achieved tremendous circulation, not the least because of a Poster Law obliging all public offices and means of transportation to display them (H. F. Dahl 1982, 176).

A postcard showing a Nazi soldier tearing down one anti-Nazi poster, while another is being glued up reading Long Live the King. From *12-milorg-karikaturer,* n. d. Norges Hjemmefrontmuseum.

A Nazi poster urging a "steady course" by boarding the steamship *Nasjonal Samling* and thereby being aligned with Norway's Viking past. Artist: Kaare Sörum; printer: Thon & Co., 1942.

A Nazi poster inviting Norwegian youths to live up to their Viking heritage by joining the *Norske Legion* against the "common enemy": Bolshevism. Printer: Copia Litho, 1941.

Blaming "England's Crime"—the 8 April laying of mines in Norwegian waters—
for the German invasion of Norway. Artist: Trömper; printer: Thon & Co., 1940.

A Nazi poster graphically articulating the threat and urging the rejection of Bolshevism. Artist: Harald Damsleth; printer: Thon & Co., 1943.

The Magic Formulas H–7 and VVV

The Arne Skouen essay just cited continues by observing that for every thousand times a Nazi poster appeared, King Haakon's monogram—H7—appeared *ten* thousand times

> etched with a fingernail on a Nazi poster, written with chalk on a children's hop-scotch board, . . . drawn with ski poles in the snow along the trail, incised on the walls of elevators and hallways, carved into telephone-poles and -booths, cafe tables, tree trunks, windows and tram seats. . . . [Skouen 1943, 7–8]

In the words of Per Heradstveit, the H7 took on a "strangely metaphysical significance" (1979, 14).

Never slow to realize the power of a good symbol, neither were the Nazis above borrowing one from the enemy—if they thought they could get away with it. This they tried to do with the V-symbol. Originated in Belgium early in the war and championed by Winston Churchill as a symbol of the occupied lands' indomitable will to survive, the V began appearing on mountainsides and building walls in the countries Hitler had invaded.

During the summer of 1941, however, the Germans decided to co-opt the V. The front page lead-article of the 18 July 1941 *Aftenposten* announced that the letter henceforth would stand for Viktoria, an ancient German concept connoting the victory of cultured nations over chaos.

In Oslo the printing of all magazines stopped in the presses so that the Germans could incorporate their V into the cover design, as in the pictured example from *Norsk ukeblad* (Norwegian weekly). Inside each magazine identical notices appeared proclaiming:

> The route pursued by the German defence force has always led to victory. . . . Norway, too, has seen evidence of its ultimate victory in the creation of Regiment Nordland and Den norske Legion in which Norwegian youth fight in the truest sense of the word—for Norway, home, honor and victory—*Viktoria*—the sign which today greets us everywhere. The letter V on the streets and buildings, in the press, broadcasting and films, is the symbol of Europe's victory over Bolshevism, German victory on all fronts. . . . *Viktoria* is the future of Europe and Norway.

Instituted one month after Hitler's 22 June 1941 attack on the Soviet Union, the V campaign was actually part of an enormous propaganda offensive aimed at convincing the world of Germany's

The V, standing for German Victory on All Fronts. Artist: unknown; printer: Copia Litho, 1941.

One of countless summer magazine covers incorporating the German V for victory over Bolshevism. From *Norsk ukeblad* 8 August 1941. Reprinted with permission of *Norsk ukeblad*, Oslo, Norway.

emergence as the defender of Western European culture against Bolshevism.

In most of the occupied countries of Europe, the Nazi effort to overtake the V eventually succeeded. In Norway, however, both sides continued to use the V and to argue about its meaning. As one Jössing poster put it:

> Let the Nazis say what they want: The V-symbol is ours! It is the symbol of freedom and justice and the Germans' defeat. *Vi vil vinne!* [We will win!] (undated placard, signed by *De Navnlöse* [Those without name], Norges Hjemmefrontmuseum)

The German V campaign led to the Jössing counteroffensive of filling in the German Vs with the H7 monogram, so that the entire symbol came to denote victory over Nazism. Contradicting the

The German V symbol reappropriated by the Jössings by adding Haakon's insignia and the BBC wartime signature, Morse code for V. Photo: NTB (Norsk Telegram Byrå).

German usage, circulars began to appear asserting that since the German language had no word for victory beginning with a V, the letter must instead stand for *verliehren* (lost).

Auf deutsch kan man nicht Viktoria schreiben, aber Wiktoria. Verliehren kan man aber sehr gut schreiben.
(In German the word isn't written *Viktoria*, but *Wiktoria*. *Verliehren*, on the other hand, certainly is spelled with a V.)

The underground newspaper *Hjemmefronten* (The homefront) described these circulars in its August 1941 issue and soon anti-Nazi graffiti-artists were defacing the German Vs to convey the same message by adding *-erliehren* or *-erloren* (lost) to the V or by writing "-ictory" in contrasting paint on top of it.

Naturally the V-campaign also provided grist for the humor mill. Jokes about it show popular awareness that the Nazis had stolen a British symbol.

Tyskland har "Veene", England er faren. [Schou-Sörensen]
(Germany has *veene* ["birth pangs," a homonym of "the Vs"], England is the father.)

I fjor tok de koksen, i år tar de *V*eden. [Schou-Sörensen]
(Last year they took the coal, this year they're taking *veden* ["the wood," homonym of "the V." The joke also alludes to the wartime fuel shortage.])[3]

The battle over these expressive symbols grew somewhat less intense as the war continued, but neither side gave in until the occupation ended.

Press Censorship

As already mentioned in chapter 4, censorship of the press was among the very first policies the occupiers implemented. Initially the only requirement was that the press exclusively carry reports beneficial to the German war effort. Soon more rigid "Military Guidelines for the Press" articulated the goal of convincing the Norwegian people that

1) the German nation was best suited to be the leading power of the world, and that Germany would win the war because of her cultural and material superiority.

A Jössing-defaced slogan once proclaiming, German Victory on All Fronts, now claiming English "Victory" and Germany *"Verloren"* (lost). Photo: Leif-Erik Bech.

2) Hitler's and the German Nazi party's view of right and wrong was the only correct view, and according to it:
3) the noble Germanic race should be cultivated, while the other, inferior races should yield to the guidance of the master race; therefore:
4) the erroneous principle of democracy should be destroyed. [Luihn 1981, 9]

The Nazis took over the Norwegian wire service, NTB (Norwegian Telegram Bureau), and Quisling established a State Office of the Press whose most essential duty was to supply the newspapers with material about the positive contributions of Quisling and the NS to the new pan-Germanic Norway.

Some diarists note the disparity that consequently arose between the Nazi-controlled media and other news sources. Åslaug Rommetveit's diary, for example, reports:

> February 15, 1941: At 7:30 PM the British news in Norwegian comes on the radio, over the British station. It corresponds little with Norwegian news.

Actually neither side could be totally trusted, as Slaatto notes on 13 September 1940.

> In the newspaper nothing is true anymore. Every day the Germans write that *many thousands* of British planes are missing. These are pure lies. From England we hear just the opposite, but if you average the two, it probably comes out about right.

The underground newspapers tried to keep people mindful of the dangers of German and Nazi propaganda. An article in *Norge i dag* (Norway today) urged its readers,

> Never lose sight of the fact that you are being subjected to constant mental bombardment from people making a concerted effort to conquer you, and who will go to any lengths to succeed in that effort. [Luihn 1960, 49]

These measures notwithstanding, some of the propaganda inevitably managed to penetrate, as this 12 November 1940 entry in Greta Dahl's diary fretfully predicts:

> But people gradually become poisoned by the newspapers, they are under such strict control and fill us with their propaganda. Without any sort of discussion meetings or the like, I fear the one-sided propaganda will achieve its intended effect. If only it can be stopped before it causes too much divisiveness here in Norway.[4]

Evidence of the effectiveness of NS propaganda may certainly be seen in the rise of party membership statistics from 4,200 in August 1940, to 25,000 by February 1941 (out of a wartime population of 3,000,000). Observers have traditionally concluded that most who joined: (a) sought economic or other material advantages available through party membership, (b) were impressed by the German military successes, or (c) felt that the high degree of German discipline would lead to victory (Olsen 1946, 41).[5] In the ongoing Jössing struggle to fight Nazism's appeal, jokes and anecdotes came to play a vital role.

WILLING DISTORTIONS

Keeping themselves mindful of the Nazis' less than straightforward portrayal of the truth, some diarists recorded actual incidents of their deceit.[6]

> One day a woman who lives near Ekeberg cemetery saw an officer and a private come carrying a wreath. Through binoculars she watched them place the wreath on one grave, photograph it and then move on to the next grave, place the wreath there and photograph it. This they did with all the graves. [Schou-Sörensen]

Even in honoring the dead, the anecdote suggests, the occupiers practiced fraud.

Humor about Nazi propaganda appears to have had three main functions: (a) to keep people mindful that what they were hearing indeed *was* propaganda, (b) to point out the occupiers' propensity to lie, and (c) to denigrate the image of the Germanic Übermensch. Schou-Sörensen also records the following incident which clearly serves the first function:

> After the UFA Week in Review newsreel of bombardments and the usual war footage, a man in the back row stands up and announces: "Pling, this was the advertisement."

The unreliability of the Nazi-controlled press was summarized in the well-known saying that *NTB* now signified "Not to Believe" (Schou-Sörensen).[7] A related quip held that "The Oslo radio broadcasting station is called *Hitlerjugen*" (Hitler Lie, cf., *å juge* [dialect] = "to lie"), a homonym of Hitler Jugend, the infamous Hitler Youth organization (Schou-Sörensen). The following narrative joke about a Swedish business traveler in occupied Oslo also plays on the tremendous distortions imposed by Nazi censorship:

> Toget kom sent om kvelden, så han tok inn på et hotell og gikk rett til sengs. Neste morgen, mens han i hotellets frokostsal ventet på maten, kom en kelner med dagens avis. Svensken fordypet seg i denne, men etter en tids forlöp sank avisen langsomt ned og hodet på en i alle deler desorientert svenske ble synlig. "De-de-det måste dock vara et annet krig!"—sa han hen for seg. [Kristiansen 1945, 54]
> (The train arrived late at night, so he checked into a hotel and went straight to bed. The next morning, as he waited for breakfast in the hotel dining room, a waiter came with that day's newspaper. The Swede became absorbed in it, but after some time had passed, the newspaper

sank slowly to reveal the face of a completely confused Swede. "Th -thi-this must be about a different war!"—he muttered to himself.)

People remarked that the ads were the only part of the Nazi press untainted by propaganda.[8]

Avis-guttene i Bergen ropte en dag:
"Nytt, siste nytt, 2 nye avertissementer, resten jug." En annen dag: "Nytt, siste nytt. London bombet igjen. Tolv tyske bombefly bomber London, tretten vendte uskadt tilbake." [Imsland 1946, 49]
(One day the newspaper boys in Bergen were hawking: "News, latest news, two new advertisements, the rest lies." Another day: "News, latest news. London bombed again. Twelve German bombers strafe London, thirteen returned safely.")

This tendency of the Nazi press to minimize German casualties in order to make their victories seem all the more impressive received many other humorous formulations as well.[9]

På en trikk forsökte en tysker å bibringe en nordmann det inntrykket at tyskerne hadde erobret Norge så å si uten at noe av det edle tyske krigerblod var flytt.
 -Våre tap under hele det norske felttoget utgjorde bare to mann, sa tyskeren.
 –Jaså? sa nordmannen interessert.–Ja, jeg har jo hört om han der på "Blücher", men si meg, hvor falt den andre? [Svendsen n.d., 18]
(On a street car a German was trying to impress a Norwegian with the "fact" that the Germans had conquered Norway more or less without spilling any noble German warrior blood.
 "Our losses during the entire Norwegian campaign came to only two men," said the German.
 "Really?" said the Norwegian with interest. "Well now, I've heard of the one on the *Blücher,* but—tell me—where did the other one fall?")

While some claim that as many as 1,000 German lives were lost in the Norwegian sinking of the *Blücher,* even the documented figure of 320 deaths far exceeds the number admitted by the German in this joke.[10] In the entire Norwegian campaign as many as 65,000 Germans are thought to have fallen, again a rather larger number than cited by the German.

Such blatant falsification of the casualty reports calls for appropriate reprisal, as the next two jokes suggest:

Etter feldttoget i Norge kom 100 tyskere til himmelen. "Hvor kommer dere fra?" spurte St. Peter. Jo da, de hadde falt i Norge. St. Peter måtte

inn å undersöke dette. Han forsvandt inn i himmelen. Litt etter kom han tilbake og sa: "I de tyske komunikeer står det at bare to stykker er faldt i Norge. De kan få komme inn. De andre får dra til helvete." [Slaatto][11]
(After the campaign in Norway 100 German soldiers arrived in Heaven. "Where are you coming from," St. Peter asked. They said they'd fallen in Norway. St. Peter went inside to check the records. Returning a little later he said, "According to the official German communiques, only two German soldiers fell in Norway. They can come in; the rest of you can go to hell.")

En nordlandsfisker forteller at han rodde forbi to havarerte tyskere. Den ene var ferdig, den andre ropte:
"Hjelp! Jeg drukner!"
"Men jeg rodde videre jeg," sa han, "for dom er så fæle tel å juge, så en kan'ke tru på noe av det dom sier!" [Ellingsen]
(A fisherman from North Norway tells that he rowed past two shipwrecked Germans. One of them was done for, but the other shouted:
"Help! I'm drowning!"
"But I just kept on rowing," he said, " 'cause they're such terrific liars, you can't believe a thing they say!")[12]

So inculcated in lies were the Germans, according to folk wit, that they wouldn't know how to handle the truth if given the chance.

En tysker forundret seg over at det var hel pressefrihet her för. Kunne man absolutt skrive hva man ville, spurte han, og tilföyet: Hvordan kunne man da vite hva som var sannheten? [Schou-Sörensen]
(A German was amazed to hear that there had been complete freedom of the press in Norway before the war. "Could you really write absolutely anything you wanted," he asked, adding: "How could you ever know what was the truth?")

World-Class Liars

In addition to pointing out the general proclivity of all Nazis to lie, humor identified Hitler, Quisling, and Mussolini as the champions of prevarication.

Hitler og Quisling med fölge var ute på en myr. De ble enige om å gå ut på myren og se hvem som sank dypest i for han löy mest. Hitler gikk först og sank i til halsen. Deretter Göhring ikke fullt så langt, så Göbbels litt kortere igjen, men Quisling sank bare i til livet. Forundret så de andre på ham, men han sa: "Jeg bare står på Lunde jeg." [Schou-Sörensen]

(Hitler and Quisling accompanied by their entourages were out in a swamp. They agreed to walk further out into the swamp and see which one sank deepest for he would be the worst liar. Hitler went first and sank to his neck. Then Goering went down not quite so far, and Goebbels a little less still, but Quisling sank just to his waist. The others stared at him in amazement, but he said: "I'm standing on Lunde's shoulders" [i.e., Gulbrand Lunde, his propaganda minister].)

Quisling's reply could also be interpreted to imply that he's only repeating Lunde's words, and is not culpable for them. The next item, too, deals with the Nazi leaders' lies:

Hitler og Musse skal in i himmelen og blir stanset av St. Peder som spör hvor mange ganger de har löyet. Musse har löyet 2 ganger og må til straff gå 2 ganger rundt himmelen. Da han kommer tilbake spör St. Peder om han har sett noe til Hitler. "Ja," sier Musse, "han skulle hjem og hente motorsykkelen sin." [Larsen]
(Hitler and Mussolini are stopped on their way into heaven by St. Peder who asks how many times they have lied. Mussolini has lied twice and for punishment must walk around heaven twice. When he gets back St. Peder asks if he has seen any sign of Hitler. "Yes," says Mussolini, "he went home to get his motorcycle.")

The BIG Lie: Germany as Norway's Savior

As mentioned in chapter 1, the Nazis initially tried to convince Norway that their purpose in occupying the country was to protect her from British attack. They had come as friends, they said, as helpers not as occupiers. Folk wit knew better.

Terboven er i Nordland og der snakker han med en gammel nordlending. Terboven sier at det er fælt hvordan engelskmennene har herjet osv. Nordlendingen svarer at jo dem er fæle til å juge!
"Jaså, gjör de det?" svarer Terboven.
"Ja, tror du ikke dem hadde malt hakekorset på alle flyvemaskinene sine som bombet her." [Larsen]
(Terboven is in North Norway speaking with an old north-lander. Terboven exclaims over the horrible destruction the British have wrought, etc.
The North-lander answers that the British sure are terrible liars too!
"Oh, really?" says Terboven.
"You bet. Would you believe they went and painted swastikas on all the planes they used for bombing us?")

Popular humor also expressed its opinion of German "help" by inverting the Norwegian equivalent of the proverb "It's always darkest before the dawn." The normal version of the Norwegian saying, "When trouble is greatest, help is closest at hand" [Når nöden er störst, står hjelpen nærmest], was transformed to Når hjelpen er nærmest er nöden störst. "When help is closest at hand, trouble is greatest" (Schou-Sörensen, Ellingsen). Only when German "help" arrived did Norwegians discover what real trouble was.

The next joke also ridicules the concept of Germany's "assistance":

En mann vil in på vinmonopolet, men dören er låst. Han rister i döra og roper på en tysker i nærheten og ber han hjelpe seg. Men tyskern vil ikke. Han roper flere ganger, men uten resultat. Da går han helt bort til tyskern og sier:" . . . er du ikke kommet hit for å hjelpe oss da?" [Larsen]
(A man is trying to get into the liquor store, but it's locked. He rattles the door and asks for help from a nearby German. But the German refuses. The Norwegian asks him several times, but to no avail. Now he goes over to the German and says, ". . . didn't you come here to help us?")

DEGRADING THE GERMAN ÜBERMENSCH

A major goal of German and Nazi propaganda was to discredit prewar Norwegian society and its government, now exiled in England. While undermining Norwegian self-respect, some of this propaganda also sought to cultivate a boundless admiration for the German victors, promoting the idea that the war was essentially already over and that all future European and world politics would revolve around Germany and be shaped by the National Socialists. During the summer of 1940, moreover, appearances seemed to validate these claims (Hegna 1983, 249).[13]

Working against the perception of German superiority posed a challenge, but jokes made important inroads by deprecating the occupiers, emphasizing the German Nazis' stupidity and impotency, and pointing out the consequent inaccuracy of their inflated self-image.

The Germans have reported bombing a town called Random on the outskirts of London, because English radio reported that the Germans were bombing "at random."

Sinnsykehospitalene kalles for: Höyskoler for NS'ene. [Schou-Sörensen]
(Insane asylums are called: "Institutes of Higher Education for the NS.")

En man ble dödsdömt. Han fikk velge hvordan han ville drepes. Han valgte å bli hengt opp mellom Ulrikken og Lövstakken, og så ble skutt på av det tyske luftvern. Ti dager etter, ble han tatt ned. Da var han död av sult. [Christerson]
(A man was sentenced to death. Permitted to choose his own method of execution, he chose to be suspended between Ulrikken and Lövstakken [mountains in Bergen], and then be shot at by the German air force. Ten days later he was taken down. By then he had starved to death.)

A joke with cognates in several other countries recycled itself into Norwegian currency to ridicule the blindness of Nazi ideology.

En liten gutt sitter ved fortauget å leker med nogen kattunger. Da kommer en tysk offiser forbi og sier til gutten, "Du sitter å leker med kattunger du."
"Nei," svarer gutten. "Det er nasister."
Tre uker efter kommer offiseren forbi og ser den samme gutten sitte å leke med kattungene. Han sier: "Sitter du å leker med nasistene ennå?"
"Nei," svarer gutten. Det er ikke nasister lenger nå, får nå har dem fått auer!" [Larsen, Schou-Sörensen, Rommetveit; Göring cognates in Ellingsen and Slaatto][14]
(A little boy is sitting on the sidewalk playing with some kittens. A German officer comes along and asks the boy,
"Are those kittens you're playing with?"
"No," the boy answers, "they're Nazis."
Three weeks later the officer comes by again and, seeing the same boy playing with the kittens, says, "Are you still playing with those Nazis?"
"No," answers the boy. "They're not Nazis anymore; now their eyes are open!")

Another joke on the blindness of Nazi ideology told:

A Norwegian professor was asked if he knew the origin of the Nazi salute. Was it really an Old Norse greeting?
"I don't know about that," replied the professor, "but I have heard that Magnus the Blind walked with his hands waving before him." [Vigness 1970, 256]

Portraying the average Norwegian's refusal to take the Nazis seriously, of course, also served to denigrate Hitler's intimidating image (cf. chap. 2).

Noen tyskere kom til en skole som var helt forlatt. De spurte etter vaktmesteren, men den eneste som var igjen var fyrböteren. Han svarte på en blanding av norsk og tysk: Ich bin nicht der vaktmester, ich bin der fyrer. [Schou-Sörensen, Christerson, Ellingsen]
(Some Germans came to an abandoned school. They asked for the head janitor, but the only person left was the man who minded the furnace. He answered in a mixture of Norwegian and German: *Ich bin nicht der vaktmester, ich bin der fyrer.* —"I am not the janitor, I am the *fyrer*" ["firer," "stoker," in Norwegian a homonym of Führer].)

By making a pun of Hitler's intimidating title Der Führer, the janitor refuses to be bullied just as the conductor in the next joke deflects the implicit Nazi threat of invading England (see chap. 9) embodied in the soldiers' incessant singing:

Noen tyskere satt på Laksevågsfergen og sang "Wir fahren gegen Engeland." Da kom konduktören og sa: "Dere er visst kommet på en gal ferge! Denne går nemlig bare til Laksevåg." [Christerson]
(Some Germans were sitting on the local ferry to Laksevåg [near Bergen] singing, *"Wir fahren gegen Engeland"* [We're on the way to England].[15] The conductor came by and remarked, "Then you're on the wrong ferry. This one only goes as far as Laksevåg.")[16]

This chapter has considered the powerful propaganda machine Hitler had at his disposal and demonstrated the readiness of Norwegian occupation humor to meet its onslaughts by defacing the Nazis' state-of-the-art posters, deploying anti-Nazi symbols, and otherwise deflating the image of the German Übermensch. By portraying the Nazis instead as ineffectual, blundering, and impotent, Jössing humor questioned why anyone would fear or support these buffoons. The next chapter shows how Jössing humor answered that query.

7

The Universality of Resistance and Absence of Nazi Support: Humor's View

On 4 November 1940 Marie Slaatto told her diary:

> Yesterday the 3rd (Sunday) Lillehammer received a visit from the Nazi Gudbrand Lunde,[1] who was to lecture at the bank. A large group, mostly young boys in *Hird* uniforms accompanied him.[2] Lots of posters were put up before the meeting, but were instantly torn down. When the meeting was to begin at 5 o'clock, a bunch of people had gathered in front of the bank to hiss. Lunde naturally thought everyone had come to listen to him. A loudspeaker system was set up through which his voice could be heard: "My honored assembly!" That said, everyone turned around and left.[3] Only a total of 60 people stayed to listen, and this included those from Lillehammer as well as from Gjövik and other places. The same thing has happened elsewhere, especially in Trondheim, Bergen and Oslo. But in Gjövik 50% of the people are Nazis.[4]

The next day she wrote:

> -Today the newspapers say there was a full house at the bank and great enthusiasm.

Slaatto's account tells of the lack of support for the Nazis and also of the same willingness to distort the truth seen in the previous chapter. Despite isolated areas of strong Nazi support, the total influx of Norwegians to the Nazi party was actually rather minimal relative to the overall population, a fact that Nazi propaganda did its best to conceal.

> Never has such a strong and numerous organization existed as ours (Quisling speech in Trondheim).
> NS is not a party, it is a movement that represents the will of the people (Quisling speech in Tolga).

When membership rolls failed to reach expected heights, Quisling had a ready response.

> NS has so many members now, it doesn't need any more. (Sarpsborg June 21, 1942). [Mogens 1945, 249]

Each side represented membership statistics best to suit its own needs, the Nazis inflating them and the Jössings making it seem as though no one at all had joined. In reality a total of about 60,000 joined the Nazi party, out of a wartime population of 3,000,000, the largest membership at any one time being reached in November 1943 with an enrollment of almost 43,000 (Dahl 1974, 180).[5]

Openly demonstrating nonsupport for the Nazis became a directive of the organized resistance and was encouraged by the underground press.

> Let the Nazis have all the arrangements that aim to spread the poisonous German propaganda to themselves. No respectable Norwegian goes to a German theater performance or similar event. Don't forget the cinema strike: Boycott all German films and newsreels. If you go to see a "neutral" film, don't take your seat until the German newsreel or propaganda film is over. [*Norges budstikke,* no. 1, May 1941]

As a result, the Nazis had to go to extra lengths to achieve a good audience.

> Realizing that few willingly attended their propaganda meetings, they simply barricaded the doors in a theatre, cinema or concert hall, suspended the performance and forced a political lecture on the audience. . . . In towns where the boycott of German and Nazi-controlled Norwegian pictures was most effective, the State Police would order scores of citizens to visit the cinema twice a week and to show their ticket at the police station as proof. In some cases the police ordered people to visit the church, so that the Nazi vicar could be provided with a congregation. [Thomsen 1945, 46]

In Stiklestad where the Nazis held two rallies during the occupation, the following anecdote of Nazi misrepresentation circulates:

> This time [1944] a radio broadcast was made from the rally. While the reporter announced that "thousands upon thousands are streaming to Stiklestad," a division of storm troopers marched loudly in place, so their foot steps would be heard through the microphone. [Veimo 1987, 205]

The Jössings meanwhile found their own ways to demonstrate, as Greta Dahl reports in a 12 November 1940 entry.

Despite the threat of strict punishment for destroying NS posters, you can't find a single undamaged one anywhere in town. Best of all was this incident involving the janitor at the City Hall: In broad daylight he took pail and brush and scrubbed the posters off the walls. Regulations prohibit posting bills on those walls, and he used the ruling to demonstrate his own convictions.

WHENCE COMETH MY HELP?

In the same 12 November 1940 entry Greta Dahl laments, "But worst of all is the large number of cowardly scoundrels that nevertheless do join the NS." Nazi party members came largely from the ranks of workers, farmers, and people in public service. Contrary to humor's depiction, their educational level was well above average, though most were new to politics.[6] During the first months of the occupation the party attracted members easily, but as opinion about the war changed, the view of NS membership grew more negative. The September 1941 state of emergency with its subsequent executions played a significant role in turning majority opinion against party membership, and those who joined from then on, tended to do so out of a deeper commitment.

As Germany's war fortunes worsened after her February 1943 loss of Stalingrad, NS membership flagged in spite of its material advantages. Though a few districts could show a majority of party members, in most they were decidedly in the minority and grew increasingly isolated as the occupation wore on.[7] The Nazis' high degree of organization in women's groups, youth organizations, rallies, and assemblies kept them in the public eye, however, and sometimes conveyed an impression of a larger membership.

Humor balanced this impression by claiming a total absence of Nazi support,[8] a view frequently expressed in variants of the following widespread joke (here quoted from the January 1941 issue of the underground newspaper *Hvepsen*):

I en bygd i Nord-Tröndelag mötte ingen tilhörere opp. Da NS folkene kom ut av mötelokalet fant de en mökkekjerre bundet til bilen. På kjerra var festet en plakat med inskriften: "dette har vi gjort for at dere i hvert fall skal ha *en* tilhenger."
(In a certain town in Nord-Tröndelag no one came to hear an NS lecture. When the NS members left the meeting hall, they found a

manure trailer attached to their car. On the trailer was a sign saying: "We've done this so you'd have at least *one tilhenger* [wordplay meaning both "trailer" and "follower" in the sense of "political supporter"].)[9]

The same issue of *Hvepsen* reported that

> In one place only two people came to hear [the NS lecture]. After waiting a while for more to arrive, the speaker sarcastically remarked, "I suppose the others are listening to London." This prompted one of the prospective audience members to take out his watch and exclaim, "Good God, you're right! It's time for the BBC broadcast," and with that he left.

This meeting, as *Hvepsen* also reports, was later described in the Nazi paper *Fritt folk* as "a great success; all those who came, except *one,* joined the NS."

Another joke circulating during the early war years emphasized the weakness of Nazi support in a different way.

> A man was questioning a Norwegian editor about the hoped-for (Allied) invasion of German-occupied Norway.
> "How long will it take," he asked, "for our own forces to get things under control?"
> "First of all, these Quislings will have to be liquidated," answered the editor. "That alone may take forty-eight hours."
> "Oh, no!" said the man. "They're not that numerous. Twenty-four hours will be more than enough for that job!" [Olav and Myklebust 1942, 38]

THE NAZIS: YOUNG AND NAIVE TO OLD AND DECREPIT

In an effort to increase their ranks, the Nazis created especially attractive terms for recruiting young people. They allowed minors to join Regiment Nordland and to set out for the German front without their parents' permission. These measures and the youthfulness of the Hird invited Jössing humor to mock the Nazis' immaturity, and to imply that the party, being forced to accept whatever members it could entice, had to settle for the young and naive, since they alone would be dumb enough to fall for its ideology.

> Kunngjöring: Dun er frigjitt, —hirden har begynt og barbere seg. [Ellingsen]
> (Notice: Down [i.e., peach fuzz] will no longer be rationed; the *Hird* is now old enough to shave.)

Tyskland har bedt om våpenstillstand, for 7 tyske divisj. på Vestfronten skal stå til konfirmasjon. [Ellingsen]
(Germany has asked for a cease-fire to allow for seven German *Hird* divisions on the West Front to participate in Confirmation exercises.)

Quisling tör ikke gå ut om formiddagen for hirden er på skolen. [Ellingsen]
(Quisling doesn't dare go out in the morning because the *Hird* is still in school.)[10]

Hird Heimen kalles for barnehjem for gutter i slyngelalderen. [Schou-Sörensen]
(The *Hird* Home is called a home for boys at *slyngelalderen.* [*Slyngel-alder* means "an awkward age," but *slyngel* also means "scoundrel" or "villain" so they are also boys ripe to become villains].)

When Hitler signed a decree on 26 September 1944 establishing a people's army to defend German soil by means of conscripting every able-bodied man between the ages of sixteen and sixty, folk wit found particular amusement in the upper age-limit, regarding it as proof of Nazi desperation.

Metusalem var nede på jorden men kom forbausende fort opp til himmelen igjen. "Jeg var i Berlin," sa han til Vår Herre, "og der holdt de på å innkalle min årsklasse." [Schou-Sörensen]
(Methusala was down on Earth, but returned to Heaven surprisingly soon.
"I was in Berlin," he said to the Lord," and they were about to call up my age group.")

To gamlinger möttes:
"Er du innkalt du, og?"
"Ja."
"Var ikke du med i forrige krig?" (1914–1918)
"Nei, jeg var for gammel!!" [Ellingsen]
(Two old timers meet:
"Have you been called up too?"
"Yes."
"Weren't you in the last war?" (1914–1918)
"No, I was too old!!")

Norway's own Nazi party was similarly scrambling for support, according to folk wit, and would just as gladly take anyone it could get its hands on.

March 1943: Forskjellen mellom Quisling og en bank. Banken tar innskudd og Quisling tar utskudd. [Schou-Sörensen]

(The difference between Quisling and a bank. The bank takes *innskudd* [deposits] and Quisling takes *utskudd* [the dregs].)[11]

GRASSROOTS RESISTANCE

Popular humor emphasized the enormous numbers of those who opposed the New Order.

Det er innført papirrasjonering for NS har skrevet liste over alle jössingene. [Ellingsen]
(Now paper will have to be rationed; the Nazi party's made a list of all the Jössings.)[12]

By portraying defiance as a characteristic of both ends of the age spectrum, the humor suggested that resistance prevailed throughout Norwegian society.[13]

During the war in southern Norway the Germans twice captured a 74-year-old farmer who was wearing a makeshift uniform and carrying an antiquated rifle. Because of his age, the man was immediately released and told to go home. But the old gentleman was captured a third time.
"When are you going to give up this nonsense?" demanded the Germans, now furious. "This is a war for young men, not for you and your old blunderbuss."
The old man smiled grimly and said: "This old blunderbuss has done good work so far and I don't intend to put it away until the Norwegian flag flies over Berlin!" [Olav and Myklebust 1942, 8]

Aiming not only to wrest Norway back from the Nazis, the man intends to take Germany. Nor do the Nazis intimidate his junior counterpart:

A little boy was on his way home. His face was scratched and battered, and an elderly lady stopped to ask him if he had been in a fight.
"Of course I have!" answered the lad. "If you grown-ups don't put these storm troopers in their place, then we youngsters have got to take matters into our own hands." [Olav and Myklebust 1942, 31]

In addition to covering both extremes of the age spectrum, Jössing jokes depict public officials approving and promoting ostensibly illegal resistance tactics, thereby placing their loyalty to an independent Norway above all else, including their jobs.[14]

When venturesome young Norwegians set out for England to join their country's fighting forces, they do not hesitate to "borrow" any conveniently located boat. Thus a fisherman called on the sheriff to report that his boat had been stolen the preceding night. The sheriff looked at him disapprovingly:

"Shame on you!" he said. "You might have at least waited a week before reporting it." [Olav and Myklebust 1942, 35]

As noted earlier (chap. 5), a comparison with Eastern Bloc humor provides an instructive contrast. While the Norwegian material emphasizes the large number of like-minded resisters, the Communist jokes tend to highlight the ubiquity of traitors and the impossibility of trusting others.

While waiting for the bus at an overcrowded bus stop, Ionescu starts a conversation with a stranger. A beautiful Chevrolet races by.

-That Volga is really beautiful isn't it?

The stranger doesn't answer. After a while, a Mercedes passes by and Ionescu exclaims:

-Oh look at that beautiful Zil.

Now the stranger can't stand it any longer.

-You don't seem to know very much about cars, he says.

-I know a lot about cars, *it's you I know nothing about.* [Banc and Dundes 1986, 24, emphasis mine]

Two Rumanian policemen were standing on guard together. One asked the other:

-What do you think of our regime?

-The same as you.

-In that case it is my duty to arrest you. [Banc and Dundes 1986, 30]

While jokes from the former Communist regimes tend to reveal the presence of informers where they're least expected, in the Norwegian humor, it is the resisters who appear in unexpected quarters, such as the sheriff in the boat joke and the asylum director in the one that follows:

One evening several inmates of the Reitgjerde hospital for the insane escaped and managed to tear the swastika from the flagpole at Kristiansten Fort before being apprehended. Greatly worried, the director of the asylum called on the highest civil official in Trondheim for help in avoiding German reprisals.

"I can give you no advice officially," said this Norwegian, "but— well, it's too bad all of us aren't crazy." [Olav and Myklebust 1942, 39]

Perhaps the most extreme example of humor accentuating Norway's high degree of anti-Nazi sentiment appears in Oddmund Kristiansen's postwar humor collection. It tells of a Swedish journalist who decided that getting arrested would provide him with the best opportunity to observe firsthand the conditions in Oslo's Grini concentration camp. Thinking a streetcar conductor as an employee of the state would have Nazi sympathies, he determined to provoke one in order to be placed under arrest.

When the conductor put out his hand to receive payment for the ticket, the Swede raised a clenched fist and said rather loudly, "Red Front!" The conductor brightened, nodded a whispered "You ride free!" and continued his rounds.

The journalist tried again, this time a policeman. He showed him the same gesture and said "Red Front"—and almost had a heart attack when the constable began talking about a bottle of cognac he had at home and wouldn't the Swede come over that evening, say around 7 o'clock?

Perspiring with disbelief, the Swede decided to make one last try and presently spotted a German officer: What if he tried him? It could have serious consequences, but nothing ventured, nothing gained. He leaned over to the officer and said quite softly: "Red Front." The German knitted his brow, pointed his thumb over his shoulder and said, "Shhh, *vorsicht* [be careful]. The fellow sitting behind me is a Nazi!"

The journalist fainted. [Kristiansen 1945, 60–61]

HIGH PROFILE RESISTANCE

Even greater than the impact of made-up jokes, says Finn Bö, was the effect of actual Nazi put-downs uttered spontaneously by well-known Norwegian citizens. Beyond amusement, Bö asserts, these replies offered evidence of a personal conviction and courage to resist (55). Several such quick-witted responses made by prominent Norwegians became treasured currency in occupied Norway, like the following one made by the poet Arnulf Överland:[15]

One day the prisoners of Oslo's Grini Prison Camp[16] had to stand at attention as the commandant expressed his wish to make a garden. He asked if there were a gardener present. As no one stepped forward, he repeated his wish a little more sharply. No one answered. Then Arnulf Överland stepped forward, put his finger in the air and said very sweetly: "I propose that we arrest a gardener." [Thomsen 1945, 34]

Though Överland himself was subsequently deported from Grini to Germany's Sachsenhausen concentration camp where he remained for the duration of the war, his wry denunciation of the Nazis' punitive methods stayed behind to cheer and embolden others.

The author of Norway's national anthem, Björnstjerne Björnson (1832–1910), had two sons, one who joined the NS and another who most emphatically did not. About the latter, the actor and theater director Björn Björnson (1859–1942), it was told that when the Quisling paper *Fritt folk* (Free people) telephoned to request an interview, he replied: "Dritt Folk" (Shit People) and hung up (Schou-Sörensen).[17]

Schou-Sörensen also records an anecdote told about Gen. Johan Henrik Rye (1864–1944)—the commander of Norway's special forces and known as the most courteous man in Norway.

A German enthusiastically complimented him for extending courtesy even to him and thanked him for his *lebenswürdichkeit* [giving the feeling of someone else's worthiness to live]. To this the General answered that there is a difference between *lebenswürdichkeit* and courtesy.

While Rye might treat him with courtesy, the quip implied, he didn't necesarily feel the German had a right to exist.

About an even more famous military man, Gen. Otto Ruge (1882–1961), commander of the two-month Norwegian military resistance following the 9 April invasion, it was told:

A German general was explaining to General Ruge how highly the Germans regarded the Norwegians, how fond they were of them and how much they wanted to be their friends. To this General Ruge responded dryly: "Yes, and rape is also a form of love." [*Hvepsen*][18]

The distinguished geologist and University of Oslo professor of geography Werner Werenskiold (1883–1961) also figured in several anecdotes.[19]

Professor Werner Werenskiold sto på plattformen på trikken. En hirdmann kom på, og professoren måler han fra topp til tå på en måte som ikke er til å ta feil av. Hirdmannen trekker opp sin notisbok og forlanger navnet. "Mitt navn, ja det er prof. Werner Werenskiold det, men hvad heter pappaen din da, gutten min?" [Slaatto]
(Professor Werner Werenskiold was standing on the platform of a streetcar. A member of the *Hird* got on and the professor eyed him

from top to toe with unmistakable disgust. The *Hird* member took out his notebook and demanded his name.
"My name is Professor Werner Werenskiold, and what's your daddy's name, little boy?")

A related Werenskiold anecdote similarly ridicules the naïveté of the Hird, while also denigrating the Nazi salute.

Proff W W står inne i en forretning da det kommer en hirdgutt inn. Han hilser med "Heil og sæl." W W snur seg brått mot gutten og sier: "Knoll og Tott"!
Gutten blir rasende og spör W W om hans navn og stilling. Han får vite dette, og så sier W W: "Hva heter pappan din da, gutten min?" [Ellingsen]
(Prof W W is standing in a store when a *Hird* boy comes in. He salutes and says, *"Heil og sæl."* W W turns abruptly toward the boy and says, *"Knoll og Tott!"* [Hans and Fritz, the Katzenjammer Kids in the comics]. Furious, the boy demands W W's name and position. W W tells him, then asks, "And what is your daddy's name, my boy?")

An entire cycle of jokes featured Einar Rose (1898–1979), one of Norway's most popular revue artists. He most frequently appeared at Oslo's Chat Noir cabaret theater, which made a special point of smuggling anti-Nazi barbs into its performances.[20] Rose showed particular daring in this regard, and several of his jokes subsequently found their way into wartime notebooks.[21] Frequently employing visual gags, his witticisms play on many of the themes already discussed, such as contempt for the Nazis and the wishful visualization of the occupation's end.

Inne på scenen. Veggene er fulle av billeder. Rose holder 2 i hånden av Mussolini og Hitler og sier: Disse to skulle absolut vært "hengt opp." [Christerson][22]
(On stage: The walls are full of pictures. Rose holds two in his hand—of Mussolini and Hitler—and says, "These two should definitely be 'hung.'")

Rose står og selger inne på scenen. Kunden spör om *det,* om *det,* om *det.* Rose sier: "Har det ikke." "Har dere ingenting i denne butikken?" "Ja, bare vent til vi får "pakket" ut. [Christerson]
(Rose stands on stage pretending to be a store clerk. The customer asks about this, that and the other. Rose says, "Don't have any."
    "Don't you have anything in this store?"
    "Yes, just wait till we get *pakket ut.*" [*pakket ut* means "unpacked," i.e., "unloaded," but Rose's entire reply suggests "until we get rid of the *pakk* = 'rabble or riffraff,'" i.e., the occupiers].)

As noted in chapter 1, puns equating the occupiers with trash and vandals occurred frequently, so this witticism appears in many variants.

> Einar Rose kommer inn på scenen med en ryggsekk full av hermetikk og alle vil ha noe. Vent, ikke mas, sier han, dere skal få så meget dere vil når jeg bare får "pakket" ut. [Schou-Sörensen][23]
> (Einar Rose comes on stage with a backpack full of canned goods and everyone wants some. "Wait, don't worry," he says, "you'll get as much as you want as soon as I get *pakket ut*" [get "unpacked"/ /"rid of the riffraff"].)[24]

Using a different wordplay, the next joke also makes the point that the occupiers are trash:

> Rose inne på scenen. Han går helt ut til kanten, ser nedover tyskerne som sitter på förste benk. Sier: "Så nær rampen har jeg ikke vært för." [Christerson]
> (Rose on stage: He goes right up to the edge, looks down upon the Germans sitting in the first row and says, "Never before have I been so near *rampen*" [i.e., *rampelysene* = "the footlights," but *rampen* also means the "scum" or "vulgar people"].)[25]

Some of the Rose jokes ridicule individual Nazi leaders, such as the following item that led to his arrest:

> Inne på scenen. Rose klapper en terrier. Sier, "Så, så terrivovfen. Du er ikke noe poppulær her blandt folket. Ut med deg, din kjöter, ditt utyske." [Christerson]
> (On stage: Rose pets a terrier and says, "There, there *terrivovfen*" ["terrier-doggy" also a homonym of Terboven, Norway's Reichskommissar]. You aren't very popular here. Get out, you mongrel you *utyske* ["brute, monster, ugly dangerous person"; the word also contains the element *tysk* = "German"].)[26]

The Trondheim diary reports that this incident led to Rose's arrest, and it tells how Rose used his incarceration in a follow-up act.

> Efter löslatelsen optrer Rose igjen og kommer inn på scenen med terrieren sin. Han klapper hunden og sier: "Nei, er du der . . . nei, jeg tör ikke si det!! [20 September 1940]
> (After his release Rose makes another appearance. Coming on stage with his terrier, he pets the dog and says, "Is that you. . . . No, I'd better not say it!!")

Christerson also records an item referring to his arrest.

Rose på scenen med en röd rose i knapphullet: Sier: "Du holder deg godt, rose, enda du har sittet tre dager i hullet." [Christerson]
(Rose on stage with a red rose in the button hole of his lapel. He says, "You're looking good, Rose, even though you've spent three days in the hole" [i.e., jail].)

Other Rose jokes served alternative functions such as:
* denigrating the Hitler salute:

Rose lager hail med armen. Det tyske publikum svarer med det samme. Rose: "Så höyt hoppet jeg da jeg var ung." [Christerson][27]
(Rose raises his right arm in the Nazi salute. The Germans in the audience respond with the same gesture. Rose says: "That's how high I could jump when I was young.")[28]

* telling how it feels to be an occupied nation:

Chat Noir: Einar Rose utkledt som Jossa Seeberg, går ned og setter seg på fanget til en tysker og sier: Nå kan De kjenne hvordan det er å være okkupert, nå. (JS var svært tykk.) [Schou-Sörensen, Larsen]
(Chat Noir: Einar Rose dressed up as Jossa Seeberg [who was very obese], goes down and sits on the lap of a German and says: Now you can feel what it's like to be occupied.)[29]

* commenting on the Nazi repression of news, rights, and freedoms:

Rose kommer inn, stor applaus. Sier ingenting, bukker, går ut. Gjör det samme flere ganger. 3. gang bukker han, stor applaus. Han sier: "Dette var nyhetene fra Norge." [Christerson]
(Rose comes in, much applause. Says nothing, bows, goes out. Does this several times. The third time he bows, much applause. He says, "Well, that's the news from Norway.")

Inne på scenen. Rose ser utover de mange grönnklette. Sier: "Når hjelpen er nermest, er nöden störst." [Christerson]
(On stage: Rose looks out at the many green-clad [German soldiers]. He says, "Trouble is greatest, when help is closest at hand.")[30]

* Expressing the desire for a return to the prewar government:

Rose kom inne på scenen med en helt ny, flott sykkel med et gammelt rustent styre og sa at han likte det gamle styret best. [Trondheim diary, 28 June 1941]
(Rose came on stage with a very nice, brand new, bicycle that had

old, rusted-out handlebars [*styre*], and said he preferred the old *styret* [meaning both "handlebars" and "government"].)[31]

Alluding to the frequent Nazi interrogations experienced by occupied Norwegians, one joke portrays Einar Rose being similarly subjected.

Terboven inkaller Rose og spör om han har laget alle vitsene sine selv. "Ja," sier Rose. Terboven sier at han godt kan vitse om tyskerne, men ikke om Hitler, "For vet du ikke," legger han til, "at han har 800 mill. mensker bak seg?" "Nei, den er ikke min," sier Rose. [Larsen, Christerson][32]

(Terboven summons Rose and asks if he has made up all his jokes himself.

"Yes I have," Rose replies.

Terboven says it's all right if he jokes about the Germans, but not about Hitler, because—he asks—"Don't you know he is loved by 800 million people?"

"No," Rose replies, "that's not one of mine, [but it sure is a good story!"]

As in humor, so in reality, Rose did not escape punishment for his witticisms, as we have seen. The diarist Greta Dahl records that he had gotten twenty days for "his Nazi greeting" (20 October 1940).

* * *

Jokes about the universal rejection of Nazism no doubt helped dissuade the hesitant and unsure from joining the party and in this way made a valuable contribution to the development of the resistance. At the same time, however, this humor obscured the existence of a sincerely committed element within the NS who genuinely believed in the European New Order and wanted Norway to be a free partner in it. What these individuals failed to perceive until too late, was the lack of German sympathy with their goal of Norwegian sovereignty. While stringing Norway's Nazi party along with promises of eventual Norwegian independence, Hitler and his henchmen actually regarded such an eventuality as mere rhetoric. In addition to verbal persuasion they used material advantages to attract and keep adherents, sparing them from the shortage-induced hardships suffered by the rest of the population. The next chapter will show how Norwegians coped with the absence of even the most basic essentials and how they endured other challenges of occupied daily life.

8

Daily Life in Reality and in Humor

Occupation jokes provide valuable insights into the realities and frustrations of wartime daily life because of their intimately observed detail. Two items in particular dominate this humor: the elec*tric* streetcar known as the *trikk,* and the trying wartime shortages of food and other necessities.

SHORTAGES
OH YES, WE HAVE NO POTATOES

In peacetime, Norway had supplied about 80 percent of its grain consumption and about 50 percent of its other daily needs through imports. Now goods could only be obtained from Germany and German-occupied countries or from neutral countries, a circumstance that severely restricted the amount and availability of food and fiber. At the same time Hitler's policy of making Norway bear the cost of her own occupation meant that she not only had to pay high taxes but also had to share her limited resources with the occupying forces, who came to number some 300,000 (a 10-percent addition to Norway's wartime population of 3,000,000). For urban Norwegians the occupation immediately lowered the standard of living, which gradually declined even farther through wage freezes and reductions (Olsen 1946, 38).[1] Many city-dwellers turned to various forms of self-sufficiency farming to stretch their food supply,[2] and the theme of *matauk* (food augmentation) increasingly characterized all phases of occupied life, not least its humor.

Conditions worsened substantially as Christmas 1941 approached, when only fish, vegetables, and fruit remained unrationed (though also in short supply). On 11 November 1941 the underground newspaper *Fri fagbevegelse* (Free labor movement) reported:

138

Now we are really noticing the lack of food. Potatoes can't be found. The bread ration is insufficient. On the job workers must submit to a diet of salt herring. The margarine ration is being further reduced, and producers have been told that its manufacture will gradually cease so they'd better start looking for other employment. Milk is disappearing. Cheese is already gone. The meat ration, which at this season of large-scale slaughter ought to be generous, is steadily dwindling. Fresh fish is now among the rarities. Eggs are not seen.

Just as the year 1941 marked a turning point in the conditions themselves, however, it also signaled a change in the Norwegians' attitude toward them. An increasing consciousness of Nazi oppression was accompanied by an expanding awareness among non-NS members that they shared a common view of their fate; this awareness in turn awakened a growing willingness and resolve to laugh together in defiance. All of these factors contributed to a noticeable growth of anti-Nazi solidarity.[3]

Anti-Nazi Card-Tricks

That year's Christmas cards provide some of the best insights into the shortages themselves and into the developing attitude of anti-Nazi defiance (see also chap. 5 about other aspects of these cards).[4]

One card, titled "Julen 1941" (Christmas 1941) shows three stocking-capped *nisser* viewing a rather unappetizing fish in a combination of surprise and disappointment, yet also with good humor. The pork delicacies normally integral to the traditional holiday feast have become mere memories, captured in the drawings—labeled *pölse* (sausage) and *gris* (pig)—placed on either side of the fish. Behind the *nisser* hang other drawings of now absent Christmas staples: sugar, bread, shortening, and soap. The Norwegian flag hangs there too, like the other items, now but a dream, since the November 1941 Flag Ordinance reserved its display exclusively to members of the Nazi party.

Despite the shortages, people got together and shared what little they could assemble.[5] These gatherings often featured group-singing, including improvised song-parodies about the shortages, like this one from the diary of Åslaug Rommetveit sung to the tune of the well-known folk song *Pål sine höner* (Paul's chickens):

Nå kan du tro det er moro å stelle
Kjökkenet mitt er blitt kunstnernes hus.

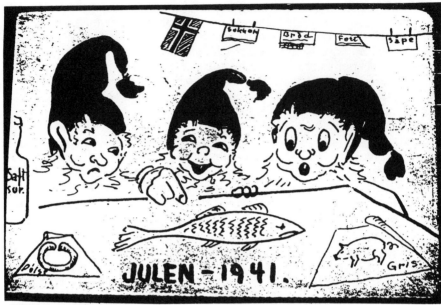

"Christmas 1941." The *nisses* react to the absence of pork products along with that of other essentials: the Norwegian flag, "sugar," "bread," "shortening," and "soap." Artist and publisher: unknown. University of Oslo Krigtrykkssamlingen.

För var det lett nok å koke og skrelle
nu er det en kunst å få noe i krus.
Kornet det *var* her - men melet er borte
Kan du forstå hvad det er som har gjort det?
Vil du ha mel må du jammen deg forte
Se å få kjöpt - ja du kan da vel *det???*

Melet har nu slik en nydelig farve
det må da sikkert ha höyfjellsol fått.
Kanskje du i det kan finne en larve
men i en kake det gjör seg så godt.
"Klukk," sier höna - men egget er borte.
Kan du forstå hva det er som har gjort det?
Vil du ha egg må du jamen deg forte
Kjöp deg en höne, ja, du kan da vel det???

Maten vi kokte i dag på en spiker
Den blei så feit og så kraftig og god.
Tilsatt en terning - hvis smaken du liker
savnes ei flesket - ja *det* kan du tro.
"Nöff," sier grisen, men flesket er borte.
Kan du forstå hva det er som har gjort det?

Vil du ha flesk må du jammen deg forte
Kjöp deg en gris, ja, du kan da vel det???

Snart kan du lage de fineste retter
kokt på en tanke og litt fantasi.
Næringsverdien blir kanskje deretter,
men hva har *det* nu for tiden å si.
Litt etter litt er det meste blitt borte.
Kan du forstå hva det er som har gjort det?
Tenk ikke på det - for *Det* skal bli borte
Vær optimist - ja, du kan da vel det???

(Now there is really such joy in my cooking,
My kitchen's become a creative workshop.
Once it was no trick to find food worth cooking.
Now there's no way to find a stocked shop.
The grain was grown, but the flour's all gone now.
Can you imagine how this has happened?
If you want flour, you'd better get a move on:
Buy up a carload, sure *that's* easy to do!!!

Now all the flour has such delightful color.
Somehow it's managed to get a suntan.
In it are larvae and other creepy-crawlers
To make up for all of the missing protein.
"Cluck," says the hen, but eggs are all gone now.
Can you imagine how this has happened?
If you want eggs, you'd better get a move on:
Buy a good hen, sure *that's* easy to do!!!

Dinner today was made out of thin air,
So filling and healthy, so tasty and good.
Just add a broth cube to give it some flavor
And no one will see there's no meat in the stew.
"Oink," says the pig, but pork is all gone now.
Can you imagine how this has happened?
If you want pork, you'd better get a move on:
Buy your own pig, sure *that's* easy to do!!!

Soon you'll be making the finest of dishes
Stewed up on dreams and pure fantasy.
All the nutrition maybe is missing,
But in *these* times, how important can that be?
Bit by bit, most things are all gone now.
Can you imagine how this has happened?
Don't think about it—*They'll* soon be gone too [i.e., the occupiers].
Be an optimist, sure *that's* easy to do!!!)

CRISIS FLOUR

Lauded in the song for its "delightful" suntan, *krise-mel* (crisis flour) was a dark-brown mixture of underprocessed, coarsely ground grain and chalk. The flatulence it caused also figured prominently in occupation humor. The well-known entertainer, Leif Juster, for example, made popular a song called "Have You Heard the New Bread?"[6] and its title soon became a standing joke (Elvsås 1980). There was also the story of the propaganda minister Gulbrand Lunde who gave a bombastic speech proclaiming that "a new wind (is) blowing over Norway!" only to be interrupted by a heckler's call that it was "just the new bread" (Ramfjord 1945, 30).

Other jokes about the so-called *fisebröd* (fart-bread) suggested that the flour consisted of wood rather than grain.

Krisetid: Barna står i kö foran Heimdalsgatens hövleri for å få kjöpt kakesmuler. [Ellingsen]
(Time of crisis: Children lining up in front of the Heimdal Street Sawmill to buy cake crumbs.)

Det var kö utenfor Mandalsgatens hövleri for å samle brödsmuler. [Hjeltnes 1987, 100]
(There was a line outside the Mandal Street Sawmill to gather bread crumbs.)

A March 1941 ordinance decreed that white flour be reserved to children under two years and the sick, prompting this joke:

Vet du at baker Samson er arrestert?
-Nei, hvorfor?
-Han hadde blandet mel i brödet. [Hjeltnes 1987, 100][7]
(Do you know that Samson the baker has been arrested?
No, why?
He added flour to his bread dough.)

ENDLESS LINES TO NOWHERE

Obtaining the materials necessary to conduct daily life became increasingly difficult, and by summer 1942, lines had become the most characteristic feature of urban life all over the country. Anywhere people sensed goods were available, a line would form and people would wait for hours. Several entries from the diary of Greta Dahl give an impression of the situation.

Dec 21, 1941:
A woman standing in the line asked: "What are they selling here?" Another woman who just came out answered: "I don't know what it is, but you can get a bag of it for one *krone*." That ought to be a joke, but unfortunately it's today's reality.

April 30, 1942:
Oh, how we froze as we stood there from 11:30 AM until 3:30 PM, when we finally got in. A policeman was there to regulate the line, letting in only 10 at a time. The jokes, however, flowed in a steady stream![8]

November 7, 1942:
There just isn't enough time for all these lines, nor is there much to stand in line for: no flour, no margarine, no surrogate coffee; still we have to wait for hours, because of all the writing and clipping [in the ration books and coupon books].

November 12, 1942:
It makes you both sad and angry, and everything seems so hopeless, for we have no recourse but to take the pittance we get and shuffle off to the next line.

March 4, 1944:
A teacher was telling about the children's conception of the 17th of May parade. She had told them about how we used to celebrate Constitution Day. These second-graders had no recollection of May 17, 1939, of course. "Oh," asked one little girl, "did you walk down the street standing in line?"

In this little girl's experience, standing in line was far more comprehensible than marching in a parade.

Shortages and Corruption

Many diarists made food a main theme, describing fantasy meals or, as Schou-Sörensen has done in the following example, recording actual incidents that reflect an underlying uneasiness about the Nazi control of foodstuffs and suspicions about fellow Norwegians profiting in the black market:

A woman from the country sold 2000 eggs to a shop. An hour later she went back in and asked to buy some eggs over the counter. She was told they had no eggs. Then she asked to talk to the manager, who told her that they had orders not to sell eggs over the counter because the Germans were to have them all.

A woman bought a can of fish balls and when she got home discovered it was full of butter. After that she bought more, saying nothing to the merchant but telling her friends, who all bought the cans and either got butter or coffee.

Norwegian dock workers who unload foodstuffs have bags inside their work clothes which they fill with food for later distribution among their own families.

The black market offered a respite to the shortages for those who could afford to pay the exorbitant prices. Farmers had to deliver a certain quantity of their produce to the Nazis, but could give the excess to friends and family or sell it at a profit. To city dwellers their standard of living seemed to far exceed their own, arousing the suspicion that the farmers were profiting from the misfortune of others. While the suspicion probably outweighed the reality, it certainly led to some good stories.

Nazilensmannen i en Östfoldbygd arresterte en bonde for svarthandel og kjörte ham i sin bil til Moss. Det lyktes under dette for den smarte svarthandler å smugle en kalveskrott inn i bilen og få den med til byen. [*Karikaturens krigs-humor* n.d., 22]
(The Nazi sheriff in an Östfold town arrested a farmer for selling on the Black Market. As he was being driven to Moss for booking, the Black Marketeer managed to smuggle a calf carcass along in the car, thereby getting it transported to town for free.)

En annen smart svarthandler fra opplandene skjenket på toget noen tyske soldater, og da de kom til Oslo, bar de hans velfylte kofferter gjennom kontrollen på Östbanestasjonen. [*Karikaturens krigs-humor* n.d., 22]
(Another smart Black Marketeer from the hinterlands shared his whiskey with some German soldiers on the train. Upon arriving in Oslo, they obligingly carried his well-stocked suitcases through the East Railway Station's duty check-point.)

About the black market, Greta Dahl notes on 12 March 1944:

I hear there's quite a Black Market in Oslo. [She quotes the high prices being charged]—I can't imagine where people get the money. But we don't hear anything from those who can't afford it. They can be found in the over-crowded doctors' offices.

While anecdotes of the black market derived from the suspicion of fellow Norwegians, more often it was the occupiers who attracted distrust and blame. On 14 September 1940, an outraged fourteen-year-old Marie Slaatto reported:

> Now I've heard something that *really* makes me mad. What do you think of this—Else's uncle was standing on the pier in Oslo watching the Germans loading some large crates into a boat. He asked a German what it was, and he answered, "the bodies of German officers being sent home to Germany." Suddenly the top fell off of one of the crates and out rolled Norwegian ham, butter, cheese, etc. Those were the German bodies! How do you like that! Sending *our* food to Germany. It really makes me mad![9]

Summing up the disparity in access to the food supply, this widely circulated postcard, graphically contrasting "Den magre og den fete" (The skinny one and the fat one), was drawn by the well-known illustrator Ridley Borchgrevink[10] in 1942 and preserved in the diary of Schou-Sörensen:

"Skinny and fatso," commenting on the differential availability of foodstuffs according to Nazi party affiliation. Artist: Ridley Borchgrevink; publisher: Eberhard Oppi Forlag, 1942.

Probably the most common way people coped with food shortage was the barter system *(byttehandel)*, advertising in the paper the items they had in excess and asking for those for which they would trade.[11] Among the countless authentic ads that filled the newspapers, *Aftenposten* allegedly carried one saying, "I have whiskey, what do you have?" The next day the following answer appeared: "I have seltzer, where do you *live?*" [*Karikaturens krigshumor* n.d., 22]

JOKES ABOUT THE FOOD SHORTAGES

Because the food shortages were the source of increasing tension and anxiety, this topic underlies many other occupation jokes as well.

På kino. Det vises fram en tysk propagandafilm. Man ser et skib i norsk havn som blir lasset for oster og andre födevarer. Da roper en stemme fra salen: "Dere kjörer filmen den gærne veien." [Larsen, Ellingsen, Schou-Sörensen]
(At a movie theater they're showing a German propaganda film. We see a German ship in Norwegian harbor unloading cheeses and other foodstuffs. Suddenly a voice yells from the audience, "You're running the film backwards!")[12]

I ei avis vart det dröfta kor stor avstand potetene skal ha. Personlig har jeg innsilt meg på en ukestid mellom hver. [Rommetveit]
(A newspaper was discussing how far apart potatoes should be. Personally I'd prefer no more than a week.)

"Vet du at hver familie må ha en tysker hver hos seg på Julaften?"
"Hva—?"
"Vi får vel ikke noget annet svin." [Larsen]
("Did you know that each family must invite a German guest for Christmas Eve?"
"What—?"
"Well, we won't be having any other swine.")

Slaughtered at Christmastime, the pig provided the basis for the traditional Christmas meal, but was, as the joke emphasizes, in short supply during the occupation.[13]

Food shortages also provided the theme for one of Arne Taraldsen's December 1943 mock stamps.[14] This one shows a fat German who has raided the livestock and crops belonging to a fair, bunad-clad young Norwegian woman. Its text: *Alt for Tyskland* (Everything for Germany), sardonically twists King Haakon's official motto: *Alt for Norge* (Everything for Norway).

Among the most popular witticisms of 1941 were those about

A mock stamp depicting a fat German officer stealing the defenseless Norwegian's food and livestock following the motto Everything for Germany. Artist: Arne Taraldsen, December 1943.

Norway's Nobel Prize-winning author Knut Hamsun (1859–1952), who championed the NS in his speeches and writing throughout the occupation.[15] Hamsun's unconditional support of their cause prompted the Nazis to reprint several of his novels for free distribution, a situation that provoked this joke:

> Hamsuns böker skal deles: England skal ha "Victoria"
> Tyskland skal ha "Markens gröde"
> Norge skal ha "Sult" [Ellingsen, Schou-Sörensen]
> (Knut Hamsun's books are to be distributed: England will receive *Victoria*, Germany will have *Growth of the Soil*, and Norway will get *Hunger*.)[16]

Several underground newspapers printed the joke, such as the 9 August 1941 issue of *Hjemmefronten*, which carried the following variant:

> The Germans have decided to divide Hamsun's works between themselves and the Norwegians. The Germans will get *The Growth of the Soil* and *Victoria*, while Norwegians will keep *Hunger*.

Three weeks later the news sheet *Alt for Norge* reported this item, portraying Hamsun's personal involvement in assigning the books' distribution.

Knut Hamsun it is said has sold *The Growth of the Soil* to the Germans, but has reserved *Hunger* for Norway. [27 August 1941][17]

The latter variant's suggestion of Hamsun's more active role reflects growing disgust with Hamsun and increasing righteous indignation over any pro-Nazi attitude, signaling the population's developing resistance mentality. The next joke captures this mounting resentment of their world-famous author:

På en auksjon i Oslo ble Hamsuns samlede verker ropt opp.
  -Ti öre, böd en nede i salen.
  -Ti öre er buden, ti öre, ingen bedre, sa auksjonarius, og hammeren falt. [*Karikaturens krigs-humor* n.d., 28]
(Hamsun's collected works were being offered at an auction in Oslo. "One cent," bid someone in the audience. "One cent is bid, will anyone bid more? Going, going, gone for one cent," called the auctioneer as he let the gavel fall.)

To this day Hamsun remains a highly controversial figure in Norway, his worldwide literary acclaim notwithstanding.

* * *

Two extended puns sum up the harshness of daily life and the previously unimagined conditions facing most Norwegians. The first is based on the Nativity scene and displays the previously noted mechanism of wartime meanings intruding on concepts that previously had more pleasant associations.

De feiret ikke jul i Tyskland (1941) fordi:
Josef var ved fronten, Maria var i arbeidstjeneste og Barnet var evakuert, Krybben var tom, Stjernen var blendet, Asenet var i Berlin, Oksen var i Italia, De Vise var i konsentrasjonsleir og De Hellige Tre Konger var i London. [Schou-Sörensen]
(They didn't celebrate Christmas (1941) in Germany because: Joseph was at the front, Mary was performing compulsory work service, the Child was evacuated, the manger was bare, the star was blacked out, the ass was in Berlin, the ox was in Italy, the wise men were in concentration camps and the Three Kings were in London.)

"Joseph" refers to Stalin, whose country Hitler had invaded the previous summer; "work service" refers to Quisling's conscription of Norwegian men and women to labor in support of the German war effort;[18] the "evacuated Child" reflects the breakup of many wartime families necessitated by sending children away for safety; the "bare manger" alludes to the food shortages, while the "darkened star" suggests the blackouts; Hitler is the "ass in Berlin" and Mussolini the "ox in Italy"; the "wise men" represent the intellectuals who were sent to prison camps for openly objecting to Nazism, and the "three kings" in London alludes to the several crowned heads of occupied countries who had protested by exiling themselves in England's capital, including Haakon VII of Norway, George II of Greece, and Peter II of Yugoslavia.

The other extended pun draws upon playing card imagery for its allusions to wartime hardships and restrictions (see also the related pun in chap. 3).

Nå kan man ikke spille bridge for: Essen er bombet, Kongen er i England, Damene flyr med tyskerne, Knektene sitter på Grini og resten av kortene har Churchill på hånden. [Schou-Sörensen]
(You can't play bridge anymore because: Essen [the German city, but also "the ace"] is bombed, the king is in England, the ladies [also playing card "queens"] are going out with the Germans, the knights [jacks] are imprisoned at Grini and the rest of the cards are in Churchill's hand.)

THE *TRIKK*

That so many jokes concern the *trikk* (from *elektrikk vogn* = "electric carriage," "streetcar") demonstrates what a pervasive part of daily life this means of transit had become in occupied Norway.[19] Fuel shortages caused more people than ever to travel collectively, and this in turn made the *trikk* a great leveler, bringing people from all social sectors into close proximity. Both in reality and in humor, the *trikk*'s intimately shared space provided individual Norwegians with a public forum in which to demonstrate their views, whether in conflict or harmony with others.

Some of the *trikk* jokes arose for linguistic reasons; the double meaning of *tilhenger* as both "following car" on the *trikk* and a "follower" in the sense of "supporter" of a political cause, for example, suited the *trikk* to articulating the theme of lacking Nazi support (as also seen in chap. 7).[20]

-Kan du si meg likheten mellom Singsaker trikkan og Nasjonal Samling?

Postcard depicting the overcrowded streetcar, from a series of 8 "Muntre krise-bilder" (cheerful scenes of crisis). Artist: Willy Bahr (b. 1901). Date and publisher: unknown. Norges Hjemmefrontmuseum.

---?
-Begge skjelver og har små tilhengere. [Kristiansen 1945, 9]
(Can you tell me the similarity between the Singsaker *trikk* and the Nazi Party?
---?
Both tremble and have only a small *tilhenger.*)

Quisling har beslaglagt alle trikkene i byen får han mangler tilhengere. [Larsen, Schou-Sörensen, Ellingsen]
(Quilsing has confiscated all the *trikk*s in town because he needs *tilhengere.*)

Hva er likheten mellom Quisling og Nordnæs trikken. Ingen har til-hengere. [Christerson]
(How is Quisling like the Nordnæs *trikk?* Neither has a *tilhenger.*)

Another pun associated with the *trikk* plays on the word *förer,* which in the context of the *trikk* means "driver." As first noted in chapter 2, such puns served to undercut the intimidating image of

The *trikk*, like the Nazi party, having only a small and trembling *tilhenger*. Artist: Oddmund Kristiansen. From *Jöss!* 1945. Reprinted with permission of Lærdal Medical, Stavanger, Norway.

the Führer (Norwegian *förer*), the title NS members used both for Quisling and for Hitler.

Har du hört at Hitler er i byen? - Overalt står det "Forstyr ikke föreren." [Schou-Sörensen]
(Have you heard that Hitler's in town? There's signs on all the *trikks:* Don't disturb the *förer.*)

The *Trikk* as Public Forum

One survivor of the occupation has identified the *trikk* as

the place we were forced to rub elbows, not only with the German occupiers but also with the dregs of our own society—the Nazis. This provided many possibilities for confrontation and numerous episodes ensued that subsequently circulated as more or less true jokes. [Steinar Floan Halse, letter to author, 18 January 1993]

As already noted in chapter 1, the Jössings found this contact with Germans and NS members particularly well-suited to practicing

the *is-fronten* (ice-front or cold-shoulder) tactic, a point Oddmund
Kristiansen also captured in his drawing from 1943 titled "the
New Uniform."

**A recent Nazi recruit in "The New Uniform" feeling the public's scorn. Artist:
Oddmund Kristiansen, in 1943, later published in Kristiansen, *Jöss!* 1945. Reprinted with permission of Lærdal Medical, Stavanger, Norway.**

Anecdotes about the *trikk* also portrayed the opposite situation,
i.e., showing deference to a fellow Jössing.

> Overfyllt trikk i Storgaten. En liten visergutt, fullastet med pakker, så
> ynkelig etter plass. Da ropte han i ytterste nöd innover vognen:
> -Er det ikke en bitte liten plass til en liten jössing der da?
> Han fikk romslig plass! [Svendsen n.d., 10]
> (Overcrowded *trikk* in Storgaten Street. A little delivery boy, loaded
> down with packages, was looking desperately for a seat. Struggling
> with his packages, he urgently called out:

"Isn't there a tiny bit of room for a little Jössing in there?"
Everyone made sure he got a comfortable seat.)

As seen in chapter 4, the *trikk* might also play backdrop to encounters provoked by the controversial *nisselue* (red stocking cap).

På Holmenkolbanen. Det er fullt på plattformen. En ung pike med rödt skjerf, röd topplue og röde strömper. En hird måler henne opp og ned og sier: "Nisse!"
Piken svarer kjapt: "Dessverre, jeg kan ikke hjelpe Dem!" [Ellingsen]
(On the Holmenkol-line. The platform is crowded. A young girl with a red scarf, red stocking cap and red stockings. A boy *hird*-member eyes her up and down and says, "Nisse!"
Without losing a beat, the girl replies, "Sorry, I can't help you.")

By intentionally misinterpreting the boy's epithet Nisse to be the euphemism for *tisse* (pee), the girl relegates the Hird member to the status of a child who needs adult supervision of his bathroom functions, and the joke thus plays on the earlier-mentioned theme of Nazi naïveté.

The drawings on the next two pages and more elaborate versions of this joke emphasize the role of the *trikk* in providing an arena for displaying a united front of resistance to the Nazis as the entire ridership joins in laughter at the Nazi's expense.

På trikken stod en liten blek pusling av en guttehird i full mundur. Da kommer det på en frisk, kraftig sportsjente, som demonstrerer kjekt med sin nisselue. Puslingen skuler stykt til henne, men tör ikke foreta seg noe. Hele trikken blir oppmerksom, men jenta later som ingen ting. Så skal småhirden av, og på stigbrettet fatter han mot, snur seg og hveser mot henne,—*Nisse!*
-Nei, skal du det du da, småen? sier jenta, mens hele trikken vreler av latter. [Imsland 1946, 117]
(On the *trikk* stood a small, pale, shrimp of a boy *hird*-member in full uniform. On board came a well-toned, athletic young lady, demonstratively wearing her *nisselue*. The shrimp stares at her with disdain, but doesn't dare take any action. Everyone on the *trikk* is following the exchange, but the young lady pretends not to notice. Soon the little storm trooper prepares to get off; on the step he gathers courage, turns toward the young lady and hisses: "*Nisse!*"
"Oh, do you have to, little one?" she says, while the whole *trikk* roars with laughter.)[21]

The degree of solidarity reflected in these jokes and drawings exceeds that which actually existed. Not only was there the matter

**Streetcar riders joining to ridicule the young Nazi Hird member. From Henry Ims-
land, *Jössingvitser*, 1946. Reprinted with permission of Lærdal Medical, Stavanger, Norway.**

of the sixty thousand Norwegians who joined the Nazi party (see
chaps. 6 and 7), but even the resisters failed to agree on wartime
strategy or on what Norway's postwar fate should be.[22] Yet the
appearance of universal accord was vital to the development of a
resistance mentality, and found particularly effective expression in
the imagery of the *trikk*.

   Jokes played out in the forum of public transport offer variations
on several other general themes of occupation humor, including
* the universality of illegal listening (cf., chap. 4):

A united front of streetcar riders and a conductor resembling King Haakon VII ridiculing the repugnant Nazi. Artist: Jens R. [Nilssen] (1880–1964). From *Karikaturens krigs-humor,* n.d.

En liten gutt satt på bussen og så en tysk soldat som hadde öreklemmer på grunn av kulden.
   -Hörer du på London du da? utbröt han. [Imsland 1946, 28]
(Sitting on the bus, a little boy saw a German soldier wearing ear muffs because of the cold.
   "Are *you* listening to London, too?" he exclaimed.)

Earphones were often used to listen illegally to the BBC. The joke suggests that the boy, being so used to seeing this done, misinterprets the soldier's head gear; it further implies that the practice is so widespread, even German soldiers might be thought to engage in it.
* wartime shortages (cf., chap. 8):

En full mann kommer inn på trikken og oppdager en gutt i hirdedrakt. Han kvekker til, letter på hatten og sier: "Takk for koksen." [Schou-Sörensen; Larsen, who has added the note, "This really happened."] (A drunk man comes into the *trikk* and discovers a boy in *Hird* uniform. He snaps to attention, lifts his hat and says, "Thanks for the coal.")

This joke with its ironic expression of gratitude circulated during the winter of 1940–41, one of the coldest in memory, whose misery was exacerbated by the shortage of home-heating fuel, which was strictly regulated by the Nazis.

* contempt for the Nazis:

A farmer got on the *trikk* where a *Hird* member was sitting in full uniform.
"Who do you think you are, all fancied up with all those braids and shining buttons?" the farmer asked.
"Don't you know?" the *Hird* man answered. "I am the cream of Norway's youth."
"Oh, is that what they call *krisekrem* (crisis cream)? [*Karikaturens krigs-humor* n.d.]

Just as the surrogate *krisekrem* was no match for the real thing, the joke implies, neither could the *Hird* members be mistaken for real soldiers.

* Jössings outsmarting the Nazis:

På trikken igjen. På plattformen står en hirdmann, en herre kommer på og naturligvis av "vanvare" kommer han til å skanyse til hirdmannen. Denne blir rasende og skjeller og smeller, men den andre står som om han intet forstår og sier til slutt: "Ich verstehe nicht." Hvorpå hirdmannen strammer seg. Neste holdeplass går hirdmannen av og når trikken er kommet i gang, roper den andre triumferende etter ham— "Du bet på den lell!" [Slaatto, January 1941]
(On the *trikk* again. A member of the *Hird* is standing on the platform when a gentleman gets on who, by accident—of course—happens to step on his foot. The *Hird* member gets furious and hollers abuse, but the other man appears not to understand and at last says, *"Ich verstehe nicht"* [I don't understand]. Hearing this, the *Hird* member snaps to attention. When the *Hird* member gets off at the next stop, the other man yells triumphantly after him: "You bit on that one, didn't you?")

* war developments:

Later in the war when Germany was being forced to retreat— or as face-saving German propaganda termed it, when they were following the *strategy* of withdrawing according to plan *(å trekke seg planmessig tilbake)*—the following joke circulated:

En full trikk. Konduktören roper: Trekk dere tilbake der da. Ingen reagerer. Trekk dere planmessig tilbake. Alle lystrer. [Schou-Sörensen] (A full trikk. The conductor yells: proceed to the rear [literally, "withdraw"]. No one budges. *Trekk dere planmessig tilbake* [withdraw according to plan]. Everyone obeys.)

This joke, too, plays on the theme of universal resistance, suggesting that once the riders realize that the conductor shares their anti-Nazi sentiments, they willingly comply with his request.

THE *TRIKK* AS MICROCOSM

Some of these streetcar items invite seeing the *trikk* as something beyond itself, as does the following outburst of the theater director Björn Björnson (1859–1942) (cf., chap. 7):

En gang Björn Björnson kjörte hjem med trikken kom det en "hird-mann" og stilte sig ved siden av ham.
Björnson gjorde front mot ham med fremskutt underleppe og pekte på utgangen. Og så kom det med lange og harmdirrende vokaler:
    "*U-u-t av m-i-i-n trikk!*" [Bö 1946, 57]
(Björn Björnson was riding the *trikk* when a *Hird* man got on and sat down beside him.
Confronting the *Hird* man with a protruding jaw and pointing toward the exit; Björnson exclaimed with elongated vowels that shook with rage,
    "*O-u-t of m-y-y trikk!*")

Clearly Björnson wanted the Nazi to vacate his country every bit as much as he wanted him off the *trikk*. Meanwhile the following allegory explicitly identifies the *trikk* with occupied Norway:

Stil om triken: Forrest står föreren, bak ham står nogen få mennesker, resten sitter inne. [Larsen, Schou-Sörensen, Slaatto]
(An essay on the *trikk:* Up front stands the *förer* with just a few people standing behind him. All the rest *sitter inne* [meaning "are sitting inside," but also "are imprisoned"].)

Suggesting the unified repudiation of Nazism by the small number standing behind the *förer*, the allegory also emphasizes Nazi oppression by the wholesale imprisonment (sitting inside) of everyone else. The image alludes not only to the actual seizures, interrogations, and jailings occupied Norwegians routinely endured, but also to the more subtle ways their lives had become subject to forces beyond their control. Smothered under the plethora of rules and regulations, they had to cope with the tedious paperwork of ration books, milk coupons, travel passes, and identity cards—encumbrances not entirely dissimilar to the endless round of standing in line, buying tickets, then having them inspected and clipped that accompanied travel by *trikk*.

In addition to the more trivial irritations of occupied life, the *trikk* image suggests the surrender of self-determination that came to characterize the foreign policy of the nation as a whole. Since 1905 Norway had been almost exclusively concerned with the country's internal affairs, but beginning with the 9 April invasion, Norway was increasingly forced to realize that events on the Steppes of Russia and in the halls of the British Parliament had serious domestic consequences as well (Furre 1992, 202).[23] Humor about the *trikk* demonstrates its congruence with this worldview not only by containing the appropriate metaphor of relinquished individual control, but also by addressing war developments beyond Norway's borders.

> Det er på trikken: —
> Inne i vognen sitter en tysk offiser. En full mann kommer inn og dumper ned ved siden av tyskeren. Mannen sitter og mumler meget ufordelaktig om Hitler. Tilslutt fiker offiseren til ham.
> "Det er all right, det," mumler mannen.
> "Meg kan du schlå, men England schlår du aldri!" [Ellingsen]
> (The scene is the *trikk*. A German officer is sitting inside the carriage. A drunk man gets on and plops down next to him. The man sits mumbling very insultingly about Hitler. At last the officer slaps him.
> "That's all right," the man mumbles [in slurred speech], "you can beat me, but you'll never beat England.")

At its most basic level, the *trikk* imagery portrays a cross-section of Norwegians, enclosed in a single vehicle, proceeding in the same direction, toward a common goal. While exaggerating the actual degree of Norway's anti-Nazi solidarity, the image reflects an awareness that the extent of occupation solidarity that did exist, was unusually high and unique in the nation's history. Social reforms undertaken by the Nygaardsvold government during the 1930s had elevated the working class into closer accord with the rest of society and had for the first time allowed Norwegians of all classes to have common goals and interests that superseded their differences.

This solidarity intensified in the wake of the German invasion, as the perception gradually developed among the opponents of

Nazism that their common interest in opposing the occupation forces overrode any remaining distinctions based on class (Hjeltnes 1987, 268–69). Without this preinvasion rapprochement, says the historian Berge Furre, Norway's response to the Nazis might instead have been civil war, with the various classes making individual arrangements with the occupiers to achieve their own best interests (1992, 174–75). Instead, an overwhelming normative pressure in favor of collectivism arose and a resistance mentality developed which cut across previous divisions. This reality, too, finds particularly apt expression in the image of the overcrowded wartime *trikk* uniting under one roof individuals of all kinds, irrespective of their previous social status or political affiliation.[24]

The *trikk* image further expressed the uniquely unified aim of the Norwegian Resistance, which despite internal division, did to a far greater degree than the anti-Nazi movements of seemingly comparable occupied countries, agree on the single goal of restoring rule under Norway's Constitution. The image of a united *trikk*-ridership ridiculing the Nazi passenger suggested a consensus of values consistent with the resistance tactic of marshaling Norway's traditional democratic social ideals against the Nazis' precept of rule by the elite. Many observers credit the existence of this unified core of values with Norway's ability to emerge strengthened from the potentially destructive experience of foreign occupation and to make a smooth transition into peacetime.[25]

As employed in Norwegian occupation humor, the *trikk* image thus provides a surprisingly comprehensive view of the realities and frustrations of daily life in occupied Norway, while also reflecting the Norwegian people's attitudes toward and response to both the occupiers and the Nazis. On a conscious level, the *trikk* anecdotes grew out of the actual confrontations that occurred in the intimately shared space of the *trikk*. Unconsciously the *trikk* image became an eloquent metaphor to express the occupation period's unique cross-class unity in resistance aims and values, a perceived solidarity that not only contributed to the developing resolve to resist Nazism, but also assisted the nation in its rapid readjustment to peace. At the same time the image effectively captured the feeling that the entire nation was now operating at the behest of her occupiers and under the influence of events taking place outside her borders. The next three chapters will explore the way in which Norway's occupation humor profiled these foreign affairs.

9

A Humorous Perspective on War Developments: From the Battle of Britain to the Flight of Rudolf Hess

Occupation jokes registered war developments with seismographic speed, especially when things were going badly for Germany. This was a valuable aspect of wartime humor given the harmful psychological effects of constantly being bombarded by the pro-German Nazi propaganda, as described in chapter 6. Endless headlines trumpeted former and future German triumphs:

> NO DOUBT OF WAR OUTCOME. AGAINST A UNITED EUROPE, ENGLAND AND AMERICA HAVE NO CHANCE
> [*Aftenposten*, (The evening post) 19 May 1942][1]

To these headlines, jokes like the following provided a welcome and powerful antidote:

> -Do you know why Hitler now wears a diving suit?
> -Why?
> -So he can inspect his fleet. [Ellingsen]

THE BATTLE OF BRITAIN

Many of the jokes about war developments derived from Germany's abortive attempts to invade England during the summer and fall of 1940. Hitler had decided to attack by air first and to disarm the British air force before attempting a surface invasion, but from the outset the skill of the British pilots took the Germans by surprise. Not only did Germany's concerted bombing raids fail to defeat the Royal British Air Force, but they resulted in substantially higher German losses than British, and Jössing folk wit reveled:

> I avisene står bare bilder av tyske fly som *skal* til England og aldri av dem som reiser tilbake—for det er ingen. [Christerson]
> (The newspapers show only pictures of German planes on their way *to* England and never of the ones coming back—because there aren't any.)

> Gåte: Hvorfor bruker engelskmennene dobbelt så mye bensin som tyskerne? De flyr frem og tilbake, mens tyskerne bare flyr en vei. [Schou-Sörensen, Christerson][2]
> (Riddle: Why do the British use twice as much fuel as the Germans? They fly back and forth, while the Germans only fly one way.)

On 17 September, Hitler postponed the invasion of Britain "until further notice," and folk wit celebrated with this riddle:

> Sp: Vet du at Hitler har kjöpt radio apparat?
> Sv. Nei, hvordan det?
> Sp. Det er den eneste måten han kan "ta" England på.
> [Larsen, Christerson, Schou-Sörensen]
> (Q: Do you know why Hitler bought a radio?
> A: No, why?
> Q: It's the only way he can "get" England.)

Song-parodies also took up the theme of the German failure; the following one from Slaatto's diary was sung (in English) to the tune of "Tipperary":

> It's a long way to British Island—
> It's a long way to go.
> It's a long way for German soldiers
> in the greatest war they know.
> They are flying, they are swimming
> but they never reach the land.
> It's a long, long way to British Island.
> It's a long way to go.

Another joke, set in Oslo's Viking Ship Museum mocked Germany's failure to invade Britain while also addressing the Nazis' proclivity at denigrating the national pride of the countries they occupied.

> En tysk soldat beså Vikingeskipene, men syntes ikke de var noe særlig å skryte av. Kan så være, sa vakten, at De ikke er noe imponert av disse skipene, men det var nå dem vi tok England med. [Schou-Sörensen][3]

(A German soldier was visiting the Viking Ships, but thought them nothing to brag about. "You may not be impressed by these ships," replied the guard, "but with them, the Norwegians did after all manage to attack England.")

With annoying persistence, the German soldiers announced their impending invasion of England by marching through the streets singing *Wir fahren gegen Engeland* (We're on the way to England). Given the failure of the enterprise, this practice inevitably inspired renaming that song as the *Die Nie-gelungen-lied* (the never-succeeded-song), a takeoff on the title of the famous Germanic epic, *Die Niebelungenlied* (Schou-Sörensen).[4] Numerous narrative jokes like the next two also sprang up to ridicule the aborted mission:

> På bryggene i Bergen står en liten gutt. En tysk bil, full av soldater, kjörer i stor fart utfor brygga. Gutten later som ingen ting, og da de förste tyskerne omsider kommer opp, er de rasende på ham fordi han ikke har hentet hjelp. Hvortil gutten svarer: "Eg trodde dokker skulle til Engeland, eg!" [Ellingsen][5]
> (A little boy is standing on the dock in [the Norwegian west coast city of] Bergen. A car full of Germans speeds past him and drives right off the dock and into the sea. The boy keeps on as before, paying no attention. Some time later, when the first Germans surface, they are furious with him for not having summoned help. To this the boy replies: "Oh, I thought you were on your way to England!")

> I den tida under okkupasjonen då me endå fekk ha radioapparatene i fred, kom to tyskarar inn i eit hus på landsbygda, der kona nettopp sat og höyrde på "nyhetene frå London." Tyskarane likte sjölvsagt ikkje dette, og den eine sa: —Det sömer seg ikkje for gode nordmenn å höyre på desse propagandanyhetene frå London.
> -Nei, eg veit det, svara kona, men eg har så lenge höyrt at Tyskland ville ta England, og nå ventar eg kvar dag at eg skal höyra Hitlers stemme frå London. [Imsland 1946, 121]
> (During the early part of the occupation when we still had our radios, two Germans came into a house out in the country where the wife was listening to "news from London." The Germans didn't like this, of course, and one of them said, "It's unseemly for good Norwegians to listen to that propaganda news from London."
> "Well, I know that," answered the woman, "but I've heard so long about Germany's plans to invade England, that any day now, I expect to hear Hitler's voice on the London station.")

As time passed, the Germans in Norway became increasingly fearful of an Allied invasion. British raids on Norwegian ports had already shown the German ramparts incapable of providing 100-percent protection.[6] Angered by the range and unexpectedness of these attacks, Hitler began to talk of turning the entire stretch of the North Sea, English Channel, and Atlantic coastline under his control into an impregnable "Fortress Europe." An extensive building campaign ensued, but failed to make the occupiers feel more secure about the dreaded attack and the Norwegian ambush they thought would accompany it. While trying to maintain an intimidating appearance, the Germans' increasingly defensive posture contrasted markedly with their earlier bravado, and folk wit savored the change.

Det var i den tiden tyskerne brölte som verst "Wir fahren gegen Engeland." Et tysk·batteri holdt på å sette opp et piggtrådgjerde på gjordet til en bonde oppe i Rennebu. Bonden gikk til den tyske Oberlöytnant og spurte hva dette skulle være godt for. Löytnanten svarte at de måtte sette opp piggtrådgjerde i tilfelle det ble invasjon og engelskmennene kom. Da kom det stilt fra bonden. Å, æ hæ vel misforstått hele greia, æ da, æ trudd det va *dokk* som skul' til England. [Imsland 1946, 122] (While the Germans were still blaring their song *Wir fahren gegen Engeland,* a German battery was putting up a barbed-wire fence on a farmer's field up in Rennebu. The farmer asked the German lieutenant colonel what it was for. The officer replied that they had to put up the barbed-wire fence in case there was an invasion and the English came. To this the farmer answered quietly, "Oh, I reckon I've misunderstood the whole thing, then, 'cause I thought *you* guys were going to go to England.")

Hitler's planned "Atlantic wall," was to consist of 15,000 concrete bunkers set at 50- and 100-yard intervals, a configuration that provides the background for the following joke:

Noen tjuagutter står og ser på mens tyskerne bygger bunkers. "Hva skal dere med di, da." spör de. "Vi skal ta imot englenderne." "Hö, tror dokker englenderne kommer med trikken, då?" [Christerson] (Some street urchins stand watching the Germans build bunkers. "What are you going to do with them, then?" they ask. "We're going to meet the British." "Ha! Do you think the British are coming on the streetcar?")

Reflecting the altered perception of Germany's vulnerability, jokes like this one began portraying Hitler as inept, failing to understand the might of his adversaries, and badly in need of advice. A further mechanism of these jokes is the wordplay stimulated, as earlier noted, by the intrusion of military terminology on daily life experiences.

> Hitler har alliert seg med 1000 sydamer. . . . Hvorfor? Han vil "falle" England i ryggen. [Christerson][7]
> (Hitler has allied himself with 1000 seamstresses. . . . Why? He wants to *falle* England *i ryggen* ["to take in at the back," also "to attack from the rear," or "to ambush"].)

Comparing the German war effort to sewing trivializes it and thus removes some of its intimidation, at the same time the image of Hitler summoning seamstresses to the front suggests his misman-agement of the task at hand.[8] The next joke more specifically ad-dresses his inability to cross the English Channel to invade Britain:

> Hitler banket på Himmelens port og St. Peter lukket opp. Du slipper ikke inn her, sa han. Nei, jeg skulle heller ikke inn, jeg ville bare snakke med Moses. Ja, vent da, sa St. Peter. Litt etter kom Moses. Du Moses, sa Hitler, hvordan klarte du å skille vannet så du kunne gå tört over?[9] [Schou-Sörensen]
> (Hitler knocked on the gates of Heaven and St. Peter opened up. "You can't come in here," he said. "No, I didn't want to come in, I just wanted to speak to Moses." "Well, wait a minute," said St. Peter. After a while Moses came out.
> "Moses," said Hitler, "how did you manage to part the waters so you could walk dry-shod across?")

Hearers of the joke no doubt enjoyed both the allusions to Hitler's aborted invasion as well as the nondeferential treatment the mighty Führer receives, both in Peter's unwillingness to admit him into Heaven and, in some versions, in Moses' curt refusal to share the badly needed information about his crossing of the Red Sea.

ENGLAND—THE REDOUBTABLE ALLY

By the time the Battle of Britain was over, the British had stood up to the worst the Germans could send their way. Had Britain succumbed, says the historian James Stokesbury, it is difficult to see how the war against Hitler would ever have been won, but even as the Jössings pinned their hopes on Britain, they couldn't help criticizing the occasionally bungled British efforts. Humor reflected this impatience while also mocking the accompanying tendency to blame the British for *everything* that went wrong.

Mussolini kommer kjörende med 50 km's fart. Hitler kommer kjörende med 100 km's fart. De kolliderer. Hvem har skylden? *England.* [Christerson]
(Mussolini comes driving along at 50 km an hour. Hitler is going 100. They collide. Who's to blame? *England.*)

Dissatisfaction with the British grew out of overly optimistic, but ultimately failed expectations during the early months of the occupation that British forces would bring a quick victory. Hope had soared on 13 April 1940 when a British fleet battalion sank two and damaged three German destroyers in Narvik harbor. On the way back, the British fleet encountered the supply ship carrying all the German ammunition for the landing forces and sank *it* as well. Three days later, the British returned to finish off the rest of the German destroyers in Narvik, leaving only land forces to defend the city. A new landing at Åndalsnes occurred on 17 April and shortly thereafter Allied troops arrived in Namsos. But these British forces were small in number, poorly trained, improperly equipped, and insufficiently armed. They also lacked support from the Royal Air Force. German air battalions easily overwhelmed them, leaving the Allies unable to stop German progress through Gudbrandsdalen and thereby prevented the planned Allied capture of Trondheim. Stretching all the way from that city to Oslo, the German forces now managed to form a solid line of defense and forced the Norwegian divisions fighting in South and West Norway to capitulate. British forces were driven out of Åndalsnes on 1 May and from Namsos on 3–4 May, leaving both cities in flames.[10] In early June, Allied forces were needed to fight Hitler's forces in France and had to pull out of Narvik; the remaining Norwegian soldiers had no choice but to surrender. Disappointed and bitter, many Norwegians resented the inadequate and ineffective British effort.

> The impression [the feeble British action] made upon the Norwegian people, who were a little confused just at the time, was not the very best and it is a fact that Quisling gained the bulk of his recruits from the districts where the British troops had made their unhappy visit. [Thomsen 1945, 10]

Chapter 5 has already mentioned the allegorical impatience of Snorri the Seal with his uncle Bart's slow response, and occupation jokes, too, addressed Britain's lack of speed.

Hitler, Musse og Chamberlain satt ved en dam. I dammen var en gull-
fisk som de efter tur skulle pröve å fange. Både Hitler og Musse gjorde
forgjeves forsök. Når de stod på den ene siden av dammen svömte
fisken over på den andre siden. Så var det Chamberlains tur. Han tok
en teskje og begynte å tömme dammen. [Larsen]
(Hitler, Musse [Mussolini] and Chamberlain were sitting by a pond
containing a gold fish they were taking turns trying to catch. Both
Hitler and Musse made unsuccessful attempts: when they stood on
one side of the pond, the fish swam over to the other side. Then it
was Chamberlain's turn. He took a teaspoon and started emptying
the pond.)

Like Sælen's children's book, the joke suggests that the British
methods will eventually prevail, but, like the next item, emphasizes
that success won't come quickly:

För i tiden sa man at det trengtes 3 ting for å vinne en krig: Penger,
penger og atter penger. Nå trenger man også 3 ting: menneskemateriell,
krigsmateriell og tid. Det förste leverer Russland, det annet leverer
Amerika og tiden leverer England. [Schou-Sörensen]
(It used to be said that three things were needed to win a war: Money,
money and money. Now we still need three things: Human resources,
war material and time. Russia has the first, America has the second,
and time is provided by England.)

Another common theme of these jokes was Britain's failure to take
the initiative while hoping to benefit from the final outcome.[11]

Aftenbönn:
Hitler: Herre Gud, gjör ende på alle russere.
Stalin: "   "   "   "   "   " tyskere.
Churchill: "   "   bönnhör dem begge. [Schou-Sörensen]
(Evening prayers:
Hitler: Lord God, put an end to all Russians.
Stalin: "   ",   "   "   "   " Germans.
Churchill:"   ", hear their prayers.)

Since Britain was the goal of the flight of Rudolf Hess, this chapter
cannot conclude without considering this classic adventure undertaken by Hitler's right-hand man.

THE FLIGHT OF RUDOLF HESS

Rudolf Hess (1894–1987) had been Hitler's most trusted colleague and confidant for nearly twenty years, as well as his deputy

as Führer of the Nazi party, when on 10 May 1941, he made an apparent escape from Germany. Taking one of the army's Messerschmitt 110 planes, he left behind a letter addressed to Hitler explaining his intention to go to Britain on a personal mission to forge peace between the two nations. Embarrassed, the Germans initially reported Hess's disappearance as an accident. The 13 May *Aftenposten* carried the headline: "HESS FORULYKKET UNDER FLYTUR" (HESS CRASHES DURING PLANE FLIGHT) and reported that Hess

> whom the *Führer* had forbidden from flying because of a chronic progressive illness, has nevertheless obtained a plane and not yet returned. A garbled letter he left behind shows signs of mental disturbance, giving rise to fears that comrade Hess has crashed somewhere or had some other sort of accident.

The article aimed to acquit Hess of treachery while at the same time arousing British suspicions about him, if he should manage to land safely.

Germany's embarrassment grew with the disclosure that Hess had landed by parachute precisely at his intended destination in Scotland. The British took him directly into custody and used the situation to full advantage in their propaganda, pointing out that Hess not only was sane, but had given them important classified information. Adding that Hess was anxious for peace because he had lost faith in German victory and could no longer respect Hitler, the British left the Nazis nervously worrying about what top secret intelligence they had forced Hess to reveal.[12] In an attempt to save face, the Nazi party news agency now represented Hess as an idealist who had hoped to forward "the peace proposals that Hitler had with great sincerity already made to Britain" and that Hess was "under the delusion that his own personal sacrifice could prevent developments which could only end in the complete destruction of the British Empire." The notice concluded by emphasizing that "Germany's struggle will not be influenced by his actions and the gap in our ranks is being closed" (Balfour 1979, 218).

Not surprisingly the episode created great consternation in the German public as well. Those faithful to the Führer sympathized that Fate had certainly spared him no tribulation, while the less devoted repeated this rhyme:

> Es geht ein Lied im ganzen Land
> Wir fahren gegen Engel-land
> Doch wenn dann Wirklich einar fährt,

So wird er für verrückt erklärt.
(There rang a song throughout the land,
"We're on our way to Engeland"
As soon as someone really went,
They told us that his wits were spent.) [Balfour 1979, 221,
original and translation][13]

Members of the German resistance chimed in with this joke:

Hess ble forestilt for Churchill, som sa:
"Nå, De er altså den gale?"
"Nei," svarte Hess, "bare stedfortrederen." [Hjeltnes 1987, 115]
(Hess was introduced to Churchill, who said,
"So you're the crazy one?"
"No," answered Hess, "just his deputy.")

Jokes about Hess circulated in Norway as well, and according to
Finn Bö they inspired hope during one of the war's bleakest periods by suddenly making Germany seem less invincible. Few believed the story of Hess's mental confusion, preferring to interpret
his actions as treachery. Conjuring up the image of rats leaving a
sinking ship, the incident suggested that others might start de-
serting the Nazi party as well, and prompted the rumor that Mussolini had landed by submarine in America and surrendered to
Roosevelt (Bö 1946, 164).

Savoring the blow to Hitler's prestige occasioned by Hess's action, incidents like the following began occuring in Norway:

In an Oslo movie theater a newsreel was showing Hitler getting on a
plane. Suddenly a voice called from the audience, "Say hi to Hess!"
[Schou-Sörensen]

Other Hess quips proliferated as well.

Hitler må hilse med venstre hånd for hans höyre hånd er i England.
(Schou-Sörensen]
(Hitler has to shake hands with his left hand now because his right
hand is in England.)

Hitler vil ikke tale mer, han er redd for å bli Hess. [Schou-Sörensen]
(Hitler doesn't want to speak anymore; he's afraid of becoming *hess*
[hoarse].)

Hess heter nå bare Mr. He. Han har SS bak seg. [Schou-Sörensen]
(Hess is now called Mr. He. His SS days are over.)

Nor was Hess soon forgotten. An entry in Greta Dahl's diary dated a year and a half later attests that Jössing amusement about Hess's flight continued to threaten the German occupiers.

October 24, 1943: Just heard some news from Bergen: At a movie theater the newsreel was showing Hitler getting on a plane. A voice in the audience said: "Greet Hess!" The lights went on, but no one knows who had said it. After the performance everyone who wasn't NS or German had to remain seated in the auditorium, and they were held there and not released until two o'clock in the morning.

Daring to suggest the ultimate failure of Hitler's mighty war machine, the jokes in this chapter have dealt with themes ranging from his failed invasion of Britain to the apparent defection of his most trusted friend. The next chapter continues the theme of war developments, giving humor's perspective on Hitler's other erstwhile friends and increasingly mighty foes.

10

Further Perspectives on War Developments: Mussolini, Rommel, and Operation Barbarossa

While British issues occupy by far the largest share of Norwegian humor's wartime commentary, folk wit addressed other developments as well, not least the trials and tribulations of the Italian dictator Benito Mussolini (1883–1945)[1] with whom Hitler had joined forces in 1937 to form the uneasy alliance known as the Rome-Berlin Axis.[2]

MUSSOLINI'S TERRITORIAL ASPIRATIONS

Blithely assuming that Britain's defeat, like that of France, was a fait accompli, Mussolini declared war on both countries on 10 June 1940 hoping to share in the spoils. He especially coveted the French-owned territory in Northern Africa for his planned Italian empire that would circle the Mediterranean. Toward that end and to prevent Hitler from having a monopoly on redrawing the map of Europe, Mussolini had already in April 1939 usurped Albania, from which he invaded Greece on 28 October 1940. The latter move infuriated Hitler who regarded the attack as a major strategic error (Gilbert 1989). Jössing humorists ignored Hitler's actual reaction, however, and used the opportunity not only to mock Mussolini's ensuing difficulties but also to ridicule Hitler's failed attempts to invade Britain.

Under Mussolinis felttog mot Hellas syntes Hitler at det gikk så altfor smått. En dag ringte han til Mussolini om det ikke var slik at han skulle være i Aten om noen dager, hvortil Mussolini svarte: "Ringer du fra London du kanskje?" [Imsland 1946, 23]
(Feeling Mussolini's campaign against Greece wasn't making satisfactory progress, Hitler telephoned Mussolini one day and asked if he

170

wouldn't soon be in Athens. To this Mussolini answered, "And I suppose you're calling from London?")

Though not accurate in detail, the joke does capture Hitler's general dissatisfaction with Mussolini and his feeling that the Italian dictator and his forces contributed little to the Axis war effort. As Hitler feared, Mussolini's invasion of Greece ended in disaster, with the Italians being expelled. Jössing humor, of course, delighted in the expulsion, since the Italian invasion had threatened British control of the Mediterranean.

Italienerne sitter i fluktstol og spiser römmegröt. [Schou-Sörensen]
(The Italians are sitting in *fluktstoler* ["folding deck chairs," the word contains the syllable *flukt*—"flight, escape"] and they're eating *römmegröt* [the familiar Norwegian "sour cream porridge," a word that contains the element *römme* which as a verb means to "run away" or "desert"].)

Not only had the invasion ended in the Italians' being ignominiously forced to flee, but it made Greece an ally of Britain, who now gained an air base in Athens within range of the Rumanian oil wells, the all-important source of Germany's fuel. To protect this interest, Hitler had to withdraw some of his forces from the Battle of Britain and send them to Romania. Against that background and suffused with a large dose of wishful thinking about Hitler's death, the following joke circulated:

Vet du hvorfor Hitler har tatt Rumania?
?
Får å få den siste olje. [Larsen, Schou-Sörensen]
(Do you know why Hitler has taken Romania?[3]
?
To get *den siste olje* [literally: "the last oil" also "last rites"].)

Italy's entry into the war had opened new theaters of battle in which Britain could engage outside her shores. In November 1940 the Royal Air Force struck the Italian navy base at Taranto and crippled half the Italian fleet for the next six months, a circumstance to which folk wit responded:

Musse har kjöpt seg dykkedrakt for det er den eneste måten han kan inspisere flåten sin på. [Larsen]
(Musse has bought himself a diving suit because it's the only way he can inspect his fleet.)

On 9 December 1940 Britain attacked Italian forces on Egyptian soil. They overwhelmed 75,000 Italians with forces only half as numerous, and on 22 January 1941 British-Australian forces surrounding the Libyan desert fortress of Tobruk, entered the port and captured 25,000 Italian soldiers (Gilbert 1989). Combined, these two events gave rise to the following witticism:

> Det er ikke eggmangel i England nå for de har tatt 100.000 hvite italienerne. [Schou-Sörensen]
> (There is no longer an egg shortage in England for they have taken 100,000 white Italians.)

"White Italians" alludes to the most common species of laying hen in Norway.

Hitler had hoped to isolate the British in Egypt and Malta in order to prevent their using the Mediterranean as a base of attack. Mussolini's invasion of Greece had destroyed that plan, and on 27 March 1941, Mussolini's troops suffered the consequences of his mistake. Cruising off Cape Matopen, Greece's southern-most point, the Italian navy was caught unawares by the formidable British forces gathered there and in the ensuing battle suffered heavy losses. Meanwhile in Libya, the British were obliterating the Italian army; the combination of these events led to this jab:

> Hele den italienske hær har gått i vanne, og hele den italienske flåte ligger på land. [Larsen]
> (The entire Italian army has gone into the sea, and the entire Italian fleet is lying on land.)

Invited to be Hitler's guest at Obersalzberg on 19 June 1941, was a chastened Mussolini, whose chagrin the following quip reflects:

> Mussolini har kjöpt seg ny radio: Molefunken. [Schou-Sörensen]
> (Mussolini has bought himself a new radio: *Molefunken* [a word sounding like Telefunken, the well-known brand of electronics, but meaning "dejected, crestfallen"].)[4]

The two leaders discussed the disastrous situation of the Italian army in Libya, and Hitler agreed to help by sending German forces to Tripoli under the command of longtime Nazi party member, Erwin Rommel.

ROMMEL AND THE NORTH AFRICAN CAMPAIGN

Popularly known as the Desert Fox, Gen. Erwin Rommel (1891–1944) was one of the most colorful characters of the entire Second

World War. As field commander of the German Afrika Korps, he led persistent and usually successful battles against the British, a record that invited the salvos of Jössing humor.

> De har innkalt alle pukkelryggede i Tyskland for å danne kamelkorps til Afrika. [Schou-Sörensen]
> (They've conscripted all the hunchbacks in Germany to create a camel corps for Africa.)[5]

In all, the war in Africa took the best part of three years and was fought and refought over the same six hundred miles between Alexandria, Egypt, and Benghazi, Libya (Gilbert 1989). On 31 March 1942 Rommel had led German-Italian forces against Libya, dismantling the British front and driving it back to the Egyptian border. Rommel's success in recapturing British territorial gains in Northern Africa offered little hope to the Jössings until the Libyan port of Tobruk managed to repulse Rommel's 10 April attack. Gradually strengthened, the fort proved capable of withstanding a two-month siege. Celebrating the British resistance while also mocking Norwegian nonsupport of Quisling's fighting force, a Jössing riddle asked:

> Hvorfor tilströmningen til Regiment "Nordland" er så lite? Fordi Hitler og Quisling lover dem et bruk, mens engelskmennene lover dem Tobruk. [Schou-Sörensen]
> (Why do so few join Regiment Nordland? Because Hitler and Quisling are promising only *et bruk* [one farm] while the English promise *Tobruk* ["two farms," a homonym of "Tobruk"].)

The farm mentioned was a recruitment inducement offered by Quisling to anyone who served in Regiment Nordland for four years.[6]

Tobruk couldn't withstand the siege indefinitely, however, and on 20 June 1942, Rommel managed to take the fortress, thereby capturing not only 300,000 prisoners, but also 2,000 working-order vehicles, 2,000 tons of fuel, and 5,000 tons of rations—vital supplies in a desert war requiring all life-sustaining goods and war materials to be brought in from the outside (Gilbert 1989). During the last week of June 1942, Rommel managed to push the British forces back as far as Al-Alamein. With his forces now only sixty miles west of Alexandria, Mussolini—eager to be seen as a victorious conqueror—flew to Libya in anticipation of a triumphal entry into Cairo, and Jössing humor jibed:

Musse har fått selofanbukser forat det italienske folk skal se at han har
gjort noe stort! [Ellingsen]
(Musse has gotten cellophane trousers so the Italian people will be
able to see that he has done something great!)

With only fifty-five tanks still operating, however, Rommel could
go no farther. In a quagmire of salt and quicksand, his forces were
stopped outside Al-Alamein on 30 August 1942. With Hitler's attention now on the fighting in Russia, Rommel lacked necessary
support, and within forty-eight hours he had to withdraw from a
battle that marked the first decisive victory for British general
Bernard Montgomery. Cheated of his triumph, Mussolini returned
to Italy.
     Meanwhile at Tobruk the German-Italian forces withstood a
British counterattack on 13 September, but when the British repeated the attack in November, Rommel's reserves lasted only
two weeks, and by 13 November, Montgomery had succeeded in
expelling the last German and Italian forces from Tobruk. Though
the Nazi-controlled press tried to make Rommel's withdrawal from
Libya appear advantageous to Germany, humor mocked the loss
by associating Rommel's name with desertion, Rommel = Römmel
[cf., å römme = "to run away"] (Schou-Sörensen, December
1942).[7] Hitler's siphoning off support from Rommel's African war
to the Russian front is addressed in this November 1942 joke about
the Libyan defeat:

> Rommel telegraferte til Hitler: Ich stehe hier an Mitelmehr und habe
> keine Mittel Mehr. [Schou-Sörensen]
> (Rommel telegraphed Hitler: *Ich stehe hier an Mitelmehr und habe
> keine Mittel Mehr* [I'm standing at the *Mitelmehr*—"Mediterranean"—
> and have no *Mittel Mehr*—"more resources"].)

The Jössings needed to celebrate Rommel's expulsion, having
little else to smile about as Christmas 1942 approached, with the
Axis forces still firmly entrenched in North Africa, Russia deeply
penetrated by the German Wehrmacht, and Southern Asia overrun
by the Japanese. Little did it seem possible that the new year would
bring results favorable to the Allies on all three fronts.
     Hitler's problems had begun multiplying even as British church
bells peeled in celebration of recapturing Tobruk. The Allies landed
in Algeria and Morocco intent on attacking German-Italian forces
in Tunisia. Conquering Tripoli in January 1943, British forces
crossed into Tunisia in February. Once again battle pitted Rommel
and Montgomery against each other; both their forces fought bit-

terly, and not until 28 March did Montgomery's troops finally begin disintegrating the tough German-Italian resistance. Ordering his forces on to Tunis, Montgomery challenged them to "drive the enemy into the sea," an objective achieved on 7 May 1943, also against staunch resistance. Back in Norway, Greta Dahl notes on 9 May, that the "Germans have been rather subdued because of Tunisia's fall." By contrast the Jössings were enjoying Hitler's presumed distress over both the North African loss and his simultaneous problems on the Russian front, where his forces had recently failed in their attempts to cross the River Don.

Hitler har fått Rommel i maven fordi han har spist for meget *T U R N I P S* og veien til Don [veien til do'en] er stengt. [Schou-Sörensen] (Hitler has developed Rommel [rumbling] in his stomach because he has eaten too many *T U R N I P S* [i.e., Tunis], and the way is blocked to the *Don* [= *do'n* "the toilet" and the "Don River"].)[8]

Popular among his soldiers, Rommel's nickname of Desert Fox had derived in part from his tactic of keeping his troops in constant motion. Feinting like a basketball player in various directions before making his actual move, Rommel would confuse and distract the enemy, then attack just where they least expected. After his defeat, Jössing humor ridiculed both Rommel's tactics and the reversal of his former advances.

Ny vals, Rommels vals: 1 skritt frem og to tilbake. [Schou-Sörensen] (New waltz, Rommel's waltz: one step forward and two back.)

Hva er forskjellen mellom Rommel og en klokke? Jo, klokka går framover og sier tikk-takk, tikk-takk, og Rommel går tilbake og sier tak-tikk, tak-tikk. [Christerson] (What's the difference between Rommel and a clock? The clock goes forward and says Tick-tock, tick-tock, while Rommel goes backwards and says tock-tick, tock-tick [homonym of *taktikk*, Norwegian for "tactics," Rommel's watchword].)

In addition to mocking Rommel's retreat, the joke shows military terminology again intruding on civilian life and literally turning it upside down.

Finally, celebrating Montgomery's success in pursuing Rommel, one joke told:

Under Rommels besök i Köbenhavn hadde en stor menneskemasse samlet seg utenfor hotellet hvor han bodde. En politimann vendte seg til mengden og sa:

–Hva venter dere på? Rommel har nettopp kjört herfra.
En röst:–Det er heller ikke ham vi venter på–det er Montgomery.
Han pleier jo alltid å være i hælene på Rommel. [Ramfjord 1945, 126]
(During Rommel's visit in Copenhagen a large group of people as-
sembled outside the hotel where he was staying. A policeman turned
to the crowd and said:
"What are you waiting for? Rommel just left."
A voice: "We're not waiting for Rommel, but for Montgomery. He's
usually right on Rommel's heels.")[9]

OPERATION BARBAROSSA

On Sunday 22 June 1941 Greta Dahl told her diary:

Last night the Germans attacked Russia. They must be insane! But they
need the Soviet oil and wheat—for that matter, their entire armaments
industry as well. Their own industry has probably all been bombed out.

Dahl's incredulity was well founded. The Germans were proposing
to take on the world's largest state which had an army as large
as the rest of the world's armed forces combined; they intended,
moreover, to finish off the job in a maximum of eight to twelve
weeks, in order to be out before winter. Operating in an intelligence
vacuum, they had little idea of the size or nature of the territory
they were invading (Gilbert 1989).

As he planned the invasion, Hitler was at the pinnacle of his
power: Germany held all of Continental Europe and Rommel was
still successfully recapturing British territorial gains in North Africa. Meanwhile Russia had made a poor showing in the Winter
War (November 1939–March 1940), during which the Finns had
impressed the world with their ability to inflict heavy losses on this
giant adversary. The Norwegian public had followed that conflict
with interest and personal engagement, shipping hand-knitted
clothing, backpacks, and other necessary items to the Finnish
front. Now soldiers from Quisling's Regiment Nordland were being
deployed in Finland to assist Nazi efforts against the Soviet
Union,[10] and the juxtaposition of the two situations gave rise to
the following ironic observation:

Under den 1. krigen sendte vi ryggsekker til Finland, nå sender vi
drittsekker. [Schou-Sörensen]
(During the first war we sent backpacks to Finland, now we're sending
drittsekker ["bastards," a word whose concrete meaning, "shit bags,"

linguistically relates to the Norwegian word for "backpacks" = *ryggsekker*].)

Hitler's Russian invasion, known as Operation Barbarossa,[11] called for a simultaneous three-pronged attack against Moscow, Leningrad, and Kiev, and was launched on 22 June 1941. The operation clearly defied the Mutual Nonaggression Pact Germany had signed with Russia in August 1939. The pact's architect, German foreign minister Joachim von Ribbentrop (1893–1946), objected to the operation, but Hitler honored his counsel no more than the pact, as the following joke implies:

> Hitler og Ribbentrop er på inspeksjonen ved fronten. Hitler föler seg nödt til å avlegge en visitt på et feltdo. Like etter bröler han ut:
> -Ribbentrop! Her finnes ikke noe papir! Gi meg et par ikke-angrepspakter! [*Karikaturens krigs-humor* n.d., 14]
> (Hitler and Ribbentrop are on an inspection round at the front. Hitler needs to visit a field toilet and soon hollers:
> "Ribbentrop! There's no toilet paper. Hand me a couple of non-aggression pacts.")

Initially the Soviet invasion went according to Hitler's plan. Despite ample warnings, Stalin had been taken by surprise, and within weeks German land forces had penetrated deep into Soviet territory, and in some places were even greeted as liberators from Soviet domination. With each passing month, however, the Germans encountered increasing resistance.

Hitler had said the war with Russia would be no ordinary war, but an operation based on racial and ideological differences. It was to be conducted with unprecedented, unmerciful, and unrelenting harshness and driven by Hitler's conviction that Russians were Untermenschen (subhuman).[12] The horrendous cruelties and mass deaths[13] caused by this policy rallied the Russian people and united them in a war "for the Motherland,"[14] whose slogan of universal resistance became: Comrade, Kill Your German (Gilbert 1989). The mutual brutality of the subsequent fighting is reflected in the following witticism:

> Krigen mellom Tyskland og Russland kalles Fellesslakteriet. [Schou-Sörensen]
> (The war between Germany and Russia is being called the *Fellesslakt-eriet* ["Butchers' Co-op" or "Mutual Slaughterhouse"].)

The Germans underestimated the resources of the Soviets, whose repeated ability to counterattack grew increasingly astonishing as they constantly put new divisions and armies into place. In July 1941, the Soviet Union formed an alliance with Great Britain, who together with the other Allies soon began sending weapons and supplies to Murmansk and to other Soviet harbors.

On 16 September 1941 Hitler ordered a halt to the advance on Leningrad, deciding to starve its population into submission rather than invade. Not expecting the Soviet conquest to take more than two months, however, Hitler had not equipped his forces for winter fighting.[15] As the first snows fell at Leningrad on 14 October, German soldiers, crippled by frostbite, found themselves unable to encircle the city, an objective not realized until 8 November 1941. Jössing humor derided the Germans' slow progress in this witticism based on the pre-1 October 1941 practice followed by the Norwegian German-censored press of referring to Leningrad as Petersburg:

-Har du hört at tyskerne har erobret Petersburg?
-Hvorledes det?
-Jo, nå har de bare Leningrad igjen å erobre. [*Folkets röst* (The voice of the people, underground newspaper), no. 2, 1941.]
(Have you heard that the Germans have conquered Petersburg? Now they've only got Leningrad left to conquer.)

In other words, the Germans had failed to accomplish their aim; Leningrad remained unvanquished.

With Leningrad encircled, Lake Lagoda offered the only gap in the German fortifications, and when it froze solid, it provided an avenue of hope to the city's starving population, finally granting a route for food and fuel. Blix has captured both Russian hopes and German adversity in his drawing from November 1941, captioned, "Hitler's March on Slippery Ice: In Russia Winter is Advancing According to Plan".[16]

These winter disasters notwithstanding, Hitler made ambitious plans for the summer of 1942, aiming first to take Stalingrad on the Volga River and then, after setting up a defensive on the River Don, at last to capture the besieged Leningrad. He also intended to take the Markop oil fields in the Caucasian mountains. When his forces reached this objective on 9 August 1942, however, they found that Soviet forces had blown up this badly needed fuel supply precisely in order to prevent Hitler from obtaining it. Commenting on Hitler's resulting misery, Jössing humor quipped:

Hitler er blitt dårlig, han har fått 'Kaukasus' i öret, og "Smuts" i öyet. [Ellingsen]

"Hitler's march on slippery ice," captioned: "In Russia winter is advancing according to plan," alluding to the calculatedly disastrous effect of the Soviet winter on Hitler's army. Artist: Ragnvald Blix (Stig Höök) Göteborgs Handels- och Sjöfarts-tidning, November 1941. Republished in Blix, *De fem årene* (1945). Reprinted here with permission of Gyldendal Forlag, Oslo, Norway.

(Hitler has become ill, he's developed *Caukasus* in his ear and *Smuts* in his eye.)

Apparently the foreign name of the mountain range sounded to Norwegian ears like a disease, while the Smuts ("dirt" in German), of course, came from all the burning oil.

On 19 August 1942 Hitler defied his generals by ordering the attack on Stalingrad, the city Stalin had named for himself and considered the showplace of Russia. Deciding that his soldiers would fight harder for a living city than one that was deserted, Stalin had decided not to evacuate Stalingrad. Responding to his slogan, Not One Step Back, and motivated by a combination of fear of the Germans, ardent patriotism, and Communist zeal, the Russians defending Stalingrad barricaded the streets, transformed the buildings into unimpregnable fortresses, and in the ferocious hand-to-hand combat that ensued, gave German forces no opportunity to dislodge them. Nor could the Germans stop the arrival of reinforcements from across the river. Though Hitler claimed in an

October 1942 speech that victory over Stalingrad was almost at hand, among his soldiers it was already being called "the mass grave of the Wehrmacht" (Gilbert 1989, 370). On 19 November the Russian defenders of the city launched their decisive counterattack. They surrounded the German forces that were encircling Stalingrad and—in one of the most bitterly fought and bloodiest battles in modern military history—killed over half of the 284,000 soldiers trapped there. Finally, on 2 February 1943, what remained of the German army surrendered. On 3 February, German radio announced that Hitler's forces had fallen prey to vastly superior forces and unfavorable circumstances.

This was no ordinary defeat. There were 150,000 dead, 90,000 had been taken prisoner, and over a quarter of the Wehrmacht's arsenal was lost. Back in Norway Greta Dahl observed the German reaction.

> February 3, 1942: Stalingrad is reconquered by the Russians, so this evening the movie theaters are closed, and I've heard that a national period of mourning has been declared.

To the armies struggling against Hitler's forces and to captive peoples throughout German-occupied Europe, though, the news of the surrender of so vast a German force and of Stalingrad's liberation brought renewed hope, and Jössing humor had a field day.

> -Hvorfor måtte tyskerne gi Hitler en doktorgrad?
> -Fordi han ikke hadde greid å ta Leningrad og Stalingrad. [Kuhnle 1945, 140]
> (Why did the Germans have to give Hitler a Doctor's Degree [= doktorgrad]?)
> Because he couldn't conquer Leningrad and Stalingrad.)

Playing on the continual conscription of civilian materials for the German front, people quipped about a

> Tvangslevering av to stoler hver, tyskerne orker ikke å stå lenger foran Stalingrad. [Ellingsen]
> (Compulsory donation of two chairs each: the Germans can no longer stand before Stalingrad.)

Other jokes emphasized the German carnage.

> Tyskerne drog i korstog mot det röde sovjet, men kom tilbake i Rödekorsvogner. [Folkets röst, 1941]

(The Germans went on a *korstog* [crusade] against the Red Army, but came back in *Rödekorsvogner* ["Red cross wagons, ambulances," linguistically related to *korstog*].)

Stalin protesterer overfor Quisling at han sender norske legioner til Östfronten, fordi det smaker så tran av dem. [Ellingsen]
(Stalin protests to Quisling about his sending members of the Norwegian Legion to the Eastern Front, because they taste too much like cod liver oil.)

Criticism of the flavor of meat had become constant in occupied Norway, where shortages left only fish entrails for animals to feed on. The joke conjures up the image of the Russian Red Army literally devouring Quisling's Regiment Nordland.

The German defeat at Stalingrad became the turning point of the war in Europe. From then on, the Russian armies would hold the initiative virtually without stop until the German army capitulated in May 1945. The projected Russian success in driving back the German front, eventually all the way to Germany, was neatly summed up in this joke from February 1943:[17]

Tyskerne og russerne er blitt venner, russerne följer tyskerne hjem.
[Schou-Sörensen]
(The Germans and Russians have become friends, the Russians are following the Germans home.)

Using the pretext of a Soviet exhibit in an area of Oslo known as Tullinlökka, one joke gloated over the Russians' subsequent invasion and conquest of Germany (to be discussed in chap. 11), suggesting that the Russians have taken over every bit of that country, right down to the furniture then being exhibited as Soviet property.

Opprör i Tyskland: Folk vil ha igjen möblene sine som er utlånt til Sovjet Utstillingen på Tullinlökka. [Ellingsen]
(Uproar in Germany: People want to retrieve their furnishings that are now on display at the Tullinlökka Soviet Exposition.)

By spring 1943, battles on all three war fronts—Stalingrad, Tunisia, and Guadalcanal—had turned the tide of the war in Allied favor. In Europe the way was now paved for the invasion of Italy from which the Allies could, in Churchill's words, attack "the soft underbelly of the German Reich."[18]

THE FALL OF MUSSOLINI AND ITALY'S SURRENDER

With Churchill's plan in mind, the Allies, having successfully driven the Axis forces out of Tunisia, invaded Sicily in July 1943. Fearing Italian defeat or defection from the Axis, Hitler moved his forces to Italy under Rommel's command, and Jössing humor accompanied him.

> Byttehandel: Et brukt Tuniskart byttes med et Italiakart. [Schou-Sörensen]
> (Swap: A used map of Tunisia to trade for a map of Italy.)

Spicing up the ubiquitous newspaper barter-columns mentioned in chapter 8, this mock ad expressed the hope that Hitler's reversals in Tunisia would be repeated in Italy.

On 16 July 1943 Roosevelt and Churchill issued a joint appeal to the Italian people, asking whether they wanted to die for Mussolini and Hitler or to live for Italy and civilization. Three days later, as American bombs attacked the Roman rail yards, Hitler met with Mussolini, whom he lectured for two hours on how to fight.

> Den gang Tyskland hadde framgang—Hitler og Musse taler sammen. Musse spör hva Hitler gjör siden det går så bra. Hitler svarer: "Vi synger 'Vår Gud han er så fast en borg.'" "Jaha, men hva skal jeg synge da?!" sier Musse.
> "Du kan jo synge 2. vers!" [Ellingsen]
> (When things were still going well for Germany, Hitler and Musse were conversing. Musse asks what Hitler's forces do to make things go so well. Hitler answers, "We sing 'A Mighty Fortress is Our God.'"
> "I see" says Musse, "but what should I sing?"
> "You can sing the second verse.")

In Norwegian the phrase to "sing the second verse" (å synge annet vers) means "to be on one's last legs." While highlighting Hitler's pessimistic view of Mussolini's prospects, the joke also alludes to Hitler's Festnung Europa plans to turn the occupied countries into a fortress (see chap. 9).

Hitler's lack of confidence in Mussolini's troops motivated his order that Rommel mobilize his forces into Italy to respond to an Allied attack. On the whole, distrust characterized the relationship between the two Axis powers, a circumstance captured in the following joke:

> En franskmann, engelskmann, italiener og tysker var oppe i en luft-ballong. De kom så höyt opp at noe ballast måtte kastes ut. De trakk

lodd, og det falt på engelskmannen. "God save the king," sa han og
hoppet ut. Så måtte mere kastes ut. Loddet falt på franskmannen. Han
sa: Vive la France!" og hoppet. Så måtte ennå mere hives og nå falt
loddet på tyskeren. Han sa "Heil Hitler" og hev italieneren av.
[Christerson]
(A Frenchman, an Englishman, an Italian and a German were up in a
hot air balloon. They got so high up that some ballast had to be thrown
out. They drew lots, and it fell upon the Englishman. "God save the
king," he said and jumped out. Then more had to be thrown out. The
lot fell upon the Frenchman. He said, "Vive la France!" and jumped.
When even more had to be thrown out, the lot fell upon the German.
He said, "Heil Hitler," and threw the Italian overboard.)

When the Allies scored a major objective by entering Palermo,
the Italians gave Mussolini a vote of no confidence, stripped him
of his power, and took him into captivity. Back in Norway, Greta
Dahl both rejoiced and fretted over this development:

July 26, 1943: Musse deposed!! Shouts of congratulations and peals of
laughter. Yes, we still do have a capacity for child-like glee. But I met
four *civilian* Germans with gas masks hanging down their duster-coats;
I guess that shows what they're expecting.

Though Italy's king now declared his country's abiding allegiance to Germany, this brought little comfort to Hitler, given his
low regard of the Italians' military aptitude. In view of the same
king's simultaneous negotiations with the Allies, moreover, Hitler's
suspicions proved well-founded.
For the Allies, by contrast, prospects brightened as they discerned the first crack in the Axis. In August the Allies isolated the
island of Sicily, and on 3 September, they invaded mainland Italy,
whose leaders the same day signed an armistice agreeing not to
oppose them. One week later Hitler countered by ordering the
occupation of Italy by German troops. Feeling Mussolini could be
useful in enlisting Italy's remaining Fascists for the Nazi cause,
Hitler used armed force to have the deposed dictator "rescued"
from captivity and helped him restore a minority government in
northern Italy. When the majority Italian government, based in
Brindisi, declared war on Germany on 13 October, Italian forces
joined the Allies in trying to break through toward Rome. The
combined forces initially made good progress in dislodging the occupying German and Italian Fascist forces, but as they approached
Casino, they encountered fierce opposition. Extraordinarily
bloody combat and intense bombing raids ensued and continued

until 18 May when the Allies finally broke through. The subsequent advance to Rome proceeded swiftly, and the Allies made their triumphal entry into the city on 4 June 1944.

Now only one front remained: Germany herself. How the war concluded there and how liberation came to Norway will be told in chapter 11.

11
Germany's Bleak Prospects for Victory: High Hopes for Haakon's Return

Wishful thinking, a vital component of so much other occupation humor, logically played a particularly prominent role in the many jokes that predicted the end of German domination and the return of King Haakon.

WAITING FOR HAAKON

While Nazi propaganda, as already noted, denounced Haakon as a treacherous deserter and suppressed all hopes of the king's ever returning to an independent Norway, Jössing humor portrayed his refusal to collaborate as heroic, an image that began taking root and propagating during the summer of 1940. The increasingly favorable popular response to Haakon also benefited the government which had joined him in exile and which had borne the criticism for Norway's military unpreparedness.[1] Humorous quips and anecdotes eagerly spread the prospect that the former regime might soon replace Quisling.

Ned med Quisling og fiskepölser.
Opp med Kongen og fleskepölser. [Schou-Sörensen]
(Down with Quisling and fish sausage
Up with the King and pork sausage.)

Når enden er god—er Quisling gått. [Ellingsen]
(When the end is good, Quisling is gone, [i.e., the ending will be good when Quisling has gone].)

This gibe echoes the Norwegian version of the proverb, "All's well that ends well": Når enden er god er allting godt (When the end is good, everything is good), playing on the homonymous relationship of *godt* and *gått*.

185

A stylized king sweeps out Nazi debris including the disembodied heads of Hitler and Quisling, the swastika, and *solkors* ("sun cross," symbol of the Norwegian Nazi party), along with the slogan Germany Is Winning on All Fronts. Artist: Jens R. [Nilssen] (1880–1964); publisher: Humoristens forlag.

The theme of longing for Haakon's return also found expression in narrative jokes.

A class was assigned an essay on the subject of cats. One pupil wrote: "When Haakon VII was king in Norway, all cats were happy." [Vigness 1970, 251]
In Bodö a class was assigned to write the sentence, "Quisling is our leader" ten times. One boy wrote ten times: "King Haakon is our leader."
"What's this you're doing?" demanded the teacher.
"I can't write the letter 'Q,'" said the boy. [Vigness 1970, 256]

Det var för tvunget frammöte, pinsler og mord begynte for alvor, da NS-folkene sendte sine drabanter om med opplysende foredrag. Et sted i Tröndelag var det bl. a. også mött fram en gammel bonde. Etter foredraget stod lederen av mötet fram og sa at nå var ordet fritt, om det var noe en hadde lyst til å si eller spörre om. Bonden reiste seg.
-E det rettelig fritt, ordet, da? Kan æ si ka æ vil?
-Joda, vær så god.
-Ja, da vil æ si "Leve Kongen" da, sa han og slo ut med armene.
Det ble tumult i salen. Lederen kom fort ned, tok bonden i armen og sa han hadde å gå. Men bonden mente han hadde betalt sin krone og hadde rett til å bli til slutt.
-Du kan få att krona di, sa lederen sint og ga ham mynten.
-Bonden går mot döra, fulgt av alles blikk. I dören snur han seg mot publikum, löfter hånden med mynten i været og sier lunt:
-Ja, var det itj det æ visst", at både'n Haakon og æ får krona igjen!
[Hansen and Baggethun 1975, 19–20]
(It was before compulsory attendance, torture and executions began in earnest, when the Nazis were sending their henchmen around to give informational lectures. Somewhere in Tröndelag an old farmer was among the attendees. Following the lecture the arranger of the meeting announced that the floor was open, if anyone had something to say or ask about.
The farmer stood up.
"Can I really say what I want?"
"Of course, please go ahead."
"Well, then I want to say: 'Long Live the King,'" he declared as he dramatically threw out his arms.
Tumult broke out in the auditorium. The meeting arranger rushed down to the audience, took the farmer by the arm and ordered him to leave. But the farmer said he'd paid his money and had a right to stay until the end.
"Here's your crown [Norwegian currency] back," the arranger growled, handling over the coin.
The farmer walked toward the door, with everyone's eyes on him.

Turning toward the audience when he reached the exit, he raised the hand holding the coin and said drolly:
"Just as I thought, both Haakon and I are getting our crowns back.")

Details of just how Haakon's return actually was accomplished appear later in this chapter. Meanwhile it is worth noting the way the next joke, like the "cats" item, suggests the universality of the Norwegians' longing for this goal.

Et ektepar löper etter trikken. Konen roper: "Skynd deg Haakon! Trikken venter!"
Konduktören: "Ta det med ro frue, vi venter alle på Haakon!" [Ellingsen]
(A married couple is running to catch the streetcar. The wife yells, "Hurry up, Haakon! The streetcar is waiting!"
The conductor replies, "Take it easy, Lady, we're all waiting for Haakon!")

While Haakon had been viewed by many as distant and unknowable before the occupation (Heradstveit 1979, 13),[2] Jössing humor both shaped and reflected his developing wartime reputation as a *folkekonge* (king of the people).

·THE BEGINNING OF THE END

Already in 1941 several jokes were suggesting that the end of the war was in sight.[3]

En tysk offiser kommer inn i trikken. Han trår på den ömmeste liktå til en nordmann. Mannen blir rasende og slår offiseren i gulvet. -Ute på plattformen står en tysker og en nordmann. Da nordmannen ser at offiseren blir slått i gulvet, slår han omgående tyskeren ved siden av seg, ned for full telling.
Alle fire må bli med på "Nr 19."
Politifullmektigen kan forstå at mannen med liktåen ble rasende.
Han snur seg mot den andre: "Men De, da, mannen min. Hvilken grunn har De?"
"Ja, jeg trodde det var no det begynte, jeg." [Ellingsen]
(A German officer gets on the *trikk*. He steps on the most sensitive bunion of a Norwegian, who furiously knocks the officer to the floor. Standing on the outside platform, another Norwegian sees the officer being knocked down and he starts beating up on the German standing next to him, sending him down for the count. All four are taken to [the police station at] Möllergaten 19. The police officer can understand

why the man with the bunion got mad. He turns to the other Norwegian, "But you, Sir. What reason do you have?"
"Well, I thought it was beginning.")

What the second Norwegian thought was beginning was the general uprising against the occupiers that the Jössings assumed would accompany the occupation's conclusion. The following jocular "1941-versions" of various traditional items recorded by Schou-Sörensen also predict an imminent end of Germany's power:

The new version of The Lord's Prayer goes: *Ti riket er ditt, makten og hæren, men ikke i evighet.* (For Thine is the kingdom, and the power and the *hære* ["army," rhymes with *ære* "glory"] but not forever.)

The second verse of the popular Christmas carol *Du grönne, glitrende tre* [You Green, Glittering Tree] now begins: "The *last* Christmas in a foreign land," [replacing the original song's reference to "The first Christmas in a foreign land," i.e., Bethlehem], alluding to a hoped for absence of the occupiers by the next yuletide.

It was also said that German fairy tales, which used to begin *Es war einmal* [Once upon a time], soon would begin: *S. S. var einmal* ["S. S. once was,"—but is no more].

Hope for the war's prompt conclusion lasted into 1942.[4] In February of that year Schou-Sörensen reported seeing an illegal newspaper's masthead labeled: *2.nen og siste årgang* (second and last year of publication); since the underground press would cease to function in peacetime, the masthead suggests a pre-1943 conclusion to the war. A favorite verse by Elias Blix (1836–1909) about the springtime revival in grove *(lund)* and glen (li), became the basis of an extended pun on the names of Propaganda minister Gulbrand *Lund*e and Nazi police chief Jonas *Lie*. It apparently became quite popular, being recorded not only by Schou-Sörensen, but by Ellingsen and Christerson as well.

> No livnar det i Gulbrand Lunde
> No lauvas Jonas Lie
> No feites Vidkun Quisling
> Det lir mot slaktetid. (June 1942)
> (Now sap is rising in Gulbrand Lunde.
> Now leaves are sprouting in Jonas Lie.
> Now Vidkun Quisling's being fattened up,
> For the slaughter that's soon to be.)[5]

Germany's bleak prospects and the torture to which the occupiers would be subjected when she lost also proved a popular theme.[6]

Tre tyskere i ei ölstue. Den ene sukket. Så sukket den andre. Da avbröt den tredje og sa: "Mine herrer, la oss ikke snakke om seierssjangsene." [*Frihet*, Christmas 1940, which gives as its source the Dutch underground newspaper, *Haagsche Post*, The Haag, demonstrating the often international nature of occupation humor][7]
(Three Germans in a beer hall. One of them sighed. The second one sighed. The third one interrupted, saying: "Gentlemen, let's not talk about our chances for victory.")

En tysk soldat sitter å skryter av Tysklands storverk. Tilslutt sier han: "Når krigen er forbi skal jeg ha meg en sykkeltur rundt det Stor-tyske riket!"
Tilhörer: "Hva skal du gjöre om ettermiddagen da?" [Larsen, Christerson]
(A German soldier is bragging about Germany's great accomplishments and says at last, "When the war is over I'm going to take a bicycle trip around the Great German Realm!"
A listener asks, "And what will you do in the afternoon?")

En tysk offiser la ut for en eldre herre i kupeen om hvilken fordel det var for Norge at tyskerne var kommet: "og når krigen er slutt vil vi trekke oss tilbake så dere får landet igjen."
"Det tviler jeg ikke på," löd svaret, "men hva ville ha hendt hvis tyskerne hadde seieret?" [*Avantgarden*, 24 August 1942]
(In a train compartment a German officer was telling an older Norwegian gentleman about what an advantage it was for Norway that the Germans had come, "and when the war is over, we'll withdraw so the country will once again be yours."
"That I do not doubt," came the reply, "but what would have happened if the Germans had won?")

En jössing og en NS mann taler sammen. Jössingen spör NS mannen hva han vil gjöre hvis England vinner. Jo, da ville han ta hatt og frakk og gå.
"Ja, at du tar frakken, det kan jeg forstå, men hva skal du sette hatten på?" [Ellingsen]
(A Jössing and a Nazi are conversing. The Norwegian asks the Nazi what he'll do if England wins. "Well, then I'll just take my hat and coat and leave."
"Yes, I understand you'll take your coat, but what will you put your hat on?")

Several jokes tell of Hitler and Mussolini being arrested and sent to St. Helena, the exile of Napoleon Bonaparte.

Musse er arrestert og sendt til St. Helena. Her klager han over at det
er stykt og uopp-pusset. Vakten smiler lunt og svarer: "Ta det med ro,
"Maler'n' kommer snart." [Ellingsen]
(Musse is arrested and sent to St. Helena, which he complains is unat-
tractive and poorly maintained. The guard smiles genially and answers:
"Relax, 'the painter' is coming soon.") [The "painter" refers to Hitler,
see chap. 2]

Hvorfor Hitler ikke gifter seg? Fordi han venter på St. Helena. [Schou-
Sörensen, Rommetveit]
(Why doesn't Hitler get married? Because he's waiting for St. Helena.)

According to Rommetveit (Letter to author, 17 September 1992),
the beloved nineteenth-century poet and patriot, Björnstjerne
Björnson, had made St. Helena familiar in his poem "Mitt fölge"
(My retinue) telling of Napoleon, with victories from Moscow to
Cartigena, dying alone on St. Helena (Med seier fra Moskva til
Kartægena / han dör dog ensom på St. Helena); the witticisms
wished Hitler the same fate. Ardently longing for this outcome,
the occupied Norwegians instantly understood the reference, while
many Swedes, according to Christerson, did not—as the following
anecdote indicates:

A man was giving a lecture in Sweden recently and remarked that, "St.
Helena can yet be a *very* important political point in the great world."
Just imagine: the audience didn't get it!

Christerson indirectly suggests that the Swedes' lack of compre-
hension may be due to their less intense desire for Hitler's defeat.[8]
Though the St. Helena comparison was imaginary, several actual
parallels between the careers of Hitler and Napoleon do exist[9] and
provided the basis for several witticisms. The following calculation
recorded by Schou-Sörensen, for example, predicted Hitler's fall
in 1943:

1918 German Revolution
1789 French Revolution
 129

1933 Hitler becomes Chancellor
1804 Napoleon becomes Emperor
 129

1938 Hitler took Austria
1809 Napoleon "   "
 129

1941 June 22, Hitler invades Russia
<u>1812</u> June 23, Napoleon   "   "
129

1943   ?
<u>1814</u> Napoleon's fall in Russia
129

While the jokes in the previous chapter concerned specific war developments, other humor celebrated Germany's bad prospects in general. One of Arne Taraldsen's December 1943 stamps, for example, shows a strongly caricatured Hitler, costumed as a blond Valkyrie and wearing a lifesaver around his waist, struggling to keep afloat amid the waves, while surrounded by fish who take obvious delight in his limited swimming skills. Coupled with its text: Wir fahren gegen Engelland ("We're on our way to England), the stamp ironically contrasts that early song's boast of invading England (see chap. 9) with the ultimate failure not only of that mission, but of Hitler's entire campaign.

When things started going badly for Germany on the war front, the Norwegian population felt the consequences, as Åslaug Rommetveit's diary attests.

> September 10, 1943: Every time the Germans suffer a military defeat, things get stricter here. On these dark fall evenings we are sometimes truly terrified. . . . The day the Italians capitulated, some dairy workers celebrated on the roof of the creamery; the police appeared immediately and ordered them all to the police station.

Reflecting the heightened Nazi terrorism and intolerance in the wake of their reversals, folk wit quipped:

> Hanemarsj er forbudt for det går den veien höna sparker. [Ellingsen; Trondheim diary entry dated 8 January 1942]
> (The goose step—lit. "rooster march"—is forbidden because things are "going the way the chicken scratches" [a common Norwegian expression meaning "going downhill," i.e., not going very well].)

Another quip about Germany's reversals played on the linguistic similarity between the words *tog* (train) and *tilbaketog* (retreat, withdrawal).

> Etter at Hitler har overtatt kommandoen etter Brauchitsch sier man: "Hitler er blitt togförer på Verdens störste tilbaketog. [Schou-Sörensen][10]

A mock stamp contrasting Hitler's sinking fortunes with his troops' earlier boastful song "We're on the way to England." Artist: Arne Taraldsen, distributed by British aircraft, December 1943.

(Now that Hitler has taken over command from Brauchitsch,[11] people are saying, "Hitler has become the *togförer* [train engineer] on the world's longest *tilbaketog* [retreat].)

The following narrative joke recorded by Schou-Sörensen in January 1943 and portraying the difficult birth of a reduced Germany, celebrated the reversal of Hitler's dream of creating an enormous pan-Germanic *Reich:*

> Mutter Gross-Deutschland var syk og det ble tilkalt 3 leger, dr. Stalin, dr. Churchill og dr. Roosevelt. Den ene sa det var forspiselse, den annen at det var blokade, underernæring. Nei da, sa den tredje; Det er ingen av delene, det er Klein-Deutschland som er i anmarsj.
> (Mother Gross-Deutschland was sick and 3 physicians were called: Dr. Stalin, Dr. Churchill and Dr. Roosevelt. One of them said it was overeating, the other that it was blockage, under-nourishment. No, said the third; it's none of those things, it is Little-Deutschland about to be born.)

While humor portrayed how dreadfully it assumed Hitler must be suffering given the massive damage being inflicted upon his armies, Hitler had more and more retreated into a world of illusion having dismissed or isolated himself from his more critical advisors and listening only to the obsequious ones. Instead of the expected discouragement, therefore, those closest to him frequently noted his indomitable confidence. On the day Germany withdrew from North Africa, for example, Goebbels noted in his diary:

> May 7, 1943: The *Führer* expresses his unshakable conviction that the Reich will one day rule all of Europe. We will have to survive a great many conflicts but they will doubtless lead to the most glorious triumphs. And from then on, the road to world domination is practically spread out before us. For whoever rules Europe will be able to seize the leadership of the world. [Quoted in Gilbert 1989, 426]

Jössing humor, by contrast, persisted in portraying Hitler's sinking fortunes, as in this version of the popular Hamsun joke (see chap. 8):

> Hitler er så begeistret for Hamsun, derfor har han fått 3 av hans verker: Först fikk han Markens gröde, deretter Viktoria og til slutt Sult. [Schou-Sörensen]
> (Hitler is so fond of Hamsun that he has obtained three of his works: first he got *Growth of the soil,* then *Victoria* and finally *Hunger.*)

On 25 February 1943, a round-the-clock American and British offensive against Germany began in an effort to disable German war industry and to break the population's morale. Employing as many as one thousand bombers, the raids leveled German cities, killing almost ½ million people and wounding about 1 million. Still the German war machine rolled on virtually unhindered until 1944, when the Allied bombs destroyed essential means of transportation and communication along with vital fuel stores. Jössing humor commented on Germany's losses:

> En tysker kom inn på Vestbanen i Oslo og beklaget seg over at hans kuffert var blitt stjålet mens han var inne i stasjonens telefonkiosk. En herre som stod ved siden av ham og hörte på, henvendte seg til ham og sa: "For 2 uker siden var jeg i Berlin, jeg gikk inn i en telefonkiosk nær jernbanen. Da jeg kom ut, var både kufferten og stasjonen borte." [Christerson]
> (A German came to Oslo West Railway Station and complained that his suitcase had been stolen while he was in the telephone booth outside the station. A gentleman standing next to him overheard and turned to him saying, "Two weeks ago I was in Berlin and went into a telephone booth near the train station. When I came out, both my suitcase and the station were gone.")

Another popular witticism endowed German cities with the names of actual Norwegian cities whose names may be interpreted to suggest destruction.

> Berlin will be called *Jevnaker* [literally "flattened acre"], Köln will be called *Brandbu* ["burned dwelling"] and Essen will be called *Tomter* ["vacant lots"]. [Schou-Sörensen][12]

Reflecting the desolate results, yet another jibe held that

> Rommel er blitt överste sjef i Berlin, for han er trenet örkengeneral. [Ellingsen]
> (Rommel has been made Field Commander in Berlin because of his training in desert warfare.)

Finally this joke predicted the end of Hitler's rule:

> Forkledd som Chauffer gikk Hitler til en spåkone. Hun spådde han
> 1) at han ville slippe opp for bensin
> 2) at han ville få aksebrudd
> 3) at han ville miste förerkortet. [Schou-Sörensen]
> (Disguised as a chauffeur Hitler went to a fortune teller. She predicted
> 1) that he would run out of gas
> 2) that his *akse* [meaning both "axle" and "axis"] would break, and
> 3) that he would lose his *förerkort* ["driver's license" and license to be Führer].)

The joke neatly sums up the final plummeting of Hitler's career: by the autumn of 1944 the German ability to continue the war

depended on an uninterrupted supply of fuel, a resource that instead disappeared when Romania joined the Allies on 25 August
1944 (Hitler had "run out of gas"). Prior to that the Rome-Berlin
Axis established in 1937 had collapsed in September 1943 with
Italy's capitulation and subsequent declaration of war on Germany
(Hitler's "axle had broken"). During the final quarter of 1944,
forces were closing in from both north and south to crush Germany, and by the end of April 1945 they had joined forces and
surrounded Berlin. Hitler ensconced himself in his bunker where
he committed suicide on 30 April (and thereby certainly "lost his
license").

ROWERS

Indications of such a disastrous culmination of the German war
effort had already appeared in 1942 and grew increasingly evident
in 1943, when Germany's military failures prompted ever more
frequent traces of NS submission.[13] Even before Germany's February 1943 loss at Stalingrad, Greta Dahl told her diary:

> November 21, 1942: Now the Nazis are getting nervous, and they are
> so sorry. The idiots; it serves them right. They have been threatening
> us with everything under the sun, as though they were the ones in
> power. . . . Now the most cowardly of them are starting to disparage
> the Germans, but it won't be so easy for them to switch to Jössing
> ranks.

Quisling admitted that things had not gone as expected and began speaking of peace and tolerance among all Norwegians (i.e.,
both NS and Jössings). His followers even went so far as to admit
they had been wrong about the Jössings and to ask for forgiveness.

The Germans, too, pursued a more moderate course. "The Germans are growing more cowardly while we're growing more brave,"
Greta Dahl reports on 3 February 1943. Publicly, Terboven took
up the old refrains about Germany's not having come to oppress
the Norwegians but to cooperate with them. A certain relaxation
of terrorism was also evident, and jokes reflecting this new attitude
began to circulate.

> Hitler er begynt å lære engelsk etter Brekkes engelske lesebok. Han
> er kommet til: Fred, where are you. Come here, be quick. [Schou-
> Sörensen, Christerson]
> (Hitler has started learning English using Brekke's English Reader.

He's gotten as far as "*Fred,* where are you. Come here, be quick." [In Norwegian *fred* means "peace."])

The capitulation of Italy on 8 September 1943 brought a new urgency among many NS members to change sides. The ranks of these erstwhile Nazis, popularly known as "rowers," grew with each new defeat, and about them Åslaug Rommetveit comments on 21 March 1944:[14]

> Things are going badly for the Germans in the East, and this provokes them. The Nazis here in Norway are probably starting to shake in their boots. At any rate there are more and more who want to join the so-called "Rowers Club."[15]

The situation was tailor-made for humor. A mock swap-column advertisement played on the trade of ideologies.

> "Har hirduniform, önsker robåt med lange årer" Billmerk. "Hurtig avgjörelse." [Ellingsen]
> ("Have *Hird* uniform, want rowboat with long oars." Signed "Quick decision.")

In the Christmas 1944 issue of the illegal newspaper *Alt for Norge* this rendering of the rowers by Arne Taraldsen appeared:

Members of "The Nazi Rowing Club" led by Quisling in a desperate attempt to dissociate themselves from the Nazi party. Artist: Arne Taraldsen in *Alt for Norge,* 1944.

The drawing portrays Quisling and others rowing in hectic terror. Like Olav Tryggvasson, one of the heroic saga kings with whom the Nazi leader liked to identify, Quisling is walking on the oars in a desperate attempt to change the boat's course. But the song they sing "Ro, ro til Björneskjær" (echoing the familiar children's song "Ro, ro til fiskeskjær"—Row, row to the fishing grounds), reveals that they are bound for Björnöya, the Norwegian-owned Arctic island near Spitzbergen where—in a frequently uttered wartime threat—the Jössings swore to banish the Norwegian Nazis to suffer agonizing deaths in the brutal cold.[16]

The following gem recorded by Finn Bö captures the urgency to avoid such postwar reprisals by timely termination of Nazi affiliations:

> Har du hört at det er stilt opp premier for dem som kan skaffe NS flere tilhengere? Den som kan tegne 5 nye medlemmer får lov til å melde sig ut av partiet. Og den som kan tegne 10 nye medlemmer får skriftlig bevidnelse for at han *aldri har vært* medlem (228).
> (Have you heard they're awarding prizes to those who can increase Nazi party membership? Anyone who can get 5 people to join will be allowed out of the party. And those who can get 10 people to join will receive written documentation of *never having been* a member.)

Yet another witticism about the fluidity of Nazi party membership rolls told that photographers were extremely busy in 1944 with the police having demanded new identification cards for all NS members since their faces had changed so remarkably in recent months (Vigness 1970, 257).

In September 1944 an armistice was signed between the Soviet Union and Finland, whereupon Finland declared war on Germany. On 4 October, it was decided that German forces would make their withdrawal from Finland through northern Norway as far as Lyngen in South Troms. The Russian army followed, but stayed in Varanger, near the Russian border. Though little military action ensued, the Germans feared they would be pursued and consequently followed the burned earth tactic as they withdrew through Finnmark and Nord-Troms, destroying houses, bridges, telegraph lines, boats, piers, and everything else they thought the enemy could use. When the population refused to evacuate voluntarily in response to German tales of the horrible destruction the Russian army would inflict on them, the Germans used force to chase them out. In all fifty thousand people were driven south as their houses burned behind them. The evacuees were assembled in Tromsö and Narvik, which lacked the facilities to care for these multitudes, almost equal in size to these cities' populations (Andenæs, Riste, and Skodvin 1989).

Still many citizens had managed to stay behind, hiding out in

caves and mines, on the mountain plateaus and in forests, preferring hardship to leaving.[17] Some of the Nazi soldiers, however,
apparently regarding their mission as liberating Norway from the
terrors of both the Russians and the Western Allies, brutally
abused those who tried to remain in Finnmark. The corpses of six
civilians were found near the Nordkinn peninsula, for example,
accompanied by a printed flyer proclaiming,

> We are protecting your home against the terrorism of Bolshevism . . .
> [and] against capitalistic plunder . . . those who oppose us . . . are
> traitors against Europe and against their Norwegian fatherland, and
> will be destroyed no matter where they hide. [Bull 1979, 447–48]

Terrified that their own "liberation" might be equally violent, the
rest of Norway had to wait six more months for the occupation to
end. This last interval featured the harshest winter of the entire
war, a failed potato harvest, and a severely reduced milk ration
along with some of the worst terrorism Norwegians experienced.
The membership and activities of the organized resistance (Home
Front) grew, while the Gestapo and NS membership, having given
up all hope of gentle treatment after the war, desperately sought
to stop them by stepping up the violence of their reprisals. The
period brought continued and intense battle at the foreign fronts
as well.

GERMAN BRAVADO AND THE FALL OF BERLIN

Following the Allied soldiers' triumphal march into Rome, they
proceeded north toward Berlin which the Soviet Red Army had
been approaching from the north. By the end of 1944 Germany had
lost almost every square mile of the territory she had conquered
between 1939 and 1942; of all the capitals captured then, only Oslo,
Copenhagen, the Haag, and Warsaw remained under German control. Still Germany refused to surrender. Hitler determined that
the fighting would continue town by town, mile by mile, to the
bitter end, and the Allies had no choice but to go on fighting.[18]
    On 1 February 1945, with the Red Army less than fifty miles
away, Berlin was declared a fortress city. Young and old were set
to work building fortifications. Showing a seasoned eye for propaganda, Greta Dahl noted on 26 February 1945 that since

the papers are saying Reuter's [news service] reports of terror and panic in Germany are lies, we assume there must be terror and panic in Germany.

Hitler remained confident of averting defeat nonetheless and talked of prolonging the war by moving it either to Bavaria or to Norway, causing Greta Dahl to remark on 8 March:

Now the officers are saying they will continue the war from here and that they'll also dictate the peace treaty from here. It's enough to make you sick.

On 17 April Hitler ordered all autobahn bridges in the Berlin area to be blown up, and at a midday conference with his commanders, he declared that the Russians were in for the bloodiest defeat imaginable before they reached Berlin (Gilbert 1989, 667). When Soviet artillery nevertheless arrived three days later and opened fire on Berlin, Hitler doggedly reiterated his plan to hold Bohemia, Moravia, and Norway; he even received a birthday telegram from his Norwegian administrators promising that Norway indeed would be held (Gilbert 1989, 669). Preparations in that country bore out his claim, and Greta Dahl's diary registers the developments with grave concern.

April 25, 1945: The situation is truly terrifying now. The Germans have managed to smuggle a boat-load of SS-soldiers to Norway. They claim they'll hold "Fortress Norway" no matter what happens. . . . Demolition experts have been placed around all the towns, prepared to destroy our industries, our factories and all other important buildings. It makes my skin crawl just to think of it: Besieged together with these desperate fanatics! If only we could get our children out safely. . . .

Goebbels shared Hitler's assurances of victory and saw in Franklin Roosevelt's death on 21 April 1945 the possibility that the Allies would be thrown into disarray and thereby allow Germany to gain the upper hand. Though these hopes failed to materialize, German assurances of winning abided and became the target of Jössing humor.

Det er i krigens siste dager i Berlin. Et kumlåkk over en av kloakkene som ennu ikke er dekket av nedstyrtede hus, hever seg langsomt—et ansikt kommer til syne—det er Goebels:
"VI VINNER KRIGEN!!!!"
Pang! Kumlåkket smeller igjen. [Ellingsen]
(It is during the last days of the war in Berlin. A cover over one of the

sewers not yet inundated by the debris of bombed houses slowly rises—a face comes into view—-it's Goebbels [who proclaims]: "WE ARE WINNING THE WAR!!!!" Bang! The sewer cover slams back down.)

On 25 April Allied and Russian troops met and joined forces outside Berlin, dashing Himmler's last hopes that these two forces would turn against and fight each other affording Germany a final opportunity to prevail over both. Instead the Berlin defense perimeter which Hitler had ordered held intact at all costs, was now penetrated in several places. Sensing the end, the diarist Åslaug Rommetveit writes on 24 April 1945:

> The bloodbath in Germany must soon be over. The Allies have gathered there and are fighting in the very center of Berlin. Even German-censored newspapers are admitting that their defeat may be at hand.

Even as the papers admitted the possibility of defeat, however, Hitler continued dismissing even the closest of his generals who dared to doubt victory or urge surrender. Employing the names of once-trusted aides who suffered this fate, the following extended wordplay describes the Führer's alleged agony over their betrayal:

> Hitler befinner seg på følgende måte: Han Himler med öynene, har Hess i halsen, Rommel i magen og Göring i buksen. [Christerson] (How Hitler is feeling and behaving: He *Him*[*m*]*ler* [is rolling] his eyes, his throat is *Hess* [hoarse], he has *Rommel* [rumbling] in his stomach and is *Goering* [defecating] in his pants.)

The positions in the Third Reich of the men named in the joke and the reasons Hitler dismissed them were as follows:
Heinrich Himmler (1900–1945), the leader of the SS and Gestapo, originator of Lebensborn (see chap. 3) and chief architect of the Final Solution (to liquidate the Jews), was dismissed when Hitler learned of his April 1945 efforts to negotiate peace with the Allies. Hitler had Himmler arrested on 28 April and expelled from the Nazi party.[19]
Rudolf Hess (1894–1987) had deeply embarrassed Hitler by his 10 May 1941 flight to Scotland (see chap. 9), an episode that had also distracted attention necessary to planning the then imminent Soviet invasion. Hess remained in British captivity until the war ended.[20]
Erwin Rommel (1891–1944), the phenomenally successful leader of Germany's Afrika Korps, had become convinced by July 1944 that

Hitler must be removed from power. Preferring that Hitler be brought to trial, he refused to take part in the 20 July 1944 assassination plot, but on nevertheless being suspected of involvement (see chap. 2), he chose suicide over the threatened execution. German officials gave him a state funeral on 17 October 1944 in order to conceal from the German public the full extent of his opposition to Hitler as well as the cruelty of Hitler's revenge (Taylor and Shaw 1987, 280–81).

Hermann Goering, (1893–1946) the most prominent Nazi leader next to Hitler and head of the Luftwaffe (Nazi Air Force), sent a telegram to Hitler's bunker in April 1945 stating that since Hitler no longer possessed full freedom of command, Goering himself should replace him as Führer. Hitler regarded the telegram as treasonous and on 28 April dismissed Goering from his state offices, stripped him of all honors, revoked his membership in the Nazi Party, and ordered his arrest.[21]

In addition to marking the dismissal of both Himmler and Goering, 28 April saw the end of the fascist rule that had begun twenty-three years earlier in Italy. On that day Mussolini was shot dead by Italian partisans; a few days later Greta Dahl recorded her impressions:

> May 1, 1945: Quisling must see a terrible example of how things will go for the likes of him in Mussolini's tasteless execution. After patriots had captured him, hanged him and then carried his corpse through the larger cities, the horror has, if possible, grown even greater. I can't say I like the way Musse's body was treated: As he hung suspended, feet up, with his head down, people spat on him, and a mother fired 5 shots through his dead carcass, "one for each of her 5 assassinated sons" she said. He had earlier begged for his life, promising to establish an even greater kingdom for them if they would only let him live. Time and again those who pitilessly can send thousands to their deaths, reveal their cowardice when their own lives hang in the balance.

On 30 April, the day after the unconditional surrender of German troops in Italy, Hitler placed a gun in his mouth and fired. The next day Goebbels killed his family and himself inside the bunker. On 2 May, Berlin surrendered, and Germany subsequently capitulated on all fronts: In North Italy on 2 May, in the Netherlands and Denmark on 4 May. The final capitulations, including the liberation of Norway, came on 7 May. By the next day, the war in Europe had ended.

For several months, the government exiled in London and the

leaders of the Home Front resistance organization had harbored grave concerns about how the liberation would come to Norway. A total of 340,000 German soldiers remained in the country, including the ones who had destroyed northern Norway. Asked for reinforcements, the Allies said they had no troops to send to Norway in the event of continued fighting; there was no way the 40,000 resistance soldiers and 15,000 police officers that comprised the only opposition forces could be expected to prevail.

Fortunately the fears of prolonged combat proved unfounded. Though Terboven might have liked to fight on, he found few followers among either the Nazi security police or Wehrmacht, and in the end the Germans simply laid down their arms. The central council of the Home Front resistance organization received the authority to supervise the period of transition until the exiled government returned from England, and they urged the population to behave with calm, dignity, and discipline when the radio announced on 7 May that German forces would surrender the following day.

Describing on 7 May how she learned of the capitulation, Greta Dahl wrote:

Elna came home from school and says "peace" has come. I've got to patch the flag! Just think: Now I won't need to be nervous about you, diary, and I won't have to keep hiding you. That will seem strange after 5 years of secret writing and constant worry about how to keep you concealed. . . .

Later that day she continued:

I've patched and washed the flag, and Arild has tested the flagpole to make sure it works. . . . Lights are shining from everyone's windows; no one is thinking of blinding them tonight. It's said peace will be proclaimed all over Europe tomorrow. Oh, to have a radio!

When the Instrument of Surrender was signed the next day, Åslaug Rommetveit declared:

May 8, 1945: The greatest date in world history. Germany has capitulated. Norway is *free*. It's almost too powerful to be real. I hear the bells of Fana Church . . . Bergen is decorated as for a festival. Flags everywhere. Pictures of the King. Happy people. Everyone greeting everybody else. In a way it's an indefinable joy, for it holds so infinitely much and probably feels different to each one of us.[22]

When the king returned on 7 June 1945 she continued:

12

The Function and Legacy of Occupation Humor

By the end of the occupation, resistance had become a well-established and powerful force, easily overshadowing the earlier period, when "few were actually as brave as they think they were today" (E. Ringnes 1950, 351). Now things looked quite different than they had in the wake of Norway's crushing military defeat when the Allies had proven inept, Germany seemed unbeatable, and no organization existed to help individual citizens understand the unfamiliar experience of their nation's being occupied. Most had forgotten that in those early months, many assumed that once the armed resistance ended, a modus vivendi would be sought with the victors, as the usual postwar practice had been throughout history (Furre 1992, 177).

Fanning the flames of doubt, NS propaganda had—as we have seen—blamed the former government for the catastrophic 9 April invasion, for Norway's military unpreparedness, and for the country's inability to assert her neutrality in the war. With the king and the government having "deserted" their country, only the Nazi party would be able to make peace with Germany and establish a Norwegian government in Norway (Furre 1992, 179; Senja 1973, 11). Many had seen the wisdom in these arguments at a time when a British victory seemed highly unlikely.

The Nazi party had attracted adherents for other reasons as well. Presenting itself as the continuation of Norway's ancient agrarian tradition, the repository of pride in country and family, it drew its symbolism from Nordic mythology and its members saluted each other with a traditional Old Norse greeting.[1] The party instituted a Hird to guard their mighty förer, who promised not only to bring the country out of the war but to establish an even greater, morally healthier Norway, and—through the Führerprinzip (government by the elite)—to put an end to the "party squabbling" and "parliamentary confusion" of the past. In short, the Nazis claimed to stand for order and discipline, tradition and morality—irresistible features to many during the initial, chaotic, and confused phase of the occupation.

As the Allies had gone from defeat to defeat during the first months and years of the war, moreover, NS propaganda seemed accurate in its prediction that the old system would soon be eradicated. Against these powerful odds, anti-Nazi jokes began raising consciousness and changing minds.[2] Circulating already during the first two months after the invasion (April-June 1940),[3] occupation humor played a vital role by being among the first voices to establish and nurture the fledgling attitude of resistance.[4] Though postwar descriptions of the occupation period would make the jokes seem to be mere manifestations of an already-existing resistance mentality, wartime evidence documents no spontaneous rise in the spirit of resistance. Instead we see that resistance had to be "implanted and cultivated in the great majority of the population" (Bennett 1969, 203), as the following statement from the 18 November 1940 issue of the underground newspaper *Bulletinen* also suggests:

> More and more it is occurring to people that it is possible and worthwhile to resist.

Even as late as 1941–1942, says Ulateig, a Norwegian Nazi who fought at the German front, no concerted cold shoulder treatment could be discerned in his community, and the Nazi meetings had good attendance (1987, 98).

Backed by no organization, the initial resistance came entirely from individuals.

> People thought and acted for themselves; while their actions might have come in response to a clandestine message or a neighbor's example, the ultimate success of the resistance depended entirely on individual decisions. [Haakon Holmboe quoted in Sharp ca. 1958]

Therefore the means used to persuade people to resist also had to operate on an individual basis.

Humor, I would argue, fit the bill precisely. Its essential attributes—the ability to declare principle, educate, encourage solidarity, break down isolation, and raise morale—appealed to individuals and answered the potential resisters' felt need to be informed and involved. It is my contention that the combination of humor's intrinsic traits and the specific historical circumstances made humor a particularly effective means of developing, promoting, and imparting the nascent spirit of resistance in occupied Norway. If we consider each of humor's attributes individually, we will see the extent to which these traits specifically responded to Norway's situation.

(1) Jokes make a declaration of principle, says Joyce Hertzler in her socio-scientific analysis of humor (1970, 143). Such declarations carried crucial weight during the initial period of the occupation about which the survivor Jacob Kuhnle writes:

> Everything seemed afloat around us, with the fixed points of existence no longer visible. [1945, 82]

Humor helped identify those "fixed points" and its themes align strikingly well with the articulated principles of the resistance organizations that eventually formed, here summed up in the objectives of the Home Front Committee (ca. 1943) (Johnson 1948, 131):

a) to clear the country of every German [cf., chap. 1: contempt for the occupiers]
b) to keep the people constantly mindful of the tortures meted out against their countrymen [cf., chap. 4: Nazi cruelty and repression]
c) to refrain from ever compromising with Quisling or his helpers [cf., chap. 2: Quisling jokes]
d) to secure independence for Norway by restoring King Haakon and his government [cf., chap. 4: symbolic demonstrations of loyalty to the king and chap. 11: King Haakon's return]

Several historians have credited communication with being the cardinal factor in the developing opposition to Nazism (H. F. Dahl 1989, 220; Furre 1992, 183); humor served this vital function both by creating an early forum for articulating fundamental resistance principles and by contradicting the prevailing Nazi propaganda.

(2) Jokes educate; they not only enunciate, they inculcate their message. Studies have demonstrated the efficacy of jokes in imparting information[5] and how they contribute to the development of attitudes and values;[6] they have further revealed the existence of a human tendency to interpret jokes as personal instructions (Roos 1986, 176). Each of these mechanisms performed essential operations in occupied Norway.

> There is no recipe for resistance in an occupied country. We found ourselves in an entirely unfamiliar situation and didn't know how to respond. . . . The average person knew little about what was going on and didn't know how to interpret what they did hear. [Lunde 1982, 18]

Humor provided a framework for interpreting events. In its persistent expression of unmitigated contempt for the occupiers and consistently sympathetic portrayals of those who resisted, humor employed demonstrably effective pedagogy to teach resistance attitudes and behaviors.

(3) Jokes encourage a sense of solidarity (Hertzler 1970, 143). Jokes sanction the opinions of their tellers and strengthen a "we" feeling among their hearers. Since representatives for the in-group always get the best of it, jokes teach respect for that group at the expense of the out-group (Roos 1986, 171). Occupation humor ridiculed the occupiers and their Norwegian collaborators while, as chapter 7 shows, making it seem as though resistance were the only valid response to the situation. Once again, survivors' accounts show why this mechanism found resonance among occupied Norwegians.

> We didn't know what others were thinking or how they would act;
> [Kuhnle 1945, 27]
> little by little there grew a feeling of wanting to find ways to resist. The building up of solidarity was of primary importance. . . . It was vital to feel sure that others would do it too. [Haakon Holmboe quoted in Sharp ca. 1958, 32]

By promising the security of safety in numbers, humor helped provide self-assurance; at the same time it engendered a vital sense of community in the amorphous group of individuals who might have nothing more in common than their opposition to the New Order.

(4) Jokes help break down the isolation of the individual, says Norman N. Holland in his *Laughing, a Psychology of Humor* (1982, 172). The dread of standing alone was one of Nazism's most powerful weapons.[7] By proving that—in Holland's words—"somebody else sees what I see," jokes could allay that fear.

> Everything happened on an individual basis. The point was to convince people not to accept the "sneaking Nazification" that was underway. [Lunde 1982, 19]

Sarcastic commentary about the hardships imposed by the Nazi oppressors encouraged defiance by demonstrating that others shared similar perceptions of the circumstances. This impression was further strengthened by humor's theme of overwhelming non-support for the Nazis (cf., chap. 7), which defused the fear of standing alone by suggesting that through resisting one would actually join the majority.

(5) According to Antonin Obrdlik's classic study of gallows humor, jokes raise morale and enable people to live with fear, constant threats, and irritation, and they provide a means of persuading oneself and others that the suffering is only temporary, thereby making it possible to endure (Obrdlik 1942). The role played by Norwegian occupation humor in this regard is confirmed by a letter the author received from a leader of Milorg, the military branch of the organized resistance.

> I very much appreciate the intention of your project, for I have always felt that it was a positive attitude and humor—often in the form of gallows humor—that kept us going, and helped us to see that life wasn't utterly hopeless, or at least made us refuse to admit that it was, for *that* would have meant certain defeat. [Hasselknippe, 1 September 1989][8]

Two additional attributes of humor made it particularly effective in spreading the message of resistance in occupied Norway—its accessibility and safety.[9] Humor appeals to people of all ages and classes, in all places and walks of life.[10] As a part of normal conversational exchange, jokes better suit themselves to being shared than do political slogans and directives.[11] At the same time humor provides greater safety than more overt forms of resistance because it may be shared in private, a necessary quality in the wake of Reichskommissar Terboven's 18 July 1941 speech threatening the death penalty for any visible resistance to the New Order.[12] Add to this the capacity of jokes to be told as entertainment, without their tellers needing to take a stand,[13] and their unique potential to proliferate and to shape opinion becomes even more evident.

Common to the majority of Norwegian occupation jokes is the positive self-image they project, thereby performing two more of humor's essential functions: protecting the self-respect of the oppressed (Speier 1969, 180) and granting a measure of control in an uncontrollable situation (Abrahams and Wukash 1967, 7). The jokes depict the Norwegians consistently making fools of their occupiers, exposing the enemy's stupidity, cruelty, deceit, and pomposity while displaying their own bravery and quick-wittedness. Compared to political jokes from other oppressive regimes, moreover, the Norwegian material tends far more frequently—as demonstrated in chapters 5 and 7—to depict the oppressed unabashedly treating their oppressors to sharp-tongued, disrespectful put-downs.

Several factors may account for the "quick-witted put-down" characteristic of Norwegian occupation jokes. For one thing, the humor evoked by the quick-witted response corresponds closely with the established Nordic tradition of the sagas and folktales. *Olav den helliges saga* (St. Olav's saga), for example, portrays one of King Olav's warriors at the Battle of Stiklestad (29 July 1030) receiving his death wound and remarking, as he withdraws the fatal arrow and notices fat hanging from his heart sinews: "Godt har kongen född oss"—The king has fed us well—(Sturluson 1979, 440).

While saga replies of this type often serve to emphasize a character's heroic stoicism,[14] situations from Scandinavian folktales parallel even more closely the sharp-tongued, impudence of the occupation joke hero. Perhaps the most obvious example is "Prinsessen som ingen kunne målbinde" (The princess who had to have the last word) in which the hero wins the princess precisely because, unlike her other suitors, he consistently and imperturbably manages to make witty replies to her intimidating statements, until she at last is the one left speechless (Asbjörnsen and Moe 1982, 408–11). In another tale, "Manden og troldet i ordkamp" (The man and the troll duel with words), the man's ready response to the troll's threatening statements enable him to prevail and cause the troll to be turned to stone (Nicolaissen 1879, 85–86).[15] The Jössing jokes' predilection for portraying Norwegian unflappability in the face of German or Nazi authority carries on this Scandinavian tradition of favoring stoicism and confrontation in the face of adversity and intimidation.

At the same time the quick-witted put-down humor responded to the specific situation Norwegians faced in wartime. The frustration of daily encounters with the occupiers and the need to contradict German propaganda created both a compelling psychological desire and a strong pragmatic need to denigrate the German occupiers and to emphasize Norwegian superiority.

The jokes portray individuals refusing to be intimidated by the occupiers' domineering presence and rejecting the self-aggrandizing propaganda that promoted Germany as the seat of culture.

Inverting propaganda's glorified image, humor contrasts Norwegian common sense and groundedness with German pomp, and depicts Norwegian intellectual and cultural superiority prevailing over the occupier's stupidity, cruelty, and boorishness.

By convincingly portraying the Norwegians as unanimously engaged in a fearless degradation of the Nazi regime, the jokes cre-

A Nazi poster promoting Germany as "The Creative Nation" and celebrating her cultural triumphs. Artist: Harald Damsleth; publisher: Thon & Co., 1941.

ated a wartime feeling of solidarity that crucially assisted the resistance effort while also helping to establish a core of values that critically assisted Norwegians in making a smooth transition to peace (see also chap. 8). While the resistance fighters of other occupied countries often had varied and competing goals, an unusual degree of unity characterized the Norwegian resistance whose primary goal was the reestablishment of Norwegian constitutional sovereignty based on prewar values. Above all, these values included loyalty to a system based on a democratic outlook rather than rule by the elite. Jössing humor celebrated these prewar ideals and their symbols, such as the monarchy, the flag, and the Seventeenth of May,[16] and it opposed the "New Time" by suggesting that "good" Norwegians found their strength and vindication in Norway's traditional (prewar) society which it posited would resume once the crisis had passed. Keeping the population aware of these prewar values, Jössing humor helped the country emerge relatively unscathed from five years of occupation by a diametrically opposed regime.

At the same time the jokes helped create and promote the legend of the Norwegian population's spontaneous and unanimous resistance to Nazism, a concept that remains strong to this very day. The witticisms' efficacy in mocking the Nazis and painting the resisters as heroes invited the great majority of Norwegians to identify with humor's view and distance themselves from earlier confusion. Largely unquestioned for many years, this view began receiving closer scrutiny in the 1970s when the historian Hans Fredrik Dahl (1974) challenged the veracity of what he designated the six most cherished "myths" of the occupation. Examining these notions, one can see the role Jössing humor must have played in creating and fostering them.

(1) "On April 9 Norwegians immediately joined in resisting the German attack," says the myth while in fact Norwegians initially attempted to find a modus vivendi with the Germans. Much occupation humor, however, presents the mythical scenario.

(2) While the myth holds that "Storting stood watch and protected law and order," it actually allowed itself to be coerced into voting that King Haakon be deposed. Jössing humor, however, makes his return seem an eternal and universal longing (see chap. 11).

(3) "The entire population joined in resisting the Germans and Quisling," says the myth, and Jössing humor also emphasized the theme of universal resistance while ignoring the sixty thou-

sand Norwegians who became members of the NS (see chap. 7).

(4) "Norwegian resistance did irreparable damage to the German war effort," says the myth, but, since the Germans aimed not so much at ideological as strategic goals—such as the access invading Norway gave them to the North Sea, Atlantic ports, the Soviet Union, and Norwegian industry—the activities of the resistance, except for acts of direct sabotage, in fact did little harm. Jössing humor, however, frequently depicts symbolic resistance as being highly disruptive to the occupiers.

(5) While the myth states that "all Norwegians loyally took part in the resistance," in truth, argues H. F. Dahl, the majority of Norwegians—including the most ardent Jössings—engaged in economic collaboration merely by retaining their jobs since they thereby contributed to the German-controlled industry. The tension over this circumstance may be an underlying factor in the humor that exaggerates Norwegian resistance.[17]

(6) "We came through it well." The occupation is a fond memory for most Norwegians, who, says Dahl, tend to forget that not all their countrymen emerged unscathed, notably the approximately 50 percent of Norway's Jews who never returned (see chap. 2). Given the vital role of tension as a mechanism of humor which enables jokes to function as reliable gauges of unresolved issues, the absence of the Norwegian Jews as a theme in Jössing humor does seem to corroborate this issue's failure to grasp the hearts and minds of most Norwegians.

The romanticized notion of Norway as a unanimous nation of resisters might thus more realistically be replaced by the concept of a majority of Norwegians rallying around resistance because an active core of convinced, dedicated partisans of democracy was numerous and resolute enough to exert social pressure which radiated from the leaders to the most undecided (Andenæs, Riste, and Skodvin 1989, 90). Deserving of notice is the way this sizable core wisely and effectively used humor as one of its weapons. While the humor may consequently have contributed to an idealized view of Norwegian resistance, there is no denying the value of the forum these jokes provided for communicating courage and censored opinion, solidarity and hope.

To this day Jössing jokes and symbolic demonstrations retain inestimable value as unconsciously accurate reflections of the propaganda, shortages, tensions, fears, and uncertainty experienced by those who endured the occupation. Reaching across the fifty years that separate us from that challenging time, Jössing humor imparts essential emotional truths about the everyday life of the period that are often simply unavailable elsewhere. Nor has the type of humorous response surveyed here ceased to function in today's world. A manifestation of the human spirit triumphant, it is operating at this very moment to undermine totalitarian regimes elsewhere on the globe, and is destined to outlast them all, just as Jössing humor survived Hitler's Thousand Year Reich.

Notes

PREFACE

1. Several of those who experienced the occupation have commented on this danger. The diarist Marie Lysgaard Slaatto ruefully predicts on 13 August 1940, "If the Germans see this book I'll probably be shot." Looking back, Åslaug Rommetveit wrote in a 17 September 1992 letter to the author:

> Much of what I wrote down was *dynamite* in the eyes of the occupiers. What wouldn't I have risked of jail sentences if the "right" people had come across the books where I told off the Nazis and Germans on almost every page. . . . They ransacked our houses here in Bryne . . . then I'd often wrap the books in oil cloth and bury them beneath the apple tree in the yard until the Gestapo calmed down again.

So great was the danger that yet another survivor assumes it would have prevented the existence of any such collections.

> Unfortunately no one thought at that time that the jokes, too, were part of occupation history, so they didn't write them down or keep track of them. Part of the cause, no doubt, was the fear of landing in a concentration camp if the joke collection were found during a raid. [Letter to author from Sverre Eilertsen, 17 January 1993.]

2. As the manuscript was being completed, I found two more diaries: one in the Bergen University Library and the other in the Trondheim University Library (Avdeling for spesialsamlinger). The diary of Herman Friele (of the prominent coffee-producing family) at Bergen provided extra insights into daily life conditions, while the Trondheim diary (four volumes by Sverre Larsen titled "Attila kommer: Noen dagbokblader fra Naziveldetsdager i Trondheim," (Attila is coming: Some diary pages from the days of Nazi power in Trondheim) hereafter referred to as the "Trondheim diary" to avoid confusion with Sölvi Larsen's joke diary) contained a number of jokes, whose dates and commentary proved helpful in confirming information from the other sources, especially since the jokes in Larsen's, Ellingsen's, Christerson's, and Schou-Sörensen's notebooks bore few dates.

3. Translations throughout the manuscript are the author's own, except where otherwise indicated. Jokes quoted in Norwegian appear as found with any spelling idiosyncracies left intact.

4. Indeed, Sverre Larsen in his Trondheim diary refers to the jokes as *folkevitser* (folk jokes), a word that differs from the Norwegian word for "folk ballads" *(folkeviser)* by only one letter.

THE DIARISTS

1. Information about Sölvi Larsen has been provided by Ida Naffstad of Norges Hjemmefrontmuseum. No more is known about her.

215

2. The information about Greta Dahl was supplied by her daughters (Letter to author, 26 April 1993).

INTRODUCTION

1. Though not previously studied in depth, the humor received frequent mention in accounts from the occupation period itself.
Jacob Worm-Müller (1941):

> Our greatest reserve of forces, compared with the Germans, was our sense of humor and of the ridiculous side of the Nazis. . . . Every day new stories were told or fabricated. [47–48]

Åke Fen (1943):

> Hardly a day passes without some new joke about the Germans or Quislings. . . . When the pressure becomes dangerously great, it is laughter that saves the situation. . . . Laughter is not the least important factor in the opposition, for the enemy has nothing to meet it with. . . . [104–5]

Awareness of the importance of humor is also attested by the 1942 collection of Norwegian occupation jokes published in America under the meaningful title, *He Who Laughs . . . Lasts: Anecdotes from Norway's Homefront* by Hans Olav and Tor Myklebust. After the war, several published collections of the humor appeared in Norway. Most inclusive is Finn Bö's *Forbuden frukt* (Forbidden fruit) (1946). Some others are: Halfdan Hansen and Ivar Baggethun, *Husker De hva vi lo av?* (Do you remember what we laughed at?) (1953); Henry Imsland, *Jössingvitser* (Jössing jokes) (1946); Oddmund Kristiansen, *Jöss! Vitser, skröner og karikaturer* (Good Grief! Jokes, tall tales and caricatures) (1945); Ottar Ramfjord, *Okkupasjonshumor* (Occupation humor) (1945); Georg Svendsen, *Krigens humor samlet av Mr. George* (n. d.) (War humor collected by Mr. George); and Per Thomsen, *The German Supermentality* (1945). As the present manuscript was being completed, two further collections appeared: Jan Anderson, *Krigen på folkemunne* (The war in oral tradition) (1989) and Steinar Floan Halse, *Humöret kan ingen ta fra oss: Vitser, anekdoter og sanger fra okkupasjonstiden 1940–45* (Humor they can't steal: Jokes, anecdotes and songs from the occupation) (1993).

2. An entry in the diary of Hermann Friele notes:

> National Socialism's program contains several items which many Norwegians would perhaps like to see carried out, to correct some of what was wrong with the society we lived in before the war. [Friele's diary, vol 1, 31 December 31 1940]

The Nazi newspaper *Fritt folk* ran a series of articles in which various individuals who joined the Nazi party gave their rationale. Here are two representative examples:

> I am a member of NS because of this party's direction. I see it as the only way out of the impasse our previous leaders led us into. Our traditional culture can only be saved and continue to develop within a strong union of Germanic peoples. [Quoted in Hjeltnes 1987, 248]

> Instead of being a nation of free land holders founded on heritage and inheritance, we have been converted to a commercial state. The Norwegian people were tricked by

foreign frills and foolishness and lured by gold and trinkets. We started copying every-
thing that was foreign and forgot what was our own. We came to devalue whatever was
Norwegian and our love of country diminished to empty words and cliches. [Quoted in
Hjeltnes 1987, 253]

3. The topic of Norwegian Nazism remained too loaded with feeling to touch
during the first decades after the war and it wasn't until the 1970s and 1980s that
books appeared focusing on those who had chosen "the other side." These include
Sigurd Senja, *Quislingsgutt* (Quisling's boy) (1973); Svein Blindheim, *Nordmenn
under Hitlers fane: Dei norske frontkjemparane* (Norwegians under the banner
of Hitler: The Norwegian fighters on the German front) (1977); Haagen Ringnes,
I skyggen av solkorset (In the shadow of the swastika) (1981); Chr. Christensen,
Den andre siden (The other side) (1988); and Egil Ulateig, *Dagbok frå ein rotnorsk
nazist* (Diary of a genuine Norwegian patriot Nazi) (1987).

Chapter 1. The Humor of Contempt

1. The wreckage of the *Blücher* still lies on the bottom of the fjord, ominously
leaking oil.
2. The battle of Narvik had consequences beyond Norway's shores as well,
directly prompting the fall of British prime minister Chamberlain and his replacement by Winston Churchill (see chap. 9).
3. Adding to the confusion was the entry of German forces into Oslo led by
a brass band. Having seen Warsaw reduced to rubble during the September 1939
invasion of Poland, moreover, Norwegians were aware of the consequences of
resistance and initially wished to avoid a similar fate.
4. Of the twenty-one notes of protest Norway had sent five to Germany, ten
to England, and six to Russia (Walker 1946; 32).
5. This sentiment was perhaps best articulated by Norwegian minister Eric
Colban on 8 April.

Germany has given us the most categorical assurances that she will respect our neutrality
. . . if there is something I am afraid of right now, it is rather of some rash action by our
British friends. [Kersaudy 1987, 62]

6. In point of fact, however, Germany's invasion of Norway had been launched
several days before the British laid their mines, and came only after many weeks
of careful planning.
7. Jon Vegard Lunde has described the prevalent atmosphere of dejection.

After the invasion the Norwegian spirit was soon snuffed out. Paralyzed, disheartened
and confused, people sat with their hands in their laps and waited . . . as though anesthe-
tized. Criticism of the government was strong in all classes of the population and bitter-
ness was great. . . . The Germans, on the other hand, impressed many. [1982, 17–18]

8. The "bucket of manure" item has also circulated as a Pollack joke.
9. Christerson's version specifies people from Bergen instead of Norwegians
in general.
10. The Gulf War began on 17 January 1991 when the United States and coali-
tion forces took the offensive against Iraq over that country's incursions under
the leadership of Saddam Hussein into Kuwait.

11. These terms also came to characterize conversation and thought about the Germans, as evidenced by this 8 June 1941 entry from the diary of Greta Dahl:

Og slikt *pakk* skal noen norsker slutte seg til! (And it's with *pakk* like this that some Norwegians wish to collaborate.)

12. This popular item occurred in several variations:

Der er seperasjonering i Tyskland. Hvorfor? De har bakvasket England. [Christerson 1940]
(There's soap rationing in Germany. Why? They have *bakvasket* [been "backwashing," i.e., "slandering"] England.)
I de besatte områder er all såpe beslaglagt, den skal brukes til bakvaskelse. (Ellingsen)
(In the occupied areas all soap is confiscated, it's going to be used for *bakvaskelse* ["backwashing," i.e., "slander"].)

13. The campaign to paint Britain as the aggressor and Germany as Scandinavia's protector is well articulated in the following invasion-day placard quoted in Slaatto's diary:

Germany has determined to anticipate the British attack and has taken over protection of the neutrality of the kingdoms of Norway and Denmark, and will occupy them for the duration of the war. The German government has the sole intention of hindering Scandinavia from becoming an arena for the expansion of the British war effort. Toward this end, strong German military forces have since this morning taken control of the most important military objectives in Denmark and Norway [Slaatto, 11 May 1940].

14. The joke's washing imagery arose from the unavailability of washing supplies, a long-standing and worsening problem as Greta Dahl's diary attests.

January 5, 1940: The soap ration is being decreased. From now on only one kind of detergent and one kind of toilet soap will be available.
June 1, 1942: Ugh, washing clothes has become a terrible chore. Miserable detergent, impossible to get the clothes really clean. You have to use a washboard, and now they're hard to find, too.

15. The "gaunt German soldier growing fat in Norway" item apparently circulated even earlier since the Trondheim diary has it dated 7 October 1940.
16. To Hitler the *Altmark* incident demonstrated conclusively that the Oslo government was no longer capable of enforcing its neutrality (Kersaudy 1987, 44), and on 19 February he ordered the acceleration of Operation Weserübung, as he code-named the Norwegian invasion, in order to beat the British in taking this valuable base.
17. The diarist Åslaug Rommetveit reports on 11 November 1940:

The word *Jössing* is a popular name for Norwegians who clearly show their stance against the Germans and NS. It is like a *heidersnavn* [badge of honor].

18. According to observers from "the other side," however, it was not until after the 1943 reversal of Hitler's war fortunes that the shunning was regularly practiced (Ulateig 1987 15, 198), a circumstance the poster's 1944 date also bears out.
19. After the war, a survivor commented on the success of the ice-front.

More than once we had the pleasure of seeing the daily demonstration of contempt elicit an outburst that revealed just how deeply this tactic affected them. [Kuhnle 1945, 75–76]

During the war a German commented on the tactic.

How can one understand the Norwegians? Often one simply has the impression of dealing with spoiled children. [*Norge under hakkorset* 1940, 29–30]

Compounding the German Nazis' irritation and injury was the particular embarrassment that this coldness came from the very individuals Nazi doctrine credited with surpassing even the Germans themselves as superior specimens of the Aryan race. (*Norge under hakkorset* 29–30). About the incongruity of the roles each side was playing, the diarist Greta Dahl comments on 8 May 1941:

It must be strange for them, the Master Race, to see their underlings dressed in nice clothing, having contented wives and happy children while they themselves go like dogs, bowing and scraping for their swaggering boors of officers. Punishment exercises for the least transgression, never free, urged to hate England while having no hope of ever reaching them out on their island. And on top of all that, having to feel the disdain and hatred we show them, our pitiable overlords!

20. Ellingsen has the following variant:

Det er mange mennesker på trikken. En liten gutt er med sin mor. En fremmed löfter velvillig gutten opp på trikken. Gutten snur seg, og ser at det er en tysker.
    "Nei men, er du sånn snild svinetysker, du da?"
(It's crowded on the tram. A little boy is with his mother. A stranger kindly lifts him up into the tram. The boy turns and seeing it is a German, he says, "My, what a kind German-swine you are.")

21. Two years later she similarly reflects:

When we compare our situation with that of the Germans, it is impossible to feel deep hatred for the German soldiers; only if they're Gestapo or SS can we hate them. [G. Dahl 28 December 1942]

And on 13 April 1943, she comments about seeing a distinguished-looking German soldier in his fifties or sixties.

It was tempting to talk to him and find out who he really was. It must be terrible for these older men who seem used to better conditions than being stuffed into these old worn-out uniforms and crammed into barracks, hauled like animals in open trucks through wind and cold, commanded to run in deep snow, in short: to be a solider. [G. Dahl]

22. Humor also loses sight of the fact that not all occupying soldiers were themselves sympathetic to Nazism. Though no statistics exist about their numbers, the plight of men unwillingly drafted into the service of their country was even worse than that of the occupied Norwegians. While the Norwegians garnered strength from the growing unity of their opposition, the German opponents of Nazism had little or no support that could be openly demonstrated by their countrymen and they risked severe punishment as traitors if they opposed their own authorities. Still they had to suffer the same scorn from the Norwegians as their Nazist fellow soldiers (Walker 1946, 94–95).

23. While Denmark's decision has been understood by posterity as necessitated

by her diminished prospects for self-defense given her flat landscape and small size, Sweden's wartime actions have traditionally been less sympathetically received, to the point of straining some Norwegians' subsequent view of this neighbor, despite the indispensable role she played as a safe haven for both Norwegian and Danish war refugees.

24. Experiences like the ones described in the following entries of Greta Dahl's diary added personal relevance to the robbery image:

> January 5, 1941: [a] woman here in town was expecting her daughter home so she cleaned her living room and bought new rugs and curtains. She had just finished when two Germans arrived. They were going to take over the living room. She asked if she might remove the new rugs and curtains. Ha! All the room's inventory was recorded in a notebook, and she would have to account for any missing items.
> October 29, 1942: Now all farms are being forced to cut down their trees and give the lumber to the Germans.
> March 27, 1944: I'm looking at the sofa pillow. Embroidering a rose on it would certainly do a lot for its appearance, but I expect we'll lose it along with everything else and that dampens my enthusiasm to make improvements. I hear that everyone else feels the same way.

25. Terboven's appointment and subsequent official acts receive more detailed attention in chapter 2.

26. The image of thirty pieces of silver also figures prominently in jokes about Vidkun Quisling, as chapter 2 will demonstrate.

27. Another variant of this joke went:

> En tysk offiser i Bergen som kunne norsk, gikk sammen med en annen tysker og sa til ham: Guttene i Bergen er så slagferdige, nå skal vi stoppe en og höre hva han sier.
> "Hei du. Har du sett et lass med apekatter kjöre forbi her nylig?" "Har du dotti tur du kanskje?" [Schou-Sörensen]
> (A German officer who knew Norwegian was out walking with another German in Bergen and said to him: "The boys in Bergen are so sassy, let's stop one and see what he has to say. Hey, have you seen a load of monkeys drive by here recently?" "Why? Did you fall off maybe?")

28. Especially prominent in the Trönder jokes are *apokope* (the dropping of the final syllable) and the predominance of the *æ*-sound.

29. Ellingsen has this variant:

> Vinmonopol i Trondheim er stengt for de har ikke flere heil og sel'.
> (The Vinmonopol in Trondheim is closed for they have no more *heil og sel'* ["whole bottles to sell," again a homonym with *heil og sæl*].)

30. The church had long opposed the violence of the armed Nazi guard known as the Hird and in February 1941 a letter from the bishops (who in Norway are employees of the state) was read from pulpits all over the country. It declared that they would continue their religious activity, but do so independently of the Nazi-controlled state. In March the ministers followed suit. The Nazis reacted by replacing some of them with NS bishops and ministers, about a hundred in all, some of whom did not possess theological degrees.

31. Another joke about the Ullern organist plays on the theme of universal resistance to Nazism (see chap. 7).

En "nyorientert" prest skulle en söndag preke i Ullern kirke—til en forsamling på bare åtte sjeler. Organist Geburg Aasland var som vanlig ansvarlig for tonefölge, men da salmesangen tok til, kom det bare noen spede toner fra orgelet.

Da gudstjenesten var over, ble Aasland kalt inn på teppet i sakristiet og spurt hva slags orgelmusikk han presterte.

-Jeg har jo fått klar beskjed om ikke å overdöve menigheten, svarte Aasland. —Og da var det ikke annen utvei enn å akkompanere med én finger. [Nökleby 1986, 47]

(A minister of the "new orientation" [i.e., Nazi] was to preach in Ullern Church one Sunday—to a congregation of only eight souls. Organist Geburg Aasland was, as usual, to be the accompanist, but when the singing began, only some feeble notes came from the organ.

When the service was over, Aasland was called on the carpet in the sacristy and asked what sort of organ music that was he had played.

"As you know, I've received clear instructions not to drown out the congregation," Aasland replied, "so I had no choice but to play with one finger.")

CHAPTER 2. QUISLING AND HITLER JOKES

1. The term *quisling* was used as early as 1933, but its wartime application began in the *Times* (London) a few days after the 9 April 1940 invasion. The paper's Stockholm correspondent had employed it as a practical abbreviation to denote supporters of Quisling. The editor accepted the term and wrote an editorial about the new noun on 19 April (see note 3).

2. The historian Ole Kristian Grimnes points out that Nazism hadn't caught on in Norway because its primary emphasis on nationalism—not unlike that promoted by such nineteenth-century patriots as Björnstjerne Björnson—had lost its function in Norway after her liberation from Sweden in 1905. In Germany, by contrast, the World War I defeat and the humiliating terms of the subsequent peace treaty gave Nazism's extreme nationalism resonance and meaning (Grimnes 1983b, 27).

3. An editorial in the 19 April 1940 *Times* (London) expressed deep gratitude to Major Quisling for adding a new word to the English language, saying that the new word is a gift from the gods; a more brilliant combination of letters could not be found, it asserted, saying that it sounded like something slippery and snakelike and written with *Q*, a letter the British long had viewed with suspicion. From the *Times* (London) the term spread via news bureaus to countries around the globe (Senja 1973, 50).

4. Pierre Laval (1883–1945) worked to achieve an accord with Hitler after the French surrender to Germany. In spring 1941 he helped form the French Nazi party and in April 1942 he created the so-called Vichy government which openly collaborated with the Germans and fought the resistance movement.

5. The Norwegian caricature artist Ragnvald Blix (1882–1958) produced biting anti-Nazi drawings during the war under the pseudonym Stig Höök and published them in Sweden's *Göteborgs Handels-och Sjöfarts-tidning* (Göteborg's business and shipping news). After the war they were collected and published in Norway under the title *De fem årene* (Those five years) (1945).

6. To his followers Quisling was a man of decision, the only one who had *acted* in Norway's interests the day Germans suddenly appeared on Norwegian soil. While they regarded the escape of the king and the government as cowardice, they felt that Quisling had shown necessary leadership, filling the vacuum left by the former leaders. Quisling, they believed, had hindered a bloodbath and without him Norway would be a German slave state, like Poland. They assumed that most

Norwegians would eventually realize that only the NS could put the brakes on the occupiers' might and retain Norway's sovereignty (Senja 1973; Chr. Christensen 1988).

7. Related to these examples, Christerson records an actual incident in which some boys had hung a mock poster announcing: Vidkjent usling maser i Konsert-Palé. Idioter fri adgang (Well-known scoundrel ranting in Konsert-Palé Auditorium. Free admission for idiots). She also notes with glee that it took the authorities much longer than they liked to remove the jeering poster from its tree-perch eighteen feet above the ground.

8. See Ruksenas (1986, 11) for a Stalin cognate; Beckmann (1980, 79) for a cognate about Czechoslovakian president Novotny; and Raskin (1985, 226) for one about the Israeli leader Pinkhas Sapir.

The Elvis stamp issued in January 1993 spurred the following inversion of the joke:

> The Elvis stamp is slowing down the mail.
> Women don't know what side to lick. [Heard on San Francisco radio station KGO, 16 January 1993]

9. The London-based radio station established by the Norwegian government in exile frequently used humor as a means of raising morale, encouraging resistance, and conveying secret messages (see chap. 4).

10. The *New Time* or *New Order* were terms promoted by the Nazi party to characterize the sweeping social changes their regime would bring.

11. At approximately 10:00 P.M. on 25 October 1942, the car of Gulbrand and Marie Lunde went into the water between the ferry and the dock at the Våge ferry landing on the Romsdal Fjord. A flood of rumors followed proposing various scenarios for the accident: the driver was a member of the resistance who "forgot" to set the hand-brake; the boat's skipper backed away from the dock early on purpose in order to cause the car to go into the water; the British had arranged the "accident." Meanwhile it became known that the ferryman had distinguished himself by repeatedly diving down after the car, and this circumstance led to the following jocular exchange:

> Hvorfor tror du at fergemannen stupte uti etter bilen?
> Han ville kanskje forvise seg om at bildören var forsvarlig lukket. [Ramfjord 1945, 30]
> (Why do you think the ferryman dove in after the car? Perhaps to make sure the car door was securely locked.)

Other Lunde jokes flourished too, most frequently the corruption of his name to Tale Gudbrand (Speaking Gudbrand) (Schou-Sörensen). Mocking his inescapable propaganda speeches, the name evokes that of the legendary Dale Gudbrand for whom Norway's longest valley, Gudbrandsdalen, is named.

12. In all between 5,000 and 6,000 Norwegian citizens served on the German fronts (of 8,000 who applied), compared to the 40,000 the clandestine military resistance had mobilized by the end of the war. This recruitment of volunteers was one of the Nazi party's most important functions, and though they carried little weight militarily, Quisling attached considerable political importance to these fighting units as testimony to his reliability as a partner (Andenæs, Riste, and Skodvin 1989, 74–75).

Recent books about those who joined these units tell of many of the front soldiers' idealism and disappointed illusions that they would be fighting for Norway instead of swearing allegiance directly to Hitler (Senja 1973; Ulateig 1987).

13. Hitler had adopted the title of Der Führer in imitation of Italian dictator Mussolini's title, Il Duce, and his propaganda minister Goebbels had made it mandatory as part of his initiative to encourage unthinking worship of the leader (Taylor and Shaw 1987, 123–24). Jokes defusing its effect thus served the important function of psychological distancing. Two additional *förer* puns circulated.

Hitler er blitt redd for å kjøre bil. . . . Hvorfor? Han er redd for å miste förerkortet. (Christerson)
(Hitler's scared of driving a car. . . . Why? He's afraid of loosing his *förerkort* ["driver's license," also "license to be Führer"].)

En tysker spör fyrböteren: Er De vaktmesteren? Svarer: Nein, ich bin der Führer. (Christerson)
(A German asks the furnace stoker if he's the janitor. He answers: No, I'm the *Führer* [homonym with *fyrer*, "firer" or "stoker"].)

Some of the tram jokes in chapter 8 also incorporate this pun.
14. Variations of the traitor homonym:

Quisling inspiserte Hirdguttene sine som ropte: Vi er for föreren, og Quisling svarte: Og jeg er for eder (forræder). [Schou-Sörensen]
(Quisling was inspecting the *Hird* boys who shouted: We are for the *förer*, and Quisling answered: And I am *for eder* [*forræder* = "traitor"].)

Quisling had received help in obtaining his original December 1939 audience with Hitler from Admiral Erich Raeder, commander in chief of the German Navy from 1935–43, who saw in Quisling's plans an opportunity to achieve his own ambition of invading Great Britain using Norway as a base. The following joke puts the traitor theme in that context:

För Quisling ennå var kommet til makten og hadde vanskeligheter dermed, sa man: Stor-Admiral Raeder er for Quisling, og da er naturligvis Quisling for Raeder (forræder). [Schou-Sörensen]
(Before Quisling had yet come to power and was having difficulties doing so, people said: Admiral Raeder is for Quisling, so of course Quisling is *for Raeder* [another homonym of *forræder*].)

15. Jössing humor also applied the Judas image to Jonas Lie, Quisling's minister of justice, as Schou-Sörensen reports, "Now London Radio is talking about Prostituert statsråd *Judas Lie.*" Known for brutal cruelty, Lie acted out the role of the Nazi extremist that posterity has attributed to the actually more reserved, idealistic, and contemplative Vidkun Quisling (Kersaudy 1987).
16. Arne Taraldsen (1917–86) participated in Norway's armed resistance and was in Narvik in June 1940 when Norway surrendered. Afterward he went to Oslo and became involved in resistance work, illustrating various underground publications.
He produced four mock stamps as entries in a contest launched by the Nazi government. Though it is easy to see why they didn't select Taraldsen's stamps as winners, no one else seems to have won either, and the contest produced no stamp. Taraldsen's four stamps did circulate, however, being mass-produced in England in slightly larger than scale postage stamp format and dropped by British planes over Norwegian towns and cities. Complete with glue, they could be quickly licked and applied to fences, windows, and other available public surfaces. The British origin of the stamp accounts for the spelling of *ære* as "aere"

and of *færd* as "faerd." For descriptions of the other mock stamps, see chapters 4, 8, and 11 (Kvamsdal 1990).

17. A stamp bearing Quisling's likeness actually was issued in 1942. It had a face value of 20 öre, but cost 50 öre, the 30 extra öre being designated to support the widows and children of Norwegians who fell fighting for the Nazi cause. The "30 pieces of silver" motif probably derived from this subsidy.

18. Neither the term Statsakt nor Minister President is Norwegian, and—as Jössing humor demonstrates—the latter sounded especially strange in Norwegian ears and therefore invited ridicule.

19. Greta Dahl's dejection is well founded for the Statsakt had established a full-fledged NS state in Norway, headed by a party that was physically uniformed, economically aided, and politically directed by the Germans and which bore a striking resemblance to Germany's own Nazi party (H. F. Dahl 1989, 30).

20. As already mentioned, Terboven actually retained the power in occupied Norway. Appointing Quisling prime minister merely for the sake of appearances, he personally supervised the Quisling government and reported directly to Hitler.

21. According to Samuel Abrahamsen, the first example of the Norwegians' obedient compliance with the Nazis' anti-Jewish policy occurred on May 10–11, 1940, when the Norwegian police confiscated radios belonging to the Jews. No protest was made against this discriminatory action. By October 1942, the time of the mass arrests of Norway's Jews, effective means had been developed by the resistance leadership to alert the general Norwegian population of the impending arrests of other groups. When groups such as union members, teachers, students and clergy were threatened, directives *(paroler)* were issued to be observed by all loyal citizens. These brought a massive machinery into effect to protect these persons. No such directives, says Abrahamsen, were ever issued against co-operating with any aspect of the Jewish persecution (1991, 9). That is not to say, however, that there were not individuals of courage and moral strength who did protect and help Jews, assisting hundreds of Norway's Jews on successful escapes to Sweden, but no organized force to save the Jews existed in Norway that could counterbalance the well-organized Nazi machinery for their destruction (Abrahamsen 1991, 11–12).

22. Asylum jokes have flourished in other repressive regimes as well. For Communist asylum jokes see Ruksenas (1986, 101) and Draitser (1978, 46). The Nazi philosophy of euthanasia may also have helped prompt the asylum motif since the insane were high on the list of "defectives" it favored eliminating in order to perfect the master race.

23. Harald Fair Hair was king of Norway from about 874 to 932 and was renowned as the first monarch to unite Norway into a single realm. Quisling claimed to have been born on the date this occurred, a circumstance he felt gave him a national mission (Senja 1973, 53).

24. A collection of German anti-Nazi jokes, assembled by Friedrich Goetz, was published by Rudi Hartmann in 1983 under the title: *Flüsterwitze aus dem Tausendjärigen Reich* (Whispered jokes from the thousand year Reich). My thanks to Peter Liermann, Luther College, for this source.

25. As the existence of the Flüsterwitze attests, however, (and as noted in chap. 1) not all Germans supported Hitler, a point easily lost in the tendency of Jössing humor to use the term *Germans* as synonymous with Nazis, neglecting not only to differentiate Norwegian Nazis from the Germans, but also suggesting that all Germans were Nazis. In reality, of course, German opinion was far more complex and even after Hitler's enormously popular summer 1940 victory at

Dunkirk, many Germans continued to bitterly oppose him. Some of these were among the occupation soldiers, such as the one with whom Greta Dahl reports conversing in this 19 December 1942 entry:

> How he hated Hitler for causing all this misery. They were forced into the Nazi Party because they had to have food. When they went into a store for milk they'd be asked, "Are you a member of the Party?" "No." "Then we don't have any milk for you." It was like that everywhere.

Another indication that not all Germans supported Hitler came in the report in a May 1941 issue of the underground newspaper *Det kommer en dag* (The day will come) of a Norwegian who had just returned from Berlin saying that

> Every morning the Berlin police must go around the city washing away the following graffiti from fences and walls:
> Wir wollen nicht den langen Krieg.
>   "   "   " den hohen Sieg.
>   "   "   " das grosse Reich.
>   "   " nur der Führers Leich.
> (We don't want the long war.
>   "   "   " the grand victory.
>   "   "   " the great Reich.
>   " only want the Führer's death.)

26. Indirectly this joke captures a main issue of the occupation period, namely that both sides, Nazi and Jössing regarded themselves as good Norwegians who were doing what was best for their country while regarding the other side's course as harmful to the nation's interests. From these deeply held convictions arose the rancor that created the wounds which even today are far from completely healed.

27. Danish prime minister Thorvald Stauning (1873–1942) had a notably long, full beard.

28. The greeting *heil* predates Hitler's regime having long roots in Germany as a call of acclamation (hail, long live). Hitler coupled it with the raised-arm gesture he adopted in imitation of the Italian Fascist salute (Taylor and Shaw 1987, 149).

29. The *Heil og sæl* greeting is indeed found in old Norse literature, where it is spelled *Heill ok sæll*. Prior to its adoption by the Nazis, the greeting was quite common in the context of national romanticism. The Nynorsk poet Olav Aukrust (1883–1929), for example, used the formulation in his writing, and it may be found carved into the portal of the main building of Voss Folk High School built in 1902. Indicative of the postwar change in attitude toward the expression, however, the words were covered over by a metal plate which the school's present custodian says remained in place as late as 1959 when he first arrived there (Letter to author, 21 March 1994).

30. A cognate of this joke circulated in the United States during the 1992 election campaign.

> George Bush, Bill Clinton and Ross Perot are killed, who was saved? The country. [Heard on Tom Snyder's nationally syndicated radio program, 12 June 1992]

31. Several attempts on Hitler's life were planned during March 1943, but the best known and most nearly successful was executed on 20 July 1944 by a group of conspirators led by Count von Stauffenberg. That day von Stauffenberg placed a bomb-rigged briefcase in a room where Hitler and his generals had gathered.

Seeing the explosion detonate as he drove away, von Stauffenberg assumed Hitler was dead and word spread quickly. Not until that evening did he and others learn that someone had inadvertently moved the briefcase, and that Hitler had survived. Hitler immediately had von Stauffenberg shot and continued rounding up the other conspirators, actual or suspected, until all had been tortured and executed.

CHAPTER 3. FRATERNIZING WITH THE ENEMY

1. *Tyskertös* might be rendered "German whore." The word *tös* is a degrading term for "woman," suggesting loose morality, comparable to "wench" or "tart," but the depth of contempt these women's actions aroused suggests the stronger term.

2. In this regard, the postwar treatment of the *tyskertös* represents a notable exception. Despite a great deal of talk during the occupation about the revenge that would be taken when liberation came, citizens tended otherwise to follow the instructions of governmental and Home Front officials to refrain from exacting their own punishments. As a result of the enormous resentment being vented against these women, however, about one thousand of them were placed in what was termed *protective detention* and released only after agitation had gradually subsided (Andenæs, Riste, and Skodvin 1989, 124).

In recent years feminists and others have questioned the treatment afforded the *tyskertös*, asking why the actions of these women were punished so much more severely than those of male collaborators. Wondering if it was merely because women have traditionally been easier to punish, they also point out the similarity of the treatment given these women to that received by women suspected of witchcraft during the seventeenth century (Senja 1986).

3. Greta Dahl's diary comments on the further development of the *tyskertös* phenomenon as 1941 came to an end.

> December 21, 1941: The women seem to be utterly entranced. The other day a woman unabashedly reported that the Germans claim Norwegian women are erotically deprived. Even in that respect, apparently, their soldiers are better trained than ours. There must be something to it, since married women with grown children are throwing caution to the wind and taking up with the Germans, threatening to report their husbands to the authorities if they object. It's all so insane, it must be a nightmare. I hope we awaken from it soon.

On 19 August 1942, she tells of German soldiers

> flirting with our women and even returning to Germany to divorce their wives so they can marry Norwegian women.

4. The matchbox item was collected in Voss on 17 August 1992. Other Norwegians, too, still remember the secret code said to be hidden in the Nitedal name; a 17 January 1993 letter from Mads Almaas explains: "We tried to interpret everything that *could* be against the Germans and the Nazis. I remember hearing at school that Nitedals (spelled backwards) stood for: *Satan lovet Adolf döden efter toget i Norge* (Satan promised Adolf death for the campaign in Norway)."

These additional interpretations of the Nitedal "code" recorded by Larsen further attest to the inventiveness of occupation humor:

> *Nu i tiden er damene alle like stygge* (Now all the women are equally ugly).
> *Satan lover Adolf döden efter (terror) tyrani i Norge* (Satan promises Adolf death after the terrorism in Norway).

Store laban Adolf dömmes efter tyrani i Norge (The big lout Adolf will be condemned for the tyrany in Norway).
Norge intar Tyskland efter de allierte lands seier (Norway will consume Germany after the Allied victory).

5. Schou-Sörensen records the following variant:

En liten pike på 9 år fortalte fölgende historie til sin spillelærer: Nå får ikke damene ha pil på strömpene mere for tyskerne kunne ta feil av veien.
(A nine year old girl told her piano teacher: "Women can no longer have arrows on their stockings because [without that aid] the Germans might not find the way.")

6. Blacking out *(blending)* of all light sources that could make a population center vulnerable to bombing was a strictly regulated fact of occupation life. Streetlights had either blue bulbs or their glass coated in black with only narrow strips of clear glass remaining; trees and poles were painted with waist-high white belts to make them visible in the dark (Elvsås 1980).

The Germans' threat of British bombing raids in their propaganda and their zealous enforcement of the blackout policy could create friction between occupiers and occupied, as this 16 December 1943 entry from Greta Dahl's diary shows:

Around 4:30 PM we had a visit from a German officer. "Insufficient blinding." It galls me to the depths of my soul that these fat swines can come here and order us around. Luckily Arild came home at just that moment, so I could slam the door right in the face of that German fatso. They actually raid homes if the windows aren't dark enough.

7. A Trönder version of this popular joke tell that

To jenter i Trondheim hadde vært sammen med tyske soldater. Den ene sa: Æ likte no best han "Wiedersehen," æ. [Schou-Sörensen]
(Two girls in Trondheim had been with German soldiers. One of them said, "Well, the one I liked best was the guy named 'Wiedersehen.'")

8. It was widely believed that mackerel ate dead flesh, and some claimed that their black stripes derived from their having eaten uniformed German corpses (Christensen 1988, 45).

9. This particular joke may in addition reflect the more rapid development of a resistance mentality in West Norway than in other parts of the country, a circumstance described by Gerd Stray Gorden (1978).

10. Awareness of the Lebensborn goal of producing future soldiers for the German Reich is also reflected in this joke:

Vet du hvorfor klinikken er bombet?
?
Fordi det ikke skal bli flere soldater. (Larsen)
(Do you know why the maternity clinic has been bombed?
?
So there won't be any more soldiers.)

Chapter 4. Humor's Response to Nazi Repression and Cruelty

1. Haakon Holmboe was a schoolteacher from Hamar arrested by the Nazis on 20 March 1942 for openly expressing anti-Nazi sentiment. He was among

hundreds of "noncompliant" educators subsequently sent by ship to North Norway under extremely hazardous conditions. The Nazis sent them there on a work detail intended to discourage similar shows of defiance; instead the action served to increase anti-Nazi sentiment throughout the population.

2. Though regard for King Haakon grew steadily during the summer of 1940, in the period before the war he had not been particularly popular, being regarded as rather distant (Chr. Christensen 1988, 38). Circulators of an underground flyer titled "De ti bud for nordmenn" (The ten commandments for Norwegians) felt it necessary to urge Norwegians to support the king and to regard as traitors those who would have him deposed (Norges Hjemmefrontmuseum). Yet by his seventieth birthday on 3 August 1942, Haakon had become the focus of the occupation's largest demonstration of anti-Nazi solidarity. A large number of Norwegians marked the occasion by wearing flowers in their lapels, a demonstration to which the Hird again overreacted, arresting in Oslo alone some five hundred of these citizens and sending them to Grini Prison Camp.

3. The first anti-Royal-family article had already been ordered published on 14 June. Several newspapers tried to get around it, and for these attempts, some of the larger ones—including *Dagbladet* (The daily news) and *Arbeiderbladet* (The workers' news)—were stopped. Smaller local papers sometimes succeeded in greater daring, as the examples of *Ringerikeblad* (Ringerike news) and *Hardanger* cited later in this chapter will demonstrate.

4. Christerson recorded a pun reflecting the same sentiment of valuing the king over the Nazi party.

> En bridgespiller sa at han trodde kongen var bedre enn en ess (NS).
>
> (A bridge player said he thought the King outranked *en ess* ["an ace," but also a homonym of NS].)

5. Preoccupation with the numerous jailings is also seen in the quip recorded by Schou-Sörensen that the well-known author Ronald Fangen (1895–1946) had been jailed and so was now known as "Fangen Ronald" (*fangen* = "prisoner"). The first Norwegian imprisoned by the Nazis, Fangen had a British mother and was an enthusiastic supporter of the British-inspired religious organization known as the Oxford Movement, banned by Terboven's 25 September 1940 speech along with all other organizations, including the Scouts, women's groups, and temperance societies. These reasons would in Nazi eyes probably have been sufficient to justify Fangen's arrest, but as one who early perceived the sinister nature of Nazism, he had also written an outspoken and influential anti-Nazi article, "Om troskap" (On fidelity) in 1940, and it was actually this that precipitated his incarceration.

6. More recent assessments have, however, tended to blame the journalists for giving in too easily to press censorship, questioning why they didn't form a united front against the Nazis as did the schoolteachers and clergy.

7. A related item shown to me by several survivors was the drawing of the back of a truck, which looks innocent enough when the door is closed, reading: "Prepared beef and pork sausage, and more. N. Salomonsen Catering, 18 King Street on Market Square. Telephone 36745." When the door is opened, however, the left-hand panel spells out, "Down with NS, Long Live the King" (Bö 1946, 23).

8. Jokes were also circulated by these broadcasts and believed to signal that someone who had fled Norway by boat had safely reached England (Kuhnle 1945, 138).

9. This joke is the only one among the Norwegian materials examined that

With the door closed, the truck's lettering is an innocent advertisement. Door open, the *left-hand* panel reads, Down with the Nazi Party. Long Live the King. From Finn Bö, *Forbuden frukt*, 1946. Reprinted here with permission from Aschehoug Forlag, Oslo, Norway.

mentions the Jews (see chap. 2, footnote 21). Cognates of it circulated in several other occupied countries as well, and the joke itself probably originated in Germany. The Norwegian version makes a special point of the radio-listening rather than of the Jews' horrendous plight.

10. Greta Dahl's diary indicates that the authorities knew of most radios because of a long-standing policy requiring dealers to notify the broadcasting company when they sell a radio (29 August 1941). To this day the broadcast license, now paid for TV purchase, provides the primary funding for NRK, (the Norwegian Broadcasting Company).

11. In most other respects, however, Norway fared rather well compared to other German-occupied countries; while Poland lost 17 percent of its population, Yugoslavia 10 percent, and the Soviet Union 6 percent, Norway lost only 3 per thousand. Even including the considerable property destruction in North Norway inflicted by the Germans during their 1944–45 withdrawal (see chap. 11), Norway's material damages were not among the worst in Europe (Furre 1992, 200).

12. Elvsås tells, for example:

We had a kind neighbor [at Eknes in Osterfjorden in Nord Hordaland] who had a radio in the chicken-coop, which soon became a popular gathering place for the adults. In the quiet summer evenings, Öksenvad's reassuring, deep voice could be heard wafting across the fields: *"Dette er London"* [This is London]. Since no German soldiers were permanently stationed in the area, this usually posed no risk. Then came a raid: "Where *is* the radio at Eknes?" The iron heels came goose-stepping in through our garden gate as well, but the Germans never did find that radio!

13. The occupation period could teach us a thing or two about recycling!

14. This anecdote originated in Germany (where listening to the BBC was also forbidden, though radios were not confiscated), hence the son's capture in England.

15. One paper explained its motivation as follows:

We are publishing this newspaper for two reasons: We want to show that the battle for a free Norway is still being waged and will continue to be waged until the hour of peace has come. For the second: Norwegians today need to see in print the thoughts and feelings that live within them. [*Vi vil oss et land* (We want for ourselves a country), October 1940]

16. How much the illegal BBC broadcasts and undergroud newspapers meant to the occupied Norwegians is expressed by Cato Hambro in a 1943 *Nordmanns-Forbundet* (Norsemen's Federation) article.

But once in a while we were lucky enough to get to listen to London at the home of a friend who had kept his radio at the risk of his life; those were sacred hours. We were able to read illegal newspapers on a regular basis and we met people who were quite well informed. These things gave us new courage, like friendly little lights in the suffocating darkness that brooded over us. [195]

In general the *Nordmanns-Forbundet* magazine, normally headquartered in Norway, but published (in Norwegian) in the United States during the war years, provides a wealth of information and personal insight about daily life in occupied Norway. About the magazine's wartime fate, see Stokker 1992.

17. Conditions were particularly harsh in Rommetveit's district because it was part of the so-called Frontier Zone West, an area of varying depth along Norway's southwestern coast where German military authorities imposed special restrictions on travel and entry.

18. Some Norwegians, in fact, made a conscious determination not to be intimidated, as Greta Dahl's diary demonstrates:

March 8, 1941: Then Terboven came with his punishment. I'll say people were outraged. . . . And Terboven thinks that he can frighten the Norwegians into submission with this punishment. I don't think so. This episode has had a colossal effect on the Germans. They are angry with us because we are not afraid.

19. Slaatto, too, remarks on the lack of correspondence between punishment and crime.

[The jail at] Möllergata 19 has been jammed full the whole time, it is said. Every day *Hird* members come into Oslo by twos, each with his prisoner, who maybe has yelled "Up with the King!" or committed a similar offense. Then it's down to Möllergata, where they'll be on bread and water for a long time. [January 1941]

20. A version of this joke has also been collected from a Norwegian-American in La Crosse, Wisconsin.

A Norwegian was supplying the Nazis with eggs. Soon he began furnishing fewer eggs, and the Nazi officials wrote a letter of complaint to the farmer. Fewer and fewer eggs were supplied each time—each shipment was followed by a letter from the Nazi authorities until finally no eggs were sent out at all. A representative of the Nazis was dispatched to the farm to investigate. The Norwegian explained, "I kept putting up your letters in the hen house, but the hens refused to co-operate, so I shot them all for engaging in sabotage." [Reverend Vinge, collected by Mary Cary, letter to author, 6 June 1991]

21. Again Rommetveit records actual events that rival the cruelty of even the most sarcastic joke.

February 5, 1941: Thursday was a sad day for many inhabitants of the Time community. New demands. The farmers had to show up with all the horses they had of a specified age. The best ones were to be "bought" by the Germans. The owner had to run with his horse while two well-fed Germans studied the animals closely. Sad farewells between horse and owner.

CHAPTER 5. ANSWERING BACK

1. Ever since the 1905 dissolution of Norway's union with Sweden, neutrality had constituted the firm and undisputed basis of Norwegian foreign policy, which was characterized by an almost exclusive concern with the country's internal affairs. Norway's foremost desire and expectation of international politics was respect for her wish to be left alone (Andenæs, Riste, and Skodvin 1989, 9).

2. Reflecting the lack of trust in the Soviet Union that is typical of the times, Greta Dahl reports in a 7 May 1941 entry:

> The United States has refused to deliver various weapons of war ordered and paid for by the Soviet Union since they could not be sure these would not be used against England. So apparently no one trusts the Soviet Union. They're just as sly as the Germans, and equally lacking in conscience.

On 29 August 1941 she says:

> The only good thing the Germans have done is to attack the Soviet Union. Not that I think the Soviets would have attacked West Europe, but you never know. They probably wouldn't have been able to resist the temptation. No, I prefer the Germans to the Russians, although it is the barbarians who will ultimately prevail.

3. Their names additionally suggest the Jössing perception of the Nazis' inability to take a firm stand, as they vacillate (Swing and Sway) with the changing winds of fortune instead of acting in accordance with deeply held principles.

4. Quisling was very slow to realize this fact and as late as March 1945 had to be told by his foreign policy adviser, Finn Stören, that the German authorities were deliberately making fools of him and the NS; that Norway was by law at war with Germany despite the support the Quislings had given to Germany; and that they had exploited Norway's resources while under a pretense of friendship and cooperation having managed to make her administrators share their guilt as plunderers and oppressors (Andenæs, Riste, and Skodvin 1989, 81).

5. It is indicative of the confusion of the times that despite his first book's confiscation, Sælen could get another one, *Tre kalde karer* (Three cold fellows) published in 1942. It was in its wake that Sælen was finally called in for questioning. The second book likens the three Axis powers to three snowmen. Their enemy is the sun (the Allies), who melts the three snowmen one by one, first Italy, the weakest, then Japan and finally—reflecting the situation as it appeared in 1942—the toughest of all, Germany. Perhaps because of the second book's broader focus on world politics rather than on the specifically Norwegian situation, it never achieved the success of *Snorre sel*.

6. All ages responded to this message, even teenagers, normally disdainful of children's books. Berit Marianne Gabrielsen (b. 1922) tells of being in a high school class whose teacher grew significantly in his pupils' regard by reading *Snorre sel* aloud in class and thereby removed all doubt of his own attitude toward the New Order (Interview, 4 October 1992).

7. *Snorre sel* survived the occupation being reprinted in 1972, 1982, and 1985; by now over 140,000 copies have been sold. It has been translated into Icelandic,

Swedish, Greek (!), and English (*Snorri the Seal*. London: Blackie and Son). A feature length film of the book is being planned for 1997 (Sælen, letters to the author 25 February and 25 May 1994).

8. In response some Christmas card producers began dressing their *nisser* in green, yellow, and blue caps, and the beloved illustrator Thorbjörn Egner produced a series of cards in which the *nisse*, much to his chagrin, goes bare-headed, wears a top hat, and even dons a bowler!

9. Writing on 19 January 1943, Åslaug Rommetveit says the cover shows "Quisling in Hitler's arms on thin ice."

10. The Nazis may have been extrasensitive about this cover because of its accurate reflection of Hitler's displeasure with the situation in Norway, where Quisling had sparked so much resentment that the Germans had recently had to send him strict guidelines (Voksö 1985, 258). The cover's timing, moreover, as German forces were being hard pressed at the Russian front and with their pivotal defeat at Stalingrad fast approaching, only added insult to injury.

11. An alternate version of this joke appeared in the collection of Norwegian occupation humor published in America in 1942.

> A German soldier marched up to an elderly saleslady in an Oslo department store. "Heil Hitler!" he barked. "Where's the hosiery department?"
> "God save the King! Three fights up." [Olav and Myklebust 1942, 19]

12. The following anecdote shared by Elvsås similarly portrays a Norwegian refusing to give up even a shred of dignity before the occupier:

> My grandmother spoke fluent German owing to an extended stay in Hanover during her youth. I think she simply *relished* these confrontations with the Germans. Standing erect as a ruler at the top of the stairs, armed for battle in a white summer hat and cane, she took the offensive and launched a charming conversation about her old friend from Hamburg, Ella Stubbe, who lived on such-and-such-a street. Then it would develop that the "spokesman" for the German soldiers was *also* from Hamburg and lived on the same street! He could report that *his* house had been bombed, but that *fräulein* Stubbe's house right across the street had escaped damage. The conversation was about to take on a dangerously human character, so to be on the safe side, my grandmother fired off the following: "Ich war einmal mit einem Deutschen Offizier verlobt" [I was once engaged to a German officer.] Then the German clicked his heels together and saluted smartly! But my grandmother continued: *"Das var aber eine andere Zeit!!!"* [But things were different then!!!] With that, the "audience" was over. [Elvsås]

Despite the old woman's vulnerable position, she refuses to yield any measure of personal power to the German soldier. It is she who controls the conversation's tone and content, and she who decides when to bring the encounter to its abrupt but poignant conclusion.

13. Larsen has a variant.

> Under et flyangrep i Bergen stod en tysk offiser i nedgangen til en tilfluktsrom. Da fik han se en eldre dame spasere bortover gaten uten å bry seg om flyene som kretser over byen. Offiseren sier til dem inne i tilfluktsrommet at de må hente henne, men ingen vil. Så må han gå selv. Han sier til damen at hun må söke dekning, engelskmannen er over, farlig.
> "Farlig," sier damen, "det er ikke meg dem skal ha. Det er deg. Se å kom in i tilfluktsrommet."
> (During an air-raid in Bergen a German officer is standing in the entrance to a shelter when he notices an older woman strolling across the street without bothering about the

planes circling overhead. The officer tells the people inside the shelter to go and get her, but no one will. So he has to go himself. He tells the woman she must seek cover, the Englishman is overhead, dangerous.
    "Dangerous," the woman retorts. "It's not me they're after. It's you. Get along inside the shelter.")

14. Arne Skouen's observations from war-torn Oslo, published after the war as 66 *Skinnbrev fra Oslo: Glimt fra Norges hovedstad under okkupasjonen* (1943), under the pseudonym of Björn Stallare, provide good insights into occupied daily life and mood.
    15. Compare this joke with the first one under the heading "Beginning of the End" in chapter 11 for a further example of the submission/aggression contrast.
    16. The daring, disrespectful reply to authorities parallels the attitude articulated in the underground newspaper *Enig og tro* (Agreed and Faithful"—an allusion to words spoken at the signing of Norway's 1814 constitution) in response to the 1942 Ordinance.

Our Answer!
Never has it been so fatally dangerous to be a Norwegian as today. No one must doubt what this implies. It is obvious that underground activity, in any form, can not avoid being influenced by the new [October 1942] ordinance. Clearly our work must be conducted so as to minimize the risk and to eliminate unnecessary elements of danger. But it is equally clear that our effort must continue at all costs. We will not budge an inch from the course upon which we have embarked. As long as at all possible, *Enig og tro* will continue to be published. [*Enig og tro* (Skien), no. 5, November 1942]

17. Note in this regard also the following anecdote recorded by Ellingsen portraying the continuity of established behavior amid surrounding upheaval:

It is the night of 9 April 1940. The warning sirens howl over the town, an inebriated man stands on Egertorvet as people dash in all directions to find shelter. Not comprehending the situation but thinking he was part of a game of hide and seek, the man faces the wall and counts: "47. . .48. . .49. . .50. Ready or not, here I come."

Chapter 6. Adjusting the Image of the Übermensch

Übermensch = "superman"; German propaganda held that the noble Aryan race, being superior, should be masters over all others on Earth.
    1. This applies especially to the artist Harald Damsleth at the Oslo firm Herolden (Jensen and Dahl 1988).
    2. A standing theme in Quisling's speeches was the restoration of Norway's power to the lofty heights it had attained during the Viking age. He emphasized the longing felt by Norwegians, as an ancient Germanic people conscious of their heroic past, to unlock the potential of their eminent future, and he promised that Norway would again develop into a great political entity as it established the cultural and material foundation for a new civilization. Beyond being free, Norway would be great, if only it would support the Nazi party (Mogens 1945, 246).
    3. The V was also used to express views of other lands' response to the Nazi occupation, as in this item's summation of a great deal of wartime history:

Hva V'en betyr i de forskjellige land:
Norge: Vi Volder Vanskeligheter
Danmark: Vi Vil Vente

Holland: Vi Venter Vilhelmina
Frankrike: Vi Venter Våpen
Russland: Vi Venter Vinteren
Sverige: Vi Velger Vinneren
Italia: Vårt Vennskap Vakler
Tyskland: Vi Vakler Videre
England: Vi Vil Vinne [Schou-Sörensen]
(What the V means in various countries:
Norway: We pose problems [cf., the unexpected strength of the tiny nation's resistance].
Denmark: We will wait [cf., King Christian X's initial policy of peaceful coexistence with the occupiers].
Holland: We're waiting for Wilhelmina [their queen who escaped to England after Hitler's invasion].
France: We're waiting for weapons [cf., the country's lack of war materials].
Russia: We're waiting for Winter [i.e., the harsh weather that had dealt Napoleon his defeat, and which the Russians rightly believed would have the same effect on Hitler's troops, see chap. 10].
Sweden: We'll choose the winner [cf., Sweden's oft-criticized policy of neutrality that seemed to favor the contender with the best chances of victory; seeming to ignore Norway early in the war, the country's policy grew perceptibly warmer during 1943 as the tide turned against Germany].
Italy: Our friendship vacillates [cf., the nation's crossover from Axis power to Ally, chap. 11].
England: We will win [a prospect that seemed highly unlikely before Hitler's February 1943 defeat in the Battle of Stalingrad].

4. Right after the war, an occupation survivor, Jacob Kuhnle, similarly remarked:

> The thing that must be remembered in the evaluation of [the resistance fronts that gradually formed] and the battle they fought is that the opponent had a monopoly not only on the means of power, but also on the means of propaganda. Even though the Norwegian people exhibited a phenomenal degree of immunity to this propaganda, there is nevertheless something known as the "daily drip". [Kuhnle 1945, 15]

5. As mentioned in the introduction, recent years have seen a number of books in which NS members themselves explain their motivation. In Egil Ulateig's *Dagbok frå ein rotnorsk nazist* (Diary of a genuine Norwegian patriot Nazi) from 1987 we learn that many found the religious character of the party attractive and found ideals cultivated there that otherwise seemed lacking in contemporary Norwegian society. They looked to the NS to restore a previously existing way of life that had been lost to the external powers of capitalism and communism.

Far from being superficial opportunists as the Jössings saw them, many Nazis saw themselves as the only ones truly fighting for Norway's defense. Ulateig writes from a bunker in Yugoslavia on 25 October 1943:

> The Jössings ought to think a little longer before they call themselves "Norwegians"— think about all those who have made the supreme sacrifice for Norway and lie buried far away in a foreign country. They're the ones to whom our thoughts go when we promise to do our utmost as we continue to fight for the cause they died for. [63]

6. See also Slaatto's 4 November 1940 entry quoted in chapter 7, telling that only sixty individuals of indeterminate affiliation showed up for a demonstration while the next day's newspaper claimed there had been a full house and great jubilation.

7. This item also appears in the Trondheim diary dated 23 November 1940.

8. Actually the advertisements provided a splendid arena for anti-Nazi propaganda as they smuggled clandestine messages of the type described in chapter 4, but space limitations preclude a more thorough discussion of them here.

9. Along the same lines Slaatto reports in her diary on 21 May 1940,

Hitler is writing in the newspapers that only a few Germans have fallen in Norway, but that many have died in a natural disaster.

10. The delay of the attack on Oslo (see chap. 1) caused by the sinking of the *Blücher,* enabling the escape of King Haakon and the government, provides an additional reason for Jössing humor to recall this incident with felicity.

11. This item also appears in the Trondheim diary, dated 26 August 1940.

12. In February 1991 the following variant of this joke was still being told by a Norwegian-American living in La Crosse, Wisconsin:

A German plane crashed in Norway. One Norwegian asked another, "Did the pilot survive?" The other Norwegian answered, "Well, he says he's alive, but you know what liars the Germans are." [Collected by Mary Cary from Reverend Vinge; letter to author, February 1991]

13. Kuhnle comments on the effectiveness of Quisling-propaganda efforts to prove that the Norwegian society needed to be saved from its ongoing descent into decadence.

When the newspapers asserted on a daily basis that no one wanted a return to the good old days, with their unemployment, injustice and misery, some weak souls fell for it. Constantly presenting the former Norwegian society in the worst possible light, focusing only on its weaknesses and hiding all its strengths was, moreover, not without effect. [1945, 50]

14. For a Romanian Communist regime cognate of this joke, see Banc and Dundes (1986, 21) and for a Russian cognate, Ruksenas (1986, 13).

15. For more about this German marching song see chapter 9.

16. The following joke recorded by Ellingsen again highlights the refusal of occupied Norwegians to be intimidated and their spontaneous denigration of the occupiers:

Da de tyske tropper rykket inn i Norge, sto en bonde og så på de magre tyske hestene, og sa: "Er detta det dom kaller for Ribbentropper?"
(As the German troops were marching into Norway, a farmer stood watching the skinny German horses and commented, "Is that what they call *Ribbentropper?*")

The word used by the farmer plays on the name of the German politician Joachim von Ribbentrop (1893–1946), who as foreign minister was a familiar name in Norway at the beginning of the war (see also chap. 10). The farmer's quip suggests that the scrawny German steeds failed to meet Norwegian equestrian standards, while the fact that it is a "mere" farmer who dares to disparage the mighty invaders adds to the ridicule.

CHAPTER 7. THE UNIVERSALITY OF RESISTANCE AND ABSENCE OF NAZI SUPPORT

1. As mentioned in chapter 2, footnote 11, the name of Norway's head of Nazi propaganda was actually Gulbrand Lunde, but Marie, along with many

others spelled it Gudbrand, influenced perhaps by a widespread gibe at Lunde's constant speech-giving, calling him Tale-Gudbrand (Talking Gudbrand), a homonym of Dale Gudbrand, cf. chap 2, note 11.

2. Since the most important function of this armed support force was to fight Nazi resistance through arrests and hearings, the Hird also figures prominently in Jössing humor, as this chapter will show.

3. Walker reports a similar anti-Nazi demonstration tactic.

People adopted the simple but humiliating tactic of assembling in large crowds *outside* Quisling meetings, while only a handful of people were inside. [1946, 95]

4. As Slaatto's remarks accurately reflect, the developing resistance wasn't everywhere equally strong, and pockets of Nazism existed in various places around the country.

5. As of September 1940 the party had been fairly insignificant in size, but events of that month—the disbanding of all other political parties and the organization of the mostly Nazi Council of Commissioners—led to a period of growth. Through 1941 the trend was unsteady, but growing due to the energetic efforts of its promoters. Until midsummer 1942, the party continued to recruit about 1,000 new members per month. In November 1943, however, membership began to decline and this trend continued through the end of the occupation:

August 27, 1940	4,202
December 25, 1940	26,178
April 1, 1941	29,428
August 1, 1941	34,928
December 1, 1941	39,306
April 1, 1942	42,920

(*Om Landsvikoppgjöret* 1963).

6. Svein Blindheim went through a list of 709 Norwegians who fell at the German front and found that they were far from the outcasts Jössing humor claimed; many were from Norway's most prominent families. Some had no political motivation and did so purely for adventure, though just as many felt driven to sacrifice themselves for the cause.

Another observer pointed out that the NS leadership created an atmosphere that enabled young people to find the ideals they had been taught as children, both in the party's religious character and in the speeches of Quisling and Lunde. Adherents viewed Quisling as a man of action who alone among Norway's leaders had acted decisively on 9 April, was capable of fighting the threatening forces of Bolshevism and capitalism, and was committed to preventing Norway from being assimilated into a pan-Germanic Reich (Chr. Christensen 1988, 47, 139).

7. The Nazis' isolation led not least to their losing access to the opinion-shaping humor this book describes.

8. Some of these anecdotes also reflect a strong need on the part of their tellers to distance themselves from the NS, from which one may deduce a high degree of anxiety about the exact nature of their wartime stance. In part this tension may be due to the uncomfortable awareness that merely by retaining their jobs, all Norwegians, Jössings very much included, in fact acted as collaborators, since their work supported the German war effort (H. F. Dahl 1974, 175–77). This circumstance combined with normative pressure to oppose Nazism created tension, precisely the medium in which humor thrives best.

9. Because of this popular wordplay, Jössing humor frequently employed the streetcar's *tilhenger* (extra car) to mock the Nazis' lacking support, for example:

Quisling har beslaglagt trikkene for han trenger tilhengere.
(Quisling has confiscated all the streetcars because he needs *tilhengere*.)

This popular pun helped give the streetcar a high profile in occupation humor as chapter 8 will show.

10. Larsen has this variant:

"Hvorfor går du helt alene? Hvor blir det av tilhengerne dine?" Quisling svarer: "Skolen har ikke sluttet enda!"
("Why are you out walking all alone? Where are your followers?" Quisling answers: "School's not out yet.")

11. Like *pakk* and *ramp* (noted in chap. 1), the term *utskudd* also circulated in general conversation about the Nazis.

12. The joke probably takes its point of departure in the actual paper rationing instituted during the fall of 1942. This precarious paper situation caused some newspapers to cease being published and others to appear with fewer pages; book production was reduced to a minimum, and in the absence of wrapping paper, customers had to bring along their own bags and paper to the store for their purchases (Voksö 1985, 269).

13. See also examples of this mechanism of using the full spectrum of age in chapter 1.

14. The element of placing patriotic loyalty above one's job is particularly interesting given Hans Fredrik Dahl's observation about Norwegians' economic collaboration mentioned in footnote 8 (1974, 176).

15. Arnulf Överland (1889–1968) had already warned of the danger of Nazism long before the 9 April 1940 invasion, most profoundly in his 1936 poem "Du skal ikke sove" (You must not sleep, i.e., in the face of Nazi atrocities). For these views, Överland was detained by the Nazis in various jails and concentration camps from 1941 to 1945.

16. Norway's major center for political prisoners, Grini prison camp became a legendary center of Norwegian culture during the occupation, coming as it did to house so many of Norway's intellectual elite. About twenty thousand Norwegians spent shorter or longer periods there after its opening in June 1941.

17. See also the additional anecdote about Björn Björnson ordering Nazis off the streetcar in chapter 8. Concerning the strong feelings provoked by the pro-Nazi sympathies of Björnstjerne Björnson's other son, Erling, young Marie Slaatto comments (4 November 1940):

I guess the worst part of this [Nazi] meeting was that Björnstjerne Björnson's son offered words of thanks for the excellent speech, etc. Björnson who was a genuine Norwegian! His granddaughter is in Nils' class and she, too, is a total Nazi. Uff, it's horrible that Norwegians can be like that.

18. Ruge was taken prisoner immediately after the capitulation in North Norway (10 June 1940) and remained in German captivity for the rest of the war. His speech made just prior to departure for Germany became an important spur to resistance.

Remember that no state can elevate itself merely by waiting for something to happen, hoping that help will come from the outside. It must be ready to help itself when the time is right.

The speech was broadcast from Tromsö and also circulated illegally in printed flyers. The diarist Marie Slaatto preserved a copy which, like many other underground circulars, directs the receiver to "make copies and send to at least 10 of your friends."

19. Werner Werenskiold (1883–1961), was the son of the famous Norwegian painter and fairy-tale illustrator Erik Werenskiold and the author of a popular two-volume geography of Norway, *Norge vårt land* (Norway our country) (1937).

20. Theaters were closed during the first days after the invasion, but Chat Noir opened already on 17 April, and others later followed. It took awhile for censoring authorities to learn that even the slightest allusion to the situation would provoke enthusiastic response, so material of this nature continued to slip through with almost no objections during the first few weeks and months of the occupation. Gradually, however, conditions grew considerably more tense, and the censors began requiring that all material be submitted for review in advance of the performance. They then sat in the audience ready to intervene in case of unwarranted laughter or other reactions likely to be anti-Nazi demonstrations (Bang-Hansen 1961, 220).

In his history of Stavanger, Knut Stahl points out the role of these theater demonstrations in promoting anti-Nazi solidarity.

Within the walls of the theater people could laugh together at those in power. The humor united them; it was a shared weapon. They became active participants, even accomplices, in the daring [verbal] acts being committed on the stage . . . [and this] created a sense of co-operation [and] secret brotherhood. [1964, 200–201]

21. In fact the joke diaries provide almost the only information on wartime theatrical revues since contemporary newspapers, being Nazi-censored, report little of their subjects or actual material, nor do they describe the jubilant response it elicited. Though Einar Rose has regrettably written little about his experience during the occupation, both Christerson (living in Bergen) and Sverre Larsen (in Trondheim) devote special attention to Rose's jokes.

Sverre Larsen's Trondheim diary includes most of the Rose jokes in an entry dated 26 September 1940, and adds there a description of these jokes' popularity.

Revue actor Einar Rose has been the nation's oracle in these hard times, and countless stories are going around about him. Quite a few of his jokes have been really quite fantastic in their daring. Wherever you go lately, people are asking each other, "Have you heard the latest Einar Rose?"

22. The Trondheim diary has this related joke:

Einar Rose kommer inn på scenen med et billede av Hitler under armen. Han ser seg om etter en spiker på veggen mens han sier: Skal han henges, skal han henges - men setter så billdet mot veggen med de ord: eller skal vi stille ham mot muren?
(Einar Rose comes on stage with a picture of Hitler under his arm. He looks around for a nail on the wall while he says, "Shall he be hanged, shall he be hanged?" But then he leans the picture against the wall saying, "Or should we send him to the wall" [i.e., to be executed].)

23. The Trondheim diary has this version, dated 26 September 1940:

To landstrykere kommer inn på scenen. Den ene tykk og jovial, er Einar Rose og han bærer en pakke under armen. Den annen, en höy og tynd en, sier at han er sulten. "Ja," sier Rose, "det er mat nok, bare vi får pakket ut," og dermed begynner han å pakke ut matpakken.
(Two tramps come on stage. One of them, fat and jovial, is Einar Rose and he is carrying a package under his arm. The other, tall and thin, says he's hungry. "Yes," says Rose, unwrapping the package, "there's plenty of food, just as soon as we get *pakket ut.*")

According to the Trondheim diary, the same pair also acted out the visual gag noted in chapter 1 about the emaciated German soldier becoming fat after a few months in Norway (26 September 1940).

Rose's partner, a very thin fellow, comes on stage carrying a package labelled 1939. Then Rose comes on as an extremely fat and well-nourished soldier and he is labelled 1940.

24. Greta Dahl reports hearing a variant of this joke on the radio, 20 October 1940.

Joda, her er nok av klær og mat i Norge, bare vi får "pakket ut".
(Sure there's plenty of food and clothing in Norway, if we could only get *pakket ut.*)

25. The same wordplay appears in one of Schou-Sörensen's jokes.

Hirden marsjerer i gaten til trommemusikk. Trommene spiller Ramp, Ramp, Bareramp, Bareramp.
(The *Hird* is marching through the streets to drum music. The drums are playing *Ramp, Ramp, Bareramp, Bareramp* [Scum, Scum, Only scum, Just plain scum].)

The pun also appears in this item collected by Ellingsen:

Hirden har fått nye trommevirvler: Bare ramp, bare ramp, bare ramp, ramp, ramp.
(The *Hird* has gotten new drum-rolls: *Bare ramp, bare ramp, bare ramp, ramp, ramp.*)

26. Schou-Sörensen's variant goes:

Terboven, Terrorboven, Terrierboven. Einar Rose löper omkring på scenen med en terrier og snakker til den. "Ut med deg, terrierboven, ditt lille utyske".
(Terboven, Terrorboven, Terrierboven. Einar Rose runs around on stage with a terrier and says to it, "Get out of here, terrierboven, you little *utyske.*")

27. The Trondheim diary reports it as follows:

Einar Rose kommer inn på scenen og begynner å fortelle at så höyt hoppet han da han var liten, men så höyt hopper han nu—og plutselig löfter han armen til Hitler hilsen! [26 September 1940]
(Einar Rose comes on stage and starts telling that this is how high he could jump when he was little, but this is how high he can jump now—and suddenly he raises his arm in the Hitler salute!)

28. See also the related joke in the section about the Hitler salute in chapter 2.
29. In Larsen's version:

Rose går ned i salen på Chat Noir under en forestilling og setter seg på fanget til en tysk offiser og sier: "Nå kan du föle hvordan det er å være besatt og."

(Rose goes down into the audience at Chat Noir during a performance and sits on the lap of a German officer saying,
"Now you can feel what it's like to be occupied, too.")

30. See more about this rearrangement of the proverb in chapter 6.
31. According to Sverre Eilertsen (Letter to author, 17 January 1993) the "bicycle" number was also used by the revue artist Leif Juster in Oslo.
32. The Trondheim diary has this version:

På grunn av alle disse vitsene skal Rose ha vært opkalt til den tyske kommandant i Oslo. Kommandanten spör om det er han som morer det norske folk så godt. . . . "Ja," svarer Rose, han har da gjort hvad han har evnet for å more det norske folk. Kommandanten sier at han—Rose—fornærmer det tyske folk og spör om han ikke visste at i Tyskland var det "80 millioner mennesker som så til Hitler som en gud?"
"Nei," sa Rose, den måtte han være unnskyldt for å ha laget.
(Because of all these jokes, Rose was allegedly summoned to the German Kommandant in Oslo. The Kommandant asks if he's the one who's been giving the Norwegian people so much amusement. . . . "Well," Rose answers, he's been doing what he could to cheer them up. The Kommandant says that Rose's jokes insult the German people and asks if he didn't know that in Germany there were "80 million people who regarded Hitler like a god."
"No,'" said Rose, that wasn't one *he'd* made up. [26 September 1940]

CHAPTER 8. DAILY LIFE IN REALITY AND IN HUMOR

1. The cost of the occupation per inhabitant was several times higher in Norway than in other comparable lands, such as Holland and Belgium. It is estimated that 35 percent of Norway's GNP went to finance the occupation (Furre 1992, 192).
2. Though on a larger scale than most, the situation of Bergljot Ödemark (b. 1898) suggests the nature of the food-gathering activity in which many Norwegians engaged.

We were lucky having a good-sized house on half an acre of land. We turned the entire yard into a potato field, and converted my daughter's playhouse into a shelter for the pig. We kept 20 hens in the cellar. They had free run of the "farmyard": netting over a window. We fed the pig on potatoes and grass collected each day and on kitchen scraps. Some pigs were fed so much herring meal and cod liver oil that they ended up tasting more like fish than meat. [Dahr 1991]

She also describes some common items of the wartime diet: the rutabaga became a staple, often substituting for meat; it also served as a snack in place of oranges; *klippefisk-i-kål* (dried fish and cabbage stew) substituted for the Norwegian national dish of *får-i-kål* (mutton and cabbage stew). People regularly augmented their diets by picking wild fruit and berries; the men hunted and children raised rabbits, often trading with the neighbors at slaughtering time, "so the fricassee wouldn't be so personal" (Dahr 1991). Indicating that Ödemark's activities were far from atypical, *Aftenposten* carried during March 1941 a drawing of a "neat little house for the urban pig" (Bull 1979, 385).
3. About the Norwegians' new spirit of solidarity Cato Hambro writes in 1943:

But the reason Norwegians on the homefront can manage to keep up their courage and optimism, how they keep from despairing over the daily difficulties, is a change in spirit,

A suggestion for an urban pigpen. From *Aftenposten*, March 1941. Reprinted with permission from *Aftenposten*, Oslo, Norway.

a revolution within themselves. If they had been as they were before the war, they would have had serious problems in managing the stress of a passive resistance. [55]

4. An incident recorded by Schou-Sörensen also reflects this growing celebration of defiance.

A woman was selling eggs at the open-air market, two per buyer. A German came and demanded all of them. She said he could get just two like the others, but he insisted: he wanted them all. Finally she had to give in, and threw the egg basket at him, thereby smashing all of them. A man who had been watching gave her 10 crowns.

The Trondheim diary reports a similar incident on 8 January 1942 of a shop woman refusing a German tobacco and being offered money for this action by another customer.

5. Bergljot Ödemark shares the recipe for *krisekrem* (crisis whipped cream) used on such occasions in an attempt to give food a festive appearance despite the lack of milk and cream:

½ liter water
1 level tablespoon potato flour
1 level tablespoon wheat flour
1 rounded tablespoon dry milk
A little egg powder

Some drops of rum extract

It didn't taste like whipped cream, she says, but it looked good (Dahr)!

6. Juster himself performed the "new bread" number during the 1942 season at Oslo's Edderkoppen Revue Theater.

7. A 6 March 1941 entry in Herman Friele's diary elaborates:

Besides the decision that white flour is only to be used for the sick and for children, as of March 10 it is forbidden to use finely sifted wheat flour for cakes, pastry, white rolls, etc.

8. The unknown author of a 1944 *Nordmanns-Forbundet* article similarly identifies standing in line as a good arena for occupation humor.

It can not be denied that standing in line can be quite entertaining. The conversation is lively and folk humor flourishes. [Ur.der stövelhælen 1944, 133]

9. Apparently the food-smuggling episode became well-known, since Greta Dahl makes this comment about it in her diary (20 October 1940):

It's like the Norwegian said when the coffin with the remains of fallen Germans turned out to be hams, sausages and other meats: "These German soldiers sure are fat!"

10. The well-known painter and book illustrator, Ridley Borchgrevink (1898–1981), produced a series of animal motifs for the Eberh. B. Oppi Publishing Co. during the 1942 Christmas season. This particular one led to a summons and lengthy hearing at the Victoria Terasse Nazi headquarters for both the firm's publishing director and for Borchgrevink himself.

11. An indication of the popularity of obtaining needed goods by barter is seen in the fact that the 24 October 1944 *Bergens Tidende* carried 232 such ads; 69 of them offered or asked for tobacco, the most important trading commodity.

12. As is so often the case, the truth lies somewhere in between the joke and the German propaganda. It is Jössing propaganda that Norway was stripped bare of essentials. Though occupation forces made heavy demands on goods produced in Norway and on Norwegian labor, there were also large quantities of goods sent from Germany or elsewhere in Europe to Norway (Walker 1946, 85). To counteract the rumors of Norwegians starving to death, the Nazis produced a picture postcard showing healthy children, captioned: "Do we look like we're starving?" [Universitets Bibliotek Krigtrykkssamlingen]

13. Jokes about other shortages circulated as well.

Det er synd på visergutten for det er så dårlig med tobakk at han må ta et drag av kjerra. [Ellingsen]
(Too bad about the messenger boy: tobacco is in such short supply he has to "take a drag on his wagon".)

Hvorfor er det hull i kronestykket? Fordi den er Markstukken. [Schou-Sörensen]
(Why is there a hole in the Crown coin? Because it's mark-eaten.)

The word Mark means both "worm" and the German unit of monetary exchange; the same pun also occurs in the following joke recorded by Ellingsen:

Det er på et kontor. En av kontorpersonalet, medlem av NS har en pose med epler som han byr rundt.

"Er dette NS epler, dette da?"
"Nei," svarer en annen, som har tatt en stor bit av sitt eple. "Det er jössingepler, for det er ikke mark i dem!"
(At an office, one of the staff, an NS member, is offering around a bag of apples.
"Are these NS apples, then?"
"No," answers another who has taken a big bite. "They must be Jössing apples since they don't have any *mark* ("worms/Deutsch marks").")

14. For details of other Arne Taraldsen mock stamps, see chaps. 2, 4, and 11.

15. Herman Friele writes in his diary on 16 January 1941, "Knut Hamsun visited Reichskommissar Terboven this week, and was invited to visit Germany," and then adds in terse disappointment, "Hamsun accepted the invitation." Hamsun's pro-Nazi activity had, however, started long before. Even as Norwegian soldiers were fighting the two-month war that followed the 9 April invasion, he had sided with the Germans and appealed to Norwegian soldiers to throw down their arms and go home.

Hamsun also participated in the propaganda campaign to enlist Norwegian military support for Germany. Naturally the NS and Germans exploited his famous name to the utmost, while the majority of the Norwegian people grew increasingly distraught over his behavior.

Still, as Johs. Andenæs points out, Hamsun's trial presented a challenge. He had, after all, been 80 years old when the Germans invaded Norway and 85 when the war ended. Could an 85-year-old be put in prison? Were his actions manifestations of senility rather than treason? In the end, the trial emphasized his particular responsibilities to the country by virtue of his position as a world-famous author. On 23 June 1948 he was sentenced to pay a fine of 325,000 kroner (a significant portion of his net worth) and to be interned at a psychiatric institution, where he wrote a scathing account of his treatment in the book *På gjengrodde stier* (On overgrown paths), published in 1948 (Andenæs, Riste, and Skodvin 1989, 153–55).

16. The books mentioned in the joke appeared as follows: *Sult* (Hunger) 1890, *Victoria* (Victoria) 1892, and *Markens gröde* (The growth of the soil) 1917.

17. The Trondheim diary has the variant that Hamsun sells *Victoria* to the Germans and *Sult* to the Norwegians (dated 25 August 1941).

On 29 October 1941 Greta Dahl records hearing the following variant the day before at a sewing meeting:

Hamsun har delt sine verker mellom Norge og Tyskland. Norge fikk *Sult* og *Viktoria*, mens Tyskland fikk *Markens gröde*.
(Hamsun has divided his works between Norway and Germany. Norway got *Hunger* and *Victoria*, while Germany got *The Growth of the Soil*.)

Note that these versions, too, ascribe the active role to Hamsun.

18. In addition to controlling the government, the most urgent goal of Quisling and the occupiers had been to gain control of the Norwegian economy, and it is in this realm that their aims were most thoroughly and successfully carried out. On 12 July 1941 Quisling had issued the order for compulsory labor *(arbeidstjeneste)* on works of particular importance to the German war effort. In December 1942 his government introduced an infamous system of enforcing such work orders. Now employers were to hold back the ration cards of their employees, issuing weekly cards instead, thereby effectively preventing employees from strike actions, absenteeism, or changing jobs without permission.

Later, in February 1943, after Hitler announced a total mobilization of the work forces in occupied countries, Quisling decreed the conscription of all men between the ages of 18 and 55 and of women aged 21 to 40. Terboven supported this decree with the full authority of the German Reich. The period of forced labor was first fixed at 6 months, then extended to 9 months in January 1944. The men who refused conscription into this labor force by going into hiding became an important resistance force known as *gutta i skauen* (the guys in the woods).

19. In addition to the jokes and cartoons presented here, a further indication of the prominence of the *trikk* is the revue song written by Finn Bö and Bias Bernhoft to be performed at Chat Noir (Quoted in Hjeltnes, 1987, 113).

Concerning the transportation situation, one survivor writes:

> Even before the war, there weren't many cars in Norway—one per 1,000–2,000 people, perhaps—and no more were imported during the war. Of the few in place before 1940, some were hidden and the rest confiscated by the Germans. There was no gasoline and the few taxis being driven were propelled by wood knots [by means of an attached generator]. The few private automobiles that did exist were reserved for doctors and emergencies. [Grethe Jærkjend, Skien, letter to author, 17 January 1993]

Transportation grew increasingly scarce as the occupation wore on. On 19 August 1944 Greta Dahl comments:

> People rarely travel by car now. All ordinary driving is strictly forbidden. Permission is granted only for illness or matters of a serious nature. Besides there's never gasoline or wood knots [pieces of wood burned in the cars' wartime, rear-mounted generators].

20. This pun was still going strong during the summer of 1992, when the author observed trailers on Bergen's Hansa Beer Company trucks bearing the slogan: *Jeg er Hansa tilhenger* (I'm a Hansa *tilhenger*).

21. In a 1943 *Nordmanns-Forbundet* article Cato Hambro quotes this incident and says, "And fortunately we are still able to rejoice over clever answers and an amusing episode" (194).

22. While the exiled government emphasized constitutional continuity implying its own postwar prominence, the Home Front resistance thought Norway should begin with a clean slate after the war, with new leaders and a new national accord, free from the old party arguments (Furre 1992, 190–91). Instead of an awareness of the tug-of-war actually being waged between these two factions, however, the general public's occupation perception was of all opponents to the Nazi New Order sharing the single aim of restoring prewar conditions, the perception Jössing humor also reflects.

23. For a discussion of the same point as it relates to *Snorri the Seal* see chapter 5.

24. A good example of this wartime unity across previously sharp social divisions is seen in the numerous jokes and demonstrations favoring the return of King Haakon VII to rule in Norway (cf., chaps. 4 and 11). Though this view flies in the face of rather strong prewar republican sentiment, Haakon's refusal to accept Quisling's government or to abdicate the throne made him a unifying symbol for the great majority of Norwegians regardless of their preoccupation stance on the issue of monarchy. (Complicating this situation, however, was Haakon's explicit support of the London government from which the Home Front was actively trying to distance itself.)

25. Once again the image exaggerates the actual degree of unity, ignoring the

various factions that actually did exist. Still compared to some other occupied countries, the transition did proceed with remarkable ease.

CHAPTER 9. A HUMOROUS PERSPECTIVE ON WAR DEVELOPMENTS

1. Greta Dahl had commented just one day before, "Reading the newspapers these days can make you sick, but we've got to have them" (18 May 1942).

2. Also celebrating the British success at impeding German attack was this joke recorded by Slaatto in January 1941:

> A: Man kan sende så mange hullete strömper til Tyskland som man vil.
> B: Hvordan det?
> A: Jo, engelskmennene stopper dem på veien.
> (A: You can send as many worn-out stockings to Germany as you like.
> B: How so?
> A: The British *stopper* [darn/stop] them on the way.)

3. The January 1941 issue of the underground paper *Hvepsen* reports the incident as actually having taken place.

4. Gudrun Moen comments on the actual debilitating effect of repeatedly hearing the song.

> April 23, 1943—You can't imagine what it's like in Oslo now. . . . Soldiers constantly march in ranks through the streets singing their march and war song, causing people to rush to their windows and stand powerlessly wringing their hands.

5. See also the Laksevåg ferry joke in chapter 6.

6. Two raids in particular fanned Hitler's fears of a coming Allied invasion: the one on Svolvær described in chapter 4 and one that took place on Målöy on 27 December 1941, when the British sank five German ships.

7. Schou-Sörensen's variant even more strongly reflects the German fear of Allied invasion.

> Det er kommet 10.000 tyske syersker til Bergen som skal falle engelskmennene i ryggen. [Schou-Sörensen]
> (10,000 German seamstresses have come to Bergen in order to *falle* the English *i ryggen* ["take in at the back"/"ambush"].)

8. A related mechanism underlies the Salvation Army joke in chapter 4 and the joke quoted in this chapter's footnote 2, as well as the following joke with its English/Norwegian wordplay stimulated by the London Blitz of September 1940, when—after three weeks of bombing British command posts—Hitler aimed his bombs at the London docks:

> De engelske barna er sinte på tyskerne fordi de ödelegger "dokkene" deres. [Ellingsen]
> (The English children are mad at the Germans because they are destroying their *dokker* ["dolls" in Norwegian, also a homonym of the English word "docks"].)

The joke belies the horrifying destruction of the raid, which sent the entire harbor area up in flames and resulted in a tremendous loss of lives. On the other hand, the Blitz yielded great morale benefits as Londoners rose to meet the challenge.

It also turned the tide of American opinion in Britain's favor as photos circulated of St. Paul's Cathedral outlined against the flames of the burning city with planes battling overhead as schoolchildren and teachers looked on (Stokesbury 1980).

9. Schou-Sörensen says that when they tell the joke some people add: "Det sier jeg ikke, iallfall ikke til deg!" (I'm not telling, especially not to you!).

10. The results of the Norwegian campaign influenced developments outside Norway in a number of ways. Britain had put all its confidence in her navy and was shocked by the supremacy of German air power. Britain's disastrous showing sparked debates over the relative value of air versus sea power, discussions which, as mentioned in chapter 1, directly led to the fall of the Chamberlain government, as popular opinion judged that he had underestimated the German forces. Churchill who urged a more aggressive line came to power, though as first lord of the Admiralty, he actually had greater responsibility for the disaster than Chamberlain. The crippling of the German navy in the Norwegian campaign, moreover, was one of the factors that led to Hitler's already described failure to invade Britain later that year (Stokesbury 1980).

11. An additional irritation with Britain derived from the situation in the Balkans; Greta Dahl mentions in a 9 April 1941 entry:

Many are angry with the British for not stopping the Germans in the Balkans. Thesoloniki has fallen.

12. German authorities were particularly concerned that he would tell of the planned attack on Russia, but when interrogated by the British, Hess had said rumors of such an invasion were without foundation (Gilbert 1989, 181).

13. The German language version of this verse circulated in Norway on small slips of paper; Gudrun Moen saved one on which she wrote, "being passed among the Jössings who are finding great amusement in Hess' flight to Scotland."

CHAPTER 10. FURTHER PERSPECTIVES ON WAR DEVELOPMENTS

1. Hitler had been impressed by Mussolini's 1922 March on Rome, and he later imitated his use of slogans, uniforms, salutes, and party organization, but he was determined not to stand in the Italian dictator's shadow. Once Hitler had become chancellor in 1933, Mussolini's importance to him decreased, and by 1943 Italy was no more than a client state of Germany (Taylor and Shaw 1987, 221–22).

2. On 27 September 1940 Japan joined the Axis, concluding the Tripartite Pact which pledged each of the parties to help the others if attacked. Though Japan loomed large on the American wartime scene, Norwegian occupation humor makes little mention of it. Since humor tends to concern itself with those items about which people feel most tension, we may conclude that the Far Eastern theater did not pose as immediate a threat in Norway.

3. Romania joined the Axis in November 1940.

4. Another joke that mocked Mussolini's frustrated dreams of a Mediterranean empire plays, like one of the Quisling jokes in chapter 2, on the difficulty in urination that accompanies prostate trouble.

Mussolini skal opereres for prostata fordi han ikke kan få Nizza. [Schou-Sörensen] (Mussolini is going to have prostate surgery because he can't take *Nizza* [the French city of Nice, but the name also sounds like *nisse*, the euphemism for *tisse* = "pee"].)

5. Though Rommel actually had a good reputation even among the Allied soldiers, folk wit tends to see things in more black-and-white terms, and therefore ridiculed him.

6. About this inducement, Åslaug Rommetveit writes on 15 February 1941:

> Now Hitler and Quisling are enticing people to join "Regiment Nordland." We hope that all the local "little Quislings" around here will fall for it. If they participate for two years, they are promised German citizenship in addition to the Norwegian. If they are active for four years, they get a farm of about 75 acres.

7. Greta Dahl notes in her diary that Rommel was being called by the derogatory name of "Drummeln."

8. In all, three decisive battles were concluding badly for the enemies of the Allies: At Stalingrad the Russians were pushing German forces into retreat, in North Africa battles at Al-Alamein, Tobruk, and Tunisia had ended in German-Italian defeat, and on the Guadalcanal American forces were coercing Japanese forces to cede land over which their conquered flag recently had flown. Each of these victories was achieved at a high cost in lives and material, but each represented a decisive turning of the tide in Allied favor (Gilbert 1989, 374).

9. Rommel's career ended rather dramatically. After the defeat in North Africa he commanded in Italy until ordered to prepare for the Allied invasion in France in 1944. When German forces proved unable to check the Anglo-American invasion on D Day in June 1944 and the Allies subsequently advanced into France, he urged Hitler to end the war. Suspected of being involved in the assassination attempt on Hitler that followed one month later (see chap. 2), he was given the choice of being executed or taking his own life; on 14 October 1944 he chose the latter course.

10. Finland's prime motivation for joining the Nazi attack on Russia was to recover what she had lost in the Winter War.

11. The name comes from Holy Roman emperor Frederik Barbarossa who marched eastward with his army in 1190 to conquer the Holy Land from the infidel. Hitler's choice of the name reflects his view of the need to capture the Soviet Union's vital Caucasian oil fields from the inferior Slavs. He felt that hegemony over Europe would be decided in the battle against Russia and that the defeat of the Soviet Union would at last bring Britain to her knees (Gilbert 1989, 142–45).

12. The conquest and colonization of Eastern Europe had been one of Hitler's themes since *Mein Kampf;* all the other political moves had been stepping stones to this end, and he termed the operation a "crusade."

13. The Wehrmacht took 5.7 million Soviet prisoners; 3.3 million of them died in captivity, only three out of a hundred prisoners returned alive.

14. Besides rallying the enemy, Hitler's racial convictions ultimately weakened his own army, as orders of inhuman treatment to be meted out to Soviet captives led to the formation of strong partisan groups behind German lines.

15. To make up for this error, Hitler launched a drive throughout Germany to collect fur coats and winter clothing. For many this action provided the first indication that all was not well on the Russian Front (Gilbert 1989).

16. The blockade of Leningrad would last 880 days. On 14 January 1944 the Red Army resumed the offensive and on 29 January a line from Moscow to Leningrad was finally cleared, and the siege of the city came to an end.

17. Hitler had gone against Russia with 3,500,000 men, but returned to Berlin with 300,000 Russians.

18. Britain was convinced that attacking Italy would shorten the war; Americans preferred attacking from the North across the English Channel to Normandy, but went along with the British plan first. Though the latter operation, the 6 June 1944 (D Day) landing at Normandy, is probably the best-known single episode of World War II among Americans, it does not figure in Jössing humor.

CHAPTER 11. GERMANY'S BLEAK PROSPECTS FOR VICTORY

1. Occupation humor thus helped address what the historian Berge Furre identifies as the critical problem of how to maintain the exiled government's authority against the German and Norwegian Nazi efforts to discredit it in the eyes of the Norwegian people (1992, 187).

2. A concrete indication of Haakon's less than majority support is the underground leaflet titled "De ti bud for nordmend" (The ten commandments for Norwegians) referred to in the notes for chapter 4 which includes among its directives:

1. You shall obey KING HAAKON for whom you yourself have voted. . . . 6. You shall regard as a traitor every Storting member who votes to depose our brave KING and our legal government, who are the only ones who can freely and independently work for NORWAY'S liberation.

A population already convinced of these tenants does not need to have them spelled out in this way. (The leaflet is in the collection of Norges Hjemmefrontmuseum.)

3. In fact the occupation lasted much longer than either side anticipated, not ending until 8 May 1945.

4. With varying degrees of optimism and disappointment Greta Dahl anticipated the end of the war early and often, as the following entries show:

August 29, 1940:
It has been predicted that all the Germans would be out of Norway by the middle of September, and we all believed it, that's why we could laugh and be happy, and even talk to the Germans.
February 3, 1943:
We all think now that the war will soon be over. The country is rife with such rumors, and we swallow them whole, if only they go in our favor. . . . Just hope that we haven't started celebrating too early.
June 3, 1943:
Oh, how we wait for a change! Every time there's a loud noise, our first thought is: "Are they [the Allies] coming now?" No, I guess we have to continue waiting a while yet.

5. Blix's actual lyric goes:

No livnar det i lundar,
no lauvast det i li,
den heile skapning stundar
no fram til sumars tid.
(Now the groves are reviving,
Now leaves are sprouting in the glen,
the whole creation's longing
the summer soon to spend.)

6. War reprisals remained a hot topic of discussion, as Greta Dahl notes in this 9 May 1943 entry:

People are more vehemently debating what will be done with the Nazis when peace comes. Some think everything will be forgotten, but others argue that those whose loved ones have been lost or mistreated will demand revenge.

7. For a related Communist joke, see Ruksenas (1986, 21).

8. As mentioned in chapter 1, Sweden's policy toward Norway and the Norwegians tended toward caution and seeming unfriendliness during the first years of the occupation, owing to fears that they, too, would be invaded by Germany. From the outset, however, Norway's long border with Sweden provided an important escape route for refugees from the Gestapo. Sweden also developed into a meeting ground between resistance leaders and spokesmen for the exiled government in London. Nevertheless their experience of the war differed markedly, as Greta Dahl also notes in this 3 September 1944 entry:

The Swedish newspapers we have received recently have been an utter delight. Surely no Swede could feel the momentousness of such things in the same intense way we do.

9. Jössing humor enjoyed these comparisons between Hitler and Napoleon because Hitler came off worse. Both started their expeditions to Moscow in midsummer, Napoleon reached Moscow in September, while Hitler took more than a year and a half to get there. Napoleon invaded Russia on 23 June 1812, conquered Smolensk on 19 August, began the Battle of Moscow on 7 September, and reached the Kremlin on 14 September. Hitler invaded Russia on 22 June, took Smolensk on 1 August, began the Battle of Moscow on 1 October, but never did reach the Kremlin.

10. Ellingsen has this version.

Hitler er blitt lokomotivförer på tilbaketoget.
(Hitler has become the locomotive *förer* [= Führer // engineer] on the *tilbaketog* [= train // retreat].)

11. Walter von Brauchitsch (1881–1948) was commander in chief of the victorious German armies in the campaigns of 1939–41 in Poland, Denmark, Norway, the Netherlands, Belgium, France, and the Balkans. After the victory in France he was promoted to field marshal. But in December 1941 when the German armies failed to take Moscow, Hitler made von Brauchitsch the scapegoat and dismissed him.

12. Ellingsen has the version:

Omdöping av Berlin: 1ste Forslag: Jevnaker
2det Forslag: Fladeby
(Re-naming of Berlin: 1st suggestion: *Jevnaker* [Flattened Acre]
2nd suggestion: *Fladeby* [Flat City, The Flats].)

13. Humor does, however, register the existence also of those who refused to take a conciliatory stance.

Det er to nasister her nå, nasi og obsternasi. [Schou-Sörensen, April 1943]
(There are two kinds of Nazis here now, Nazi and *obsternasi* [= recalcitrance].)

Meanwhile Nazi propaganda during 1943 reflects the changing perceptions of the war's outcome, shifting from a focus on vanquishing Bolshevism to conjuring up nightmarish scenes of the terrible ramifications of an Allied victory.

14. Greta Dahl makes several additional observations about the Nazis' change in demeanor.

April 8, 1944:
There are a German officer and his wife here who have a different look about them now. Formerly superior and self-satisfied, they now appear depressed and avoid eye-contact. Sometimes I feel sorry for them, but that passes quickly.

June 16, 1944:
The Nazis in Bodö have asked to be moved farther inland. Yes, I'll bet they're scared now! But when they were threatening us with arrest, abuse and death, they certainly enjoyed themselves; then we were the ones forced to feel the fright and terror. Now the tables have turned.

Sept 4, 1944:
The poor Nazis! Yes, I said poor, although I really shouldn't. But even a stone would be moved to see them now. They're like beaten dogs: Gray-haired, stoop-necked, afraid to meet your eyes. No, when I think about it, I'm not sorry for them. Were they sorry for us when they willingly turned us in to the Germans on the least suspicion? No, they don't deserve any pity.

15. Discontent within the NS grew stronger with each German defeat. Most party members began to anticipate a coming day of atonement. On 25 September 1943 the ministers stayed away from the second-anniversary commemoration of the day the party had assumed power. Terboven made a speech to NS membership saying he wanted "no more nonsense from them"; Germany was in trouble, he said, and Norwegians could not expect independence until the war was won. He admitted that the idea of Norway's becoming "a free and independent realm after the war" was "taken from old democratic jargon," and was mere rhetoric. The speech moved many members to despair and they tried to get out of the party any way they could, even as the Gestapo stepped up restrictions against and reprisals for doing so. Many of those forced to remain shifted their focus from planning for the New Order to assuring themselves as favorable a position as possible when defeat came (Olsen 1946, 78).

16. Another joke on the Björnöya theme also included the device seen in chapter 8 of the *trikk*-ridership joining in united derision of a Nazi.

På en av Oslos forstadsbaner er det en stasjon som populært kalles "Björnöya". Under krigen satt en dag en ung hirdmann på denne trikken, og da konduktören kom, forlangte han med viktig mine:
-Tur-retur Björnöya, takk!
Men konduktören var kjapp nok:
-Vi selger bare tur til Björnöya.
Stor munterhet blant de övrige passasjerer. [Imsland 1946, 97]
(On one of Oslo's suburban streetcars there is a station popularly called "Björnöya." One day during the war a young member of the *Hird* was sitting on this *trikk*, and when the conductor came he demanded in a self-important voice:
"Round-trip to Björnöya, please!"
To which the conductor had a ready reply:
"We only sell one-way tickets to Björnöya."
The rest of the passengers laughed heartily.)

17. Twelve-year-old Laila Thorsen and her family were among those who chose to remain behind. Her diary of the experience was published in 1981 under the title *Finnmark brenner* (Finnmark is burning).

18. Like Hitler, Quisling refused to accept the reality of the approaching defeat. As late as January 1945 he made a final trip to Berlin persisting in the hope of Norway's being made a sovereign state and of his being her appointed ruler. Once again he asked Hitler to make peace between Germany and Norway and once again received the evasive answer that Norway would be free when Germany achieved victory.

19. After Germany's capitulation Himmler attempted to escape, but was captured by the British. Before he could be tried, he took a fatal dose of poison on 23 May 1945.

20. After the war Hess was found guilty at the Nuremberg trials and sentenced to life imprisonment; he died at Spandau Prison in 1987.

21. Goering was also tried at Nuremberg in 1946. Found guilty on all counts, he was sentenced to hang, but—like Himmler—escaped that fate by poisoning himself.

22. As Greta Dahl had done on several earlier occasions, Rommetveit expresses not only the one-sided hatred for the enemy typical of propaganda, but also a more complex view.

> May 9, 1945: Suddenly I feel it's a little difficult only to rejoice over peace. There are millions who did not get to take part in it. I'm referring to all my countrymen, of course, but these thoughts go first and foremost to the German people—even though they have been our enemies. They've suffered such tremendous losses on their own soil. Those are real people, too, and they've lost all their possessions and family.

Such sentiments remained, however, largely private in the normative pressure to oppose Nazism and everything associated with it. To mention that there might have been extenuating circumstances was regarded by many as indicating a lack of national loyalty (Andenæs, Riste, and Skodvin 1989, 124–25).

Senja (1973, 75) suggests that this normative pressure may have arisen because the world press had earlier in the war written disparagingly about the Norwegians' lack of resistance (see particularly the 6 May 1940 *Life* magazine article by the highly respected, Pulitzer Prize winning journalist Leland Stowe which told of "young Norwegians who continued to drink, laugh and flirt despite their country's fate" (96) as well as of the "bribery, treachery and betrayal" (98) by which the invasion had been accomplished) and because Quisling had achieved such notoriety as the quintessential Nazi traitor. Norway may have wanted to show the world that her population had no sympathy for Nazism. He quotes figures of the number of arrests per ten thousand Nazis in various countries, showing that Norway arrested the highest percent of them:

country	Nazis jailed per 10,000
France	99
Denmark	<300
Netherlands	>300
Belgium	596
Norway	633

23. Several dramatic events took place during the first hours and days following the liberation. Reichskommissar Terboven and his SS general blew themselves up in his bunker. Some of the most desperate NS leaders also committed suicide.

Quisling at first gathered some of his former supporters and demanded to be treated as head of state, but was told he would be forcibly arrested if he failed to surrender. On 9 May he turned himself in at the Oslo police station and was placed in custody.

Altogether some 50–60 members of the NS were charged with major offenses out of 18,000 arrested. Few death penalties followed, but all NS members were barred from municipal or state employment and from other privileges. Those who made large profits from work for the Germans received substantial fines.

The trial of Vidkum Quisling lasted from 20 August until 6 September; on 10 September 1945 he was found guilty on the following counts:

proclaiming himself head of government,
revoking the mobilization order against Germany,
calling for voluntary war efforts to support Germany,
establishing a "government" on 1 Feb 1942,
acting with complicity in the deportation of the Jews,
being responsible for the execution and death sentences passed on Norwegian patriots,
engaging in preinvasion collaboration with the Germans, including receiving
financial support and providing assistance in planning their attack on Norway.

In the early hours of 24 October, Quisling was placed before a firing squad at Akershus Castle and executed (Andenæs, Riste, and Skodvin 1989, 124–28).

CHAPTER 12. THE FUNCTION AND LEGACY OF OCCUPATION HUMOR

1. Ulateig mentions the allure of being chosen into a select group of youths who measured up to the Vikings (1989, 30–32).

2. This is not to suggest that the jokes accomplished the change of opinion single-handedly. Circumstances such as Terboven's usurping of power on 25 September 1940 and Nazi terrorism decisively changed the nature of the occupation, but humor provided a running commentary on these and other pivotal events and helped shape opinion about them.

3. Slaatto writes,

During the war [i.e., the two-month armed resistance following the invasion], lots of jokes came out that I have now gotten a hold of. [January 1941]

In the other personal diaries and notebooks, as well, it is primarily during the first year of the occupation that the humor figures most prominently.

4. Jon Vegard Lunde emphasizes the importance of the early resistance voices.

The first ones who took up the fight to arouse the people and create a resistance attitude probably made the most decisive contribution to the resistance. If they had not reacted, so many others would not have developed the attitude and the mentality that made it possible to build up a military organization. [Lunde 1982, 20]

We see an illustration of the doubts and reviving hopes characteristic of this period in the following December 1940 *Hvepsen* comment about an anti-Nazi demonstration:

A pile of *Fritt folk* lay in the entry way of an Oslo school. The newspapers were dragged out into the street and added to a bonfire. The pupils stood around shouting, "Hurray!" Passers-by smiled and nodded with satisfaction. *There still are many Norwegians after all* [emphasis mine].

5. Làszló Kürti has argued, for example, that Chernobyl jokes helped spread a new vocabulary and new knowledge of radiation among the general population (1988, 326).

6. The educator Björn Roos has pointed out how jokes promote the dissemination of ideas and attitudes among schoolchildren.

7. The illegal newspaper *Hjemmefronten* reported in 1941, for example:

The Nazis are trying to isolate certain individuals and single them out for special pressure. Make sure, therefore, . . . that no friend feels he's fighting alone.

8. Another survivor, Jacob Kuhnle, similarly comments:

Humor provided constant cheer and encouragement . . . and undoubtedly deserves a place high on the list of what saw us through [1945, 140].

9. While several researchers have emphasized the important role played by resistance slogans and directives *(paroler)* in developing anti-Nazi sentiment (Gjelsvik 1977, 31–32; Hirsch 1945, 7; Gordon 1978, 68–69, 91, 149, 157, 221), I would argue that humor superseded these means in effectiveness precisely because of its greater accessibility (proving more adaptable to sharing in everyday situations) and safety (allowing greater ease in concealing the speaker's own views).

10. Both the private wartime joke collections and the many postwar humor anthologies demonstrate that the occupation jokes traveled extensively in Norway; the same joke appears in regional variants (and dialects) in widely scattered parts of the country. Some of this variation may also be noted in the jokes collected in the present volume.

11. Several of those interviewed during fieldwork conducted by the author during the summer of 1989, mentioned the prominence of joke telling during the war, attesting that a frequent conversation opener was: "Have you heard the one about?. . ." (The *Aftenposten* journalist Berit Vikdal, interviewed by author, 5 August 1989).

Commenting on how humor's accessibility lends it potency to affect the emotions and actions of people who share it, Hertzler writes:

The infectiousness of laughter makes it socially effective. Because of it, laughter through social contact and intercourse is a prime factor in the extension, manifestation and intensification of social emotion, attitude, belief and action [1970, 32].

This power to influence feeling and belief makes laughter an especially effective means of persuasion.

12. Finn Bö suggests the danger of getting caught telling jokes, but also indicates the possibility of nevertheless managing to get them told.

Jokes often had to be told in a hurry and in the dangerous vicinity of treacherous ears. Sometimes you'd just barely had the chance to blurt out, in passing a neighbor on the *trikk* or street corner, "Good morning! Have you heard the one about?. . ." [1946, 29]

13. Several of my informants mentioned this aspect of humor during my 1989 fieldwork, pointing out that when a joke was told hearers' views could be gauged by noting their reaction; a similar point is made by Wilson.

> The ambiguity of the joke, in being both serious and trivial allows the joker to test for fellow feelings of rebelliousness. If others signal their approval in smiling or laughter, the joker can reassure himself that he is amongst like-minded people, and he and the group may graduate to the more satisfying expression of direct disparagement. [1979, 277]

14. As chapter 8 has demonstrated, stoicism was a trait also highly esteemed by the occupied Norwegians.

15. The existence of Scandinavian legends of the wizardlike Black Book minister exhibiting the motif known in Norwegian as *målbinding* (i.e., making an opponent speechless by means of one's own quick-witted responses) attests to the high regard in which this capacity was held. In some legends the Black Book minister uses *målbinding* to exorcise the Devil (Mauland 1931, 15), while in others a clever reply can save a person from losing his soul to the Devil (Opedal 1934, 102).

16. The Nazis had forbidden the open celebration of Norway's Constitution Day in order to keep the population's patriotic feelings from distracting the "national government" (Stahl 1964, 89).

17. Dahl and others point out that in some ways anti-Nazi humor may have even benefited the enemy, being tolerated and maybe even encouraged on the assumption that after letting off some steam, individuals could return to work more refreshed and able to continue working for the German war effort. Hans Speier argues, moreover, that telling clandestine jokes may well be an act of accommodation to suppression rather than an act of aggression, since it may assuage pangs of conscience caused by one's unwillingness to perform more courageous acts of resistance and may be a way of deluding oneself about the extent of one's daring or conviction to resist (1969).

Even in the light of such criticism, I find the Norwegians' use of humor admirable and inspiring. Faced with limited possibilities for alternative recourse, they resourcefully used the weapon they *could* wield and with it, developed the resistance mentality the situation demanded.

Bibliography

Abrahams, Roger, and Charles Wukash. 1967. "Political Jokes of East Germany." *Tennessee Folklore Society Bulletin* 33:7–10.

Abrahamsen, Samuel. 1983. "The Holocaust in Norway." In *Contemporary Views on the Holocaust,* edited by Randolph L. Braham. Boston: Kluwer-Nijhoff Publishing.

———. 1991. *Norway's Response to the Holocaust.* New York: Holocaust Library.

Alt for Norge (Everything for Norway—King Haakon's motto—underground newspaper). Oslo: Norges Hjemmefrontmuseum.

Andenæs, Johs., Olav Riste, and Magne Skodvin. 1989. *Norway and the Second World War.* 4th ed. Oslo: Aschehoug.

Andersen, Jan. 1989. *Krigen på folkemunne* (The war in oral tradition). Oslo: Tiden.

Asbjörnsen, P. Chr., and Jörgen Moe. 1982. *Samlede eventyr I* (Collected fairy tales). Oslo: Den norske Bokklubben.

Aftenposten (The evening news), Norway's largest daily (conservative), in existence since 1861, publishing two issues per day since 1885.

Avantgarden (underground newspaper). Oslo: Norges Hjemmefrontmuseum.

Bahr, Willy. *8 muntre krisebilder* (8 cheerful scenes of crisis) (postcard series). Oslo: Norges Hjemmefrontmuseum.

Balfour, Michael. 1979. *Propaganda in War. Organization, Policies and Publics in Britain and Germany.* London: Routledge and Kegan Paul.

Banc, C., and Alan Dundes. 1986. *First Prize: Fifteen Years! An Annotated Collection of Romanian Jokes.* London: Associated Universities Press.

Bang-Hansen, Odd. 1961. *Chat Noir og norsk revy* (Chat Noir and Norwegian revue theater). Oslo: J. W. Cappelens Forlag.

Beckmann, Petr. 1980. *Hammer and Tickle: Clandestine Laughter in the Soviet Empire.* Boulder: Golden Press.

Bennett, Jeremy. 1969. "Non-violent Action Against Aggression." In *Civil Resistance as a National Defence,* edited by Adam Roberts. Baltimore: Penguin Books.

Blindheim, Svein, 1977. *Nordmenn under Hitlers fane. Dei norske frontkjemparane* (Norwegians under the banner of Hitler). Oslo: Noregs Boklag.

Blix, Ragnvald. 1945. *De fem årene* (Those five years). Oslo: Gyldendal.

Borchgrevink, Ridley. 1942 (postcard series published by Eberh. B. Oppi). Oslo: Norges Hjemmefrontmuseum.

Brunvand, Jan Harold. 1973. "Don't Shoot Comrades: A Survey of the Submerged Folklore of Eastern Europe." *North Carolina Folklore Journal* 21:181–88.

Bull, Edvard, 1979. "Under den annen verdenskrig." In *Klassekamp og felleskap 1920–1945* (Class struggle and solidarity). Vol 13 of *Norges historie,* edited by Knut Mykland. Oslo: J. W. Cappelens Forlag.

Bö, Finn. 1946. *Forbuden frukt* (Forbidden fruit). Oslo: Aschehoug.

Christensen, Chr. A. R. 1965. *Norge under okkupasjonen* (Norway during the occupation). Oslo: Fabritius.

Christensen, Chr. 1988. *Den andre siden* (The other side). Oslo: Cappelen, 1988.

Christerson, Solveig Maj (Majsol Elvsås). Vitser fra 9. april 1940 og utover (Jokes from 9 April 1940 and afterwards). Joke notebook. Privately owned.

Dahl, Greta. 1990. *Fem tunge år. En husmors dagbok fra krigstidens Narvik* (Five difficult years. A house wife's diary from wartime Narvik). Oslo: Gröndahl.

Dahl, Hans Fredrik. 1974. "Seks myter om okkupasjonen" (Six myths about the occupation in Norway). In *Krigen i Norge* (The war in Norway). Oslo: Pax.

———. 1978. *Dette er London. NRK i krig. 1940–45.* Oslo: Cappelen.

———. 1982. *Den norske nasjonal sosialisme* (The Norwegian national socialism). Oslo: Pax.

———. 1989. "Scandinavia in the Second World War." In *Crime and Control in Scandinavia during the Second World War,* edited by Hannu Takala and Henrik Tham. Scandinavian Studies in Criminology 10. Oslo: Norwegian University Press/The Scandinavian Research Council for Criminology.

Dahr, Eva Braathen. 1991. "Villagris med sildesmak" (City-raised pork that tastes like herring). In *Weekend Aftenposten,* 13 December.

Dolgopolova, A., ed. 1982. *Russia Dies Laughing: Jokes from Soviet Russia.* London: Andre Deutsch.

Draitser, Emil, ed. 1978. *Forbidden Laughter: Soviet Underground Jokes.* Los Angeles: Almanac Publishing Company.

Eidsvoll (underground newspaper). Oslo: Norges Hjemmefrontmuseum.

Ellingsen, Elsa "Bibs" [b. Elsa Sophia Larssen]. Norges smil gjennom tårer (Norway's smiles through tears). Joke collection. Privately owned.

Elvsås, Majsol. 1980. Fortell fra krigstiden (Tell about the war years). NRK radio program 21 October (see also Christerson).

Enig og tro (Agreed and faithful) (underground newspaper). Oslo: Norges Hjemmefrontmuseum.

Fen, Åke. 1943. *Nazis in Norway.* Harmondworth: Penguin Books.

Folkets röst (The voice of the people) (underground newspaper). Oslo: Norges Hjemmefrontmuseum.

For konge og fedreland (For king and fatherland) (underground newspaper). Oslo: Norges Hjemmefrontmuseum.

Fossen, Anders Bjarne, ed. 1991. *Krig og kvardag 1940–45. Hordalendingar fortel* (War and everyday life 1940–45, as told by the people of Hordaland). Askøy, Norway: Clio Forlag.

Friele, Herman. Diary. Bergen, Norway: University of Bergen Library.

Fri fagbevegelse (Free labor movement) (underground newspaper). Oslo: Norges Hjemmefrontmuseum.

Frihet (Freedom) (underground newspaper). Oslo: Norges Hjemmefrontmuseum.

Fritt folk (Free people) (Nazi party newspaper). Oslo: Universitetsbibliotek.

Furre, Berge. 1992. *Norsk historie 1905–1990* (Norwegian history 1905–90). Oslo: Det norske Samlaget.

Gilbert, Martin. 1989. *The Second World War. A Complete History.* New York: Henry Holt & Co.

Gjelsvik, Tore. 1977. *Hjemmefronten: Den sivile motstand under okkupasjonen 1940–45* (The homefront: Civil resistance during the occupation 1940–45). Oslo: Cappelen.

Gorden, Gerd Stray. 1978. "The Norwegian Resistance during the German Occupation 1940–45: Repression, Terror and Resistance in the West Country of Norway." Ph. D. diss., University of Pittsburgh.

Grimnes, Ole Kristian. 1983a. "The Beginnings of the Resistance Movement." In *Scandinavia during the Second World War,* edited by Henrik S. Nissen. Oslo: Universitetsforlaget.

———. 1983b. *Norge under occupasjonen* (Norway during the occupation). Oslo: Aschehoug.

Halse, Steinar Floan. 1993. *Humöret kan ingen ta fra oss. Vitser, anekdoter og sanger fra okkupasjonstiden 1940–45* (Humor they can't steal. Jokes, anecdotes and songs from the occupation period 1940–45). Oslo: Gröndahl Dreyer.

Hambro, Cato. 1943. I okkupert Norge (In occupied Norway). *Nordmanns-Forbundet,* August, 191–95.

Hamsun, Knut. 1890. *Sult* (Hunger). Copenhagen: Philipsen.

———. 1898. *Victoria.* (Victoria). Kristiania [Oslo]: Cammermeyer.

———. 1917. *Markens gröde* (The growth of the soil). Kristiania [Oslo]: Gyldendal.

Hansen, Halfdan, and Ivar Baggethun. 1945. *Husker De hva vi lo av?* (Do you remember what we laughed at?) Horten, Norway: Evangs Trykkeri.

Hartmann, Rudi (Hrsg). 1983. *Flüsterwitze aus dem Tausendjärigen Reich gesammelt von Friedrich Goetz* (Whispered jokes from the thousand year reich. Collected by Friedrich Goetz). Munich: Knaur.

Hegna, Trond. 1983. *Min versjon* (My version). Oslo: Gyldendal.

Heradstveit, Per. 1979. *Kongen som sa nei!* (The King who said no). Oslo: Hjemmenes forlag.

Hertzler, Joyce. 1970. *Laughter: A Socio-Scientific Analysis.* New York: Exposition Press.

Hirsch, Trygve, ed. 1945. *Den illegale pressen. Norsk presse under hakekorset III* (The illegal press. Norwegian press under the swastika). Oslo: Tell Forlag.

Hjeltnes, Guri. 1987. *Hverdagsliv i krig. Norge 1940–45* (Everyday life in war. Norway 1940–45). Vol 5 of *Norge i kirg* (Norway in war), edited by Magne Skodvin. Oslo: Aschehoug.

Hjemmefronten (The homefront) (underground newspaper). Oslo: Norges Hjemmefrontmuseum.

Holland, Norman N. 1982. *Laughing, a Psychology of Humor.* Ithaca: Cornell University Press.

Humoristens krigs-revy (The humorist's war revue). n.d. Oslo: Humoristens forlag.

Hvepsen (The wasp) (underground newspaper). Oslo: Hjemmefrontmuseum.

Hoidal, Oddvar. 1989. *Quisling: A Study in Treason.* Oslo: Norwegian University Press.

Imsland, Henry. 1946. *Jössingvitser* (Jössing jokes). Stavanger, Norway: Åsmund Lærdal.

Jensen, Tom B., and Hans Fredrik Dahl. 1988. *Parti og plakat. NS 1933-1945* (Party and poster, the Norwegian Nazi party 1933-45). Oslo: Det norske samlaget.

Johnson, Amanda. 1948. *Norway, Her Invasion and Occupation.* Decatur, Ga.: Bowen Press.

Jössingposten (Jössing post) (underground newspaper). Oslo: Norges Hjemmefrontmuseum.

Karikaturens krigs-humor, med tegninger av Jens R. (The caricaturist's war-humor, with drawings by Jens R. [Nilssen]). n.d. (pamphlet). Oslo: Landstrykkeriet.

Kersaudy, François. 1987. *Norway 1940.* New York: St. Martins Press.

Kjendsli, Veslemöy. 1986. *Skammensbarn* (Children of shame). Oslo: Metope.

Kristiansen, Oddmund. 1945. *Jöss! Vitser, skröner og karikaturer* (Good grief! Jokes, tall-tales and caricatures). Oslo: Aasmund Engens Annonsekontor.

Kuhnle, Jacob. 1945. *Vi som ble hjemme* (We who stayed home). Bergen, Norway: John Griegs Forlag.

Kürti, Làszló. 1988. "The Politics of Joking: Popular Response to Chernobyl." *Journal of American Folklore* 10:324-34.

Kvamsdal, Nils, ed. 1990. *Fem år i krig. Krigshandling og kvardagsliv i Voss og grannebygdene 1940-45* (Five years at war. Military action and everyday life in Voss and neighboring communities 1940-45). Voss, Norway: Vestanbok Forlag.

Larsen, Sölvi M. Joke notebook. Oslo: Norges Hjemmefrontmuseum.

Larsen, Sverre. Attila kommer. Noen dagboksblader fra Naziveldetsdager i Trondheim (Attila is coming. Some diary pages from the days of Nazi power in Trondheim). Diary. University of Tronheim spesialsamlinger 21, no. 20. 4 vols. Hereafter referred to as the Trondheim diary.

London-nytt (London News) (underground newspaper). Oslo: Norges Hjemmefrontmuseum.

Luihn, Hans. 1960. *De illegale avisene. Den frie hemmelige pressen i Norge under okkupasjonen* (The illegal newspapers. The free clandestine press in Norway during the occupation). Oslo: Universitetsforlaget.

————. 1981. *Det fjerde våpen. Den hemmelige presse i Norge 1940-45* (The fourth weapon. The clandestine press in Norway 1940-45). Oslo: Universitetsforlaget.

Lunde, Jon Vegard. 1982. *Det var ei rar tid: Hjemmefronten i Gudbrandsdal 1940-45* (It was a strange time: the homefront in Gudbrandsdal 1940-45). Otta, Norway: Enger.

Mauland, Torkell. 1931. *Folkeminne fraa Rogaland II* (Folklore from Rogaland). (NFL 26). Oslo: Universitetsforlaget.

Moen, Gudrun. Scrapbooks and diaries. Oslo: Norges Hjemmefrontmuseum.

Mogens, Victor. 1945. *Tyskerne, Quisling og vi andre* (The Germans, Quisling, and the rest of us). Oslo: Utenriks Forlaget.

Nicolaissen, O., ed. 1879. *Sagn og eventyr fra Nordland* (Legends and fairy tales from Nordland). Kristiania, Oslo: Malling.

Norge idag, (Norway today) (underground newspaper). Oslo: Norges Hjemmefrontmuseum

Norge under hakkorset. Fakta och dokument (Norway under the swastika. Facts and documents). 1940. Stockholm: Trots allt.

Norges budstikke (Norway's messenger) (underground newspaper). Oslo: Norges Hjemmefrontmuseum.

Nökleby, Berit. 1985. *Nyordning* (The New Order). Vol 2 of *Norge i krig: Fremmedåk og frihetskamp* (Norway at war: Foreign yoke and the fight for freedom), edited by Magne Skodvin. Oslo: Aschehoug.

―――. 1986. *Holdningskamp* (The fight for popular opinion). Vol 4 of *Norge i kirg: Fremmedåk og frihetskamp* (Norway at war. Foreign yoke and the fight for freedom), edited by Magne Skodvin. Oslo: Aschehoug.

―――. 1989. *Da kirgen kom. Norge september 1939-juni 1940* (When war came. Norway September 1939-June 1940). Oslo: Gyldendal.

Obrdlik, Antonin J. 1942. "Gallows Humor—A Sociological Phenomenon." *American Journal of Sociology* 47:709–16.

Olav, Hans, and Tor Myklebust. [1942]. *He Who Laughs . . . Lasts: Anecdotes from Norway's Homefront*. Brooklyn: Norwegian News Company.

Olsen, Gunnar. 1946. *Norges kamp*. Copenhagen, Denmark: Det Danske Forlag.

Om Landsvikoppgjöret (About the national treason settlement). 1963. Oslo: Forbundet for sosialoppreisning.

Opedal, Halldor. 1934. *Makter og menneske. Folkeminne ifrå Hardanger II* (Forces and humanity. Folklore from Hardanger II). (NFL 32). Oslo: Universitetsforlaget.

Pausewang, Elin A. Analyse av *Snorre sel* (Analysis of Snorri the seal). Privately owned.

Ramfjord, Ottar. 1945. *Okkupasjonshumor* (Occupation humor). Stavanger, Norway, Åsmund Lærdal.

Raskin, Victor. 1985. *Semantic Mechanisms of Humor*. Boston: D. Reidel.

Ringnes, Ellef. 1950. *Bak okkupasjonens kulisser* (Behind the scenes of the occupation). Oslo: Heim og Samfund.

Ringnes, Haagen. 1981. *I skyggen av solkorset* (In the shadow of the swastika). Oslo: Gyldendal.

Rings, Werner. 1982. *Life with the Enemy. Collaboration and Resistance in Hitler's Europe 1939-45*. Translated by J. Maxwell Brownjohn. New York: Doubleday.

Rommetveit, Åslaug. Diary. Privately owned.

Roos, Björn. 1986. *Vitsen med vitsarne: Historieberättande bland skolbarn* (The point of jokes. Story telling among schoolchildren). Stockholm: Carlssons.

Ruksenas, Algis. 1986. *Is that You Laughing, Comrade? The World's Best Russian (Underground) Jokes*. Secaucus, N. J.: Citadel Press.

Röd, Else Margrete. 1943. Spirit—men nesten ingenting annet (Spirit—but almost nothing else). *Nordmanns-Forbundet*. March 55–60.

Schou-Sörensen, Cecilie. Jokes from wartime diary. Privately owned.

Senja, Sigurd. 1973. *Quislingsgutt* (Quisling's boy). Oslo: Gyldendal.

―――. 1981. *Forræder skutt* (Traitor shot). Oslo: Cappelen.

―――. 1986. *Dömte kvinner. Tyskejenter og frontsöstre 1940-45* (Condemned women: women who dated German soldiers and nurses at the German war front). Oslo: Pax.

Sharp, Gene. ca 1958. *Tyranny Could Not Quell Them.* London: Peace News Pamphlet.

Skodvin, Magne. 1969. "Norwegian Non-violent Resistance during the German Occupation." In *Civilian Resistance as a National Defense. Non-violent Action against Aggression,* edited by Adam Roberts. Baltimore: Penguin Books.

————. 1990. *Krig og okkupasjon 1939–1945* (War and occupation 1939–45). Oslo: Det Norske Samlaget.

Skouen, Arne [Stallare, Björn]. 1943. *66 Skinnbrev fra Oslo: Glimt fra Norges hovedstad under okkupasjonen* (66 parchements from Oslo: Glimpses of Norway's capital city during the occupation). Stockholm: Gustaf Lindström.

Slaatto, Marie Lysgaard. Diary. Oslo: University of Oslo Library Krigtrykkssamling.

Speier, Hans. 1969. "The Pitfalls of Political Humor." In *Force and Folly: Essays on Foreign Affairs and the History of Ideas.* Cambridge: MIT Press.

Stahl, Knut. 1964. *De lange årene 1940–45* (The five long years 1940–45). Stavanger, Norway: Stabenfeldt Forlag.

Stallare, Björn (see Arne Skouen).

Stokesbury, James L. 1980. *A Short History of World War II.* New York: William Morrow & Co.

Stokker, Kathleen. 1991. "Heil Hitler—God Save the King": Humor in Occupied Norway. *Western Folklore* 50:171–190.

————. 1992. "The Nordmanns-Forbundet Magazine Escapes the Nazis. *The Norseman,* no. 3, 4–6.

Stowe, Leland. 1940. How a Few Thousand Nazis Seized Norway. *Life,* May 6, 90–103.

Sturluson, Snorre. 1979. *Norges kongesagaer* (Sagas of Norway's kings). Oslo: Den norske Bokklubben.

[Svendsen, Georg]. n.d. *Krigens humor samlet av Mr. George* (Wartime humor collected by Mr. George). Oslo: Tell Forlag.

Sælen, Frithjof. 1941. *Snorre sel. En fabel i farger for börn og voksne* (Snorri the seal. A fable in color for children and adults). Bergen, Norway: Grieg.

————. 1950. *Snorri the Seal.* Translated by Stephen England. London: Blackie and Son.

Taylor, James, and Warren Shaw. 1987. *The Third Reich Almanac.* New York: World Almanac.

Thomsen, Per. 1945. *The German Supermentality.* Oslo: Fabritius.

Thorsen, Laila. 1981. *Finnmark brenner—minner og dagboksnotater fra 1944–45* (Finnmark is burning—memories and diary notes from 1944–45). Oslo: Tiden.

Trondheim diary (see Larsen, Sverre).

12 milorg-karikaturer (12 caricatures from milorg [the military resistance]). n.d. Postcard series. Oslo: Norges Hjemmefrontmuseum.

Ulateig, Egil. 1987. *Dagbok frå ein rotnorsk nazist* (Diary of a genuine Norwegian patriot Nazi). Oslo: Det norske Samlaget.

Under stövelhælen. (Under the heal of the boot). 1944. *Nordmanns-Forbundet,* June, 129–39.

Veimo, Morten. 1987. *Verdalsboka: Krig—okkupasjon—motstand* (The Verdal book: War—occupation—resistance). Verdal, Norway: Motstandsgruppa.

Vi vil oss et land (We want for ourselves a country) (underground newspaper). Oslo: Norges Hjemmefrontmuseum.

Vigness, Paul. 1970. *The German Occupation of Norway.* New York: Vantage Press.

Voksö, Per. 1985. *Krigens dagbok. Norge 1940–45* (War diary. Norway 1940–45). Oslo: Forlaget Det Beste.

Waal, Berit. 1981. *Kirgensbarn—en syklus i dikt og prosa* (The children of war—a cycle in poetry and prose). Oslo: Aschehoug.

Walker, Roy. 1946. *A People Who Loved Peace.* London: Victor Gollancz.

Werenskiold, Werner. 1937. *Norge vårt land* (Norway our country). 2 vols. Oslo: Gyldendal.

Wilson, Christopher. 1979. *Jokes: Form, Content, Use and Function.* European Monographs in Social Psychology, no. 16. London: Academic Press.

Worm-Müller, Jacob. 1941. *Norway Revolts against the Nazis.* London: Lindsay Drummond.

Wright, Myrtle. 1974. *Norwegian Diary 1940–45.* London: Friends Peace and International Relations Committee.

Zigderveid, Anton C. 1968. Jokes and Their Relation to Social Reality. *Social Research* 35:286–311.

Index

Note: In the Norwegian alphabet, the letters *æ, ö,* and *å* follow Z, and consequently have the same sequence in this index.